TELEVISION AND SCREEN WRITING

Third Edition

"Here is an uncommonly generous serving of useful information from an uncommonly generous writer and educator. The author presents precisely the "write" mix of theory and application. No writer—not a seasoned veteran nor a novice—could fail to find a bounty of useful material in this uniquely splendid contribution to the field."

Richard Walter, Professor and Screenwriting Faculty Chariman, UCLA

"The finest book of its kind!"

Malvin Wald, Adjunct Professor of Screenwriting, University of Southern California School of Cinema-TV

"Rick Blum's Television and Screenwriting is the best book written about the business of writing for television and film. I highly recommend it."

Ken Dancyger, Chair, Undergraduate Film & Television Department New York University

"One of the most comprehensive, informative sources for any writer looking to break into the indu

Bros.-TV Writers Workshop

OCT 97   MED

TELEVISION AND SCREEN WRITING

From Concept to Contract

Third Edition

Richard A. Blum

FOCAL PRESS

Boston • Oxford • Melbourne • Singapore • Toronto • Munich • New Delhi • Tokyo

Focal Press is an imprint of Butterworth–Heinemann

Copyright © 1995 by Butterworth–Heinemann

&. A member of the Reed Elsevier Group

Library of Congress Cataloging-in-Publication Data

Blum, Richard A.
    Television and screen writing : from concept to contract / Richard
A. Blum. —3rd ed.
      p.   cm.
    Rev. ed. of Television writing, 2nd ed. 1984.
    Includes bibliographical references and index.
    ISBN 0-240-80194-6 (pbk.)
    1. Television authorship. 2. Motion picture authorship. I. Blum, Richard
A. Television writing. II. Title.
PN1992.7.B58 1995
808'.066791—dc20   95–1958
                                                CIP

British Library Cataloguing in Publication Data
A catalogue record for this book is available from the British Library.

Butterworth–Heinemann
313 Washington Street
Newton, MA 02158-1626

10 9 8 7 6 5 4 3
Printed in the United States of America

FOR JENNIFER, JASON, EVE, AND ILENE

Contents

PART FOUR: SCRIPT VISUALIZATION

PART FIVE: SCRIPT FORMATS FOR TELEVISION AND MOTION PICTURES

PART SIX: MARKETING YOUR SCRIPT

Acknowledgments

I was pleased to learn that the first and second editions of this book have became classics in the field. They have been used widely at universities, professional workshops, and studio story conferences, and by television and film writers nationwide. I am grateful to all the readers, writers, teachers, and users of this book, and it is due to their interest and enthusiasm that this third revised edition is possible.

There have been some significant changes in the industry, and I have tried to incorporate them into this volume. It is my intention to provide you with the latest creative trends, formats, techniques, and marketplace insights. At the studios, production companies, networks, and cable and pay TV companies, I encountered many people who gave freely of their time and offered practical suggestions for this book. There are too many people to thank individually, but let me offer a collective thanks to you all.

At Focal Press, my thanks to publisher Karen Speerstra, editor Valerie Cimino, and former editor Phil Sutherland, for their helpful manuscript guidance. Thanks to Christina Mugno, my research assistant, for painstakingly reviewing and updating information in the bibliography and appendixes.

I would like to thank my family for bearing with me, once again, in the preparation of this book. I am particularly grateful to my children, Jason and Jennifer, for their understanding and patience over these many years. Eve Blum showed constant interest in the progress of this book, and I appreciate that support.

Friends and colleagues offered a strong network of support. Frank Tavares, as always, had many sound ideas and I appreciate his reliable feedback. I'd like to express my deep appreciation to Ilene Shatoff for her many helpful ideas and personal support at every stage. Friends like Norman Tamarkin, Larry Frank, Michele Orwin, Dan Wilcox, and colleagues at the University of Central Florida, among many others, have shared their professional insights and values. My gratitude to you all.

My writing students served as the initial impetus for this book. The questions asked, issues discussed, projects written, and experiences shared helped codify the concerns of talented new writers. I hope this edition fulfills some of their needs, and yours, in the pursuit of many television and film writing credits.

•   •   •

For permission to reprint excerpted materials, I would like to thank my writing partners and the following copyright owners.

"Death's Head" Episode #1 ("Circle of Fear" series), written by Rick Blum, reprinted with permission of Columbia Pictures Industries, Inc. All rights reserved.

Allan Gerson, co-writer, for permission to reprint excerpts from our story and screenplay, "Sonja's Men." All rights reserved.

Richard Lindheim, co-author, for permission to reprint excerpts from our books, *Inside Television Producing* (Boston: Focal Press, 1991) and *Primetime: Network Television Programming* (Boston: Focal Press, 1987). All rights reserved.

Ron Lux and Eugene Stein for permission to reprint excerpts from their script, "Murphy Brown: On the Rocks," written by Ron Lux and Eugene Stein. All rights reserved.

Frank Tavares, co-writer, for permission to reprint excerpts from our TV concept, "The Beltway Bandits." All rights reserved.

Frank Tavares, co-writer, for permission to reprint excerpts from our story and screenplay, "The Elton Project." All rights reserved.

Dan Wilcox, co-writer of "The Wind Chill Factor," for permission to reprint excerpts. All rights reserved.

1

Introduction

After working in the industry and analyzing industry requirements, I've concluded that writing for the small screen and writing for motion pictures share these needs: the development of producible stories, appealing and castable characters, credible dialogue, expert structure, and skillful visualization. This book shows how to fulfill each of those needs for episodic television, longform television, and theatrical motion pictures. It reveals the secret of creating a driving force for characters in the premise and demonstrates how that is the core of all successful television and motion picture scripts.

This book gives you specific techniques for writing high-quality and producible scripts. It discloses how to become a creative and marketable writer in every professional arena—including major studios, production companies, networks, cable and pay TV, interactive programs, grant agencies, and national filmwriting competitions.

When the second edition of *Television Writing: From Concept to Contract* was published (1984), the industry considered new television series proposals a logical entry point for new writers. At that point the industry had a lot of development deals in the works. Due to economics and other constraints, that situation has changed dramatically. Over the years, the costs of pilot and series production have escalated wildly, and networks, cable, and pay TV fight for survival in a raw competition for viewers. As a result, networks are much less likely to want to launch a new show—especially if the writer is not known to them.

Therefore, one of the most important skills for writers is to learn how to develop *spec* scripts ("speculative" means you don't get paid for it). That script serves as a consummate sample of your ability to write for television and film. It markets you as a professional to agents and producers.

New television writers can shine with a spec script showing an understanding of the existing story structure and character relationships in a current series. Freelancers who deliver producible scripts often find themselves hired as staff writers. If they're successful on staff, they move up the ladder to become *show runners* (writers who also produce). Show runners are worth their weight in gold, earning well over $1 million a year.

There is something very gratifying about developing new television and motion picture projects. Perhaps it relates to the writer's eternal fantasy of doing something that will have an impact on an audience. Think of the television viewer, bombarded with banality every night. Think of the frustration you feel seeing a movie with characters that are wooden or a plot that is a bomb. In a real way, this book is about how you can affect the quality of that barrage. Knowing the ground rules for success can help you notch up the quality of what millions of viewers see. It's a worthy fantasy to pursue.

The fact is that the writer who stands the best chance of making it is one with industry awareness and contacts coupled with talent, technique, and indomitable perseverance. If you're willing to confront incredible odds with highly professional scripts, perseverance might pay off. The industry consumes thousands of stories and scripts every season. It requires a horde of talented writers to keep the home fires burning and to draw audiences to see a box office smash.

This book can provide you with certain writing techniques, but only you can provide the essential ingredients of talent and creativity. Once you know the form, the demonstration of imagination and style is up to you. Why not put them to work and see what happens?

Part One details how to create quality premises that will be producible, castable, and marketable. It explains how to create a driving force for characters in the premise and analyzes successful television loglines and motion picture premises. The challenge of adaptation is explored, as are longform television and exploitive premises. Part One also covers developing projects for interactive programs and new technologies.

Another section examines how to create original series concepts, clarifying the differences among concepts, series presentations, bibles, and loglines. It demonstrates how series concepts are developed and offers samples from successful series. The art of *pitching* is also discussed. Whether you write for existing series or original features, freelancers have to learn the art of selling their ideas.

Part Two analyzes the creative process of story development. It shows how to choose the story area and the lead character and how to advance the story effectively. There is a discussion of strategies for developing convincing treatments and step outlines and a deliberation on the latest software for idea development. A sample step outline is included.

Another section examines dramatic elements and act structure in television and motion pictures. It also offers techniques for plotting audience interest in your story.

Part Three examines how to create realistic characters and dialogue. It deals with the problems of character development, and details the most effective devices for developing castable characters. It demonstrates how "Method" acting techniques can be used for creating dimensional characters in the script and how dialogue problems can be identified and corrected in the script phase of writing. Another section illustrates how character arcs are used to effectively build characterization in television and motion pictures.

Part Four is dedicated to script visualization, examining how to write effective scene descriptions for television comedy, television drama, and motion pictures. Another section provides an important checklist for script revision and the final polish.

Part Five concentrates on the specific formats involved in writing scripts for television and motion pictures. No producer, executive, or agent will pick up a script unless it's in the proper form. All worthy projects won't be produced—in fact, most scripts won't even be read—but if the project is well written in concept, style, and form, it stands a much better chance of being evaluated. Technique and form are essential for writers who seriously intend to enter the mainstream of the profession. This section scrutinizes script formats.

Part Six deals with the pragmatics of marketing your script—how, when, where, and to whom it should go. The odds against selling a new project are staggering, but without knowledge of the marketplace there's no glimmer of hope for success. This section provides the answers every writer should have to key questions. It provides a fully detailed examination of the marketplace and distinct strategies for marketing spec scripts, TV series concepts, motion picture screenplays, and interactive programs. It explains what happens if a producer is interested, what contractual arrangements can be expected, how to get an agent.

The last chapter looks at opportunities for noncommercial funding. It investigates national funding sources (CPB, PBS, NEA, NEH) and state funding sources, as well as private foundations and corporate sources. It explains how to write grant proposals and how projects are evaluated. Finally, it discusses screenwriting festivals, competitions, and professional workshops.

The *Appendixes* offer a wide range of contacts and resources for you to explore, dealing with each major subject examined in the book. There is also an *Annotated Bibliography* for further reference.

Just as an actor learns basic techniques to create effectively, so the screenwriter must learn techniques of writing, from the germination of an idea to the revision of a final draft. If the stress on form seems a bit dogmatic at times, please remember that competition is incredibly stiff and a professional-looking script can help you past that first major hurdle—getting the project read.

PART ONE

CREATING PRODUCIBLE PREMISES
FOR TV AND MOTION PICTURES

2

How to Create
Producible Premises

The Importance of a Producible Plot and Castable Characters

I studied screenwriting with Irwin R. Blacker at USC (the University of Southern California), who firmly believed in the importance of classical Greek dramatic theory as applied to screenwriting and the importance of plot, conflict, crisis, character, exposition, and dialogue in well-written scripts. He urged writers to think of a script as a blueprint for making a marketable film, with the same constructs classical playwrights used to appeal to audiences. Among Blacker's students were George Lucas, the screenwriter for STAR WARS and AMERICAN GRAFFITI, John Milius and Francis Ford Coppola (APOCALYPSE NOW), Bob Gale (BACK TO THE FUTURE), and Richard Walter (head of UCLA's [the University of California at Los Angeles] screenwriting program). Irwin Blacker's lectures were published posthumously in a valuable guidebook for writers entitled *The Elements of Screenwriting*.

Successful screenwriters and teachers may have different personal techniques, but they tend to agree that scripts should be written with marketable stories and characters in mind. Among the most well-known proponents of this theory are authors like Lew Hunter, Syd Field, Michael Haugue, Milt Josefsburg, Viki King, Carl Sautter, Linda Seger, and Richard Walter.

Some writers hold to the "auteur theory," which contends that screenwriters are the sole creative artists in film, and that others must defer to the writer's experimentation. The auteur theory does not consider marketing appeal, nor does it consider the collaborative nature of film work. Prolific screenwriter William Goldman (BUTCH CASSIDY AND THE SUNDANCE KID, ALL THE PRESIDENT'S MEN, MARATHON MAN,

A BRIDGE TOO FAR) has no patience for the auteur theory: "it sure as shit isn't true in Hollywood."[1] As he points out, a script can't be produced without input from producers, studios, actors, and directors. For a script to be marketable, it must have strong and flattering star roles; otherwise no one will want to play the parts. Big stars will only agree to do a film if they get all the good lines and all the memorable moments in the script.

How to Create Quality Premises That Will Be Producible and Marketable

My view is that writers have to create quality scripts that will be producible and marketable, or no one—actor, director, producer, studio executive—will take them seriously. After working in the industry and analyzing industry needs, I've established these working principles to help achieve that goal.

- The premise has to be unique and focused, so it can be pitched in a logline; i.e., a sentence or two, much like a *TV Guide* blurb or a high concept for a new feature film.
- The spine of the story must be clear, and the driving force of the story has to be credible to push your characters into action.
- The characters have to be strongly motivated and susceptible to give them appeal and castability.
- The story has to offer conflicts and twists for your characters to overcome.
- Your writing style must reflect an understanding of production pragmatics.

And what about "theme"? If it's too heavy, it will stick out like a sore thumb. If a writer deliberately pushes a political message, the entertainment value is lost and the ideological statement overshadows it. Theme material is most effective when it springs naturally from the integration of plot, character, and action. Incidentally, the industry uses "theme" to identify the premise of a movie, not the intellectual issues. The studio reader provides a thumbnail sketch of a writer's story—that's the story's theme.

Creating the Driving Force for Characters in the Premise

The easiest way to set up a crisis in the story is to create a *driving force* for your characters. Put them in a situation in which they need to achieve a very important goal. Any obstacle you throw in the way becomes a significant conflict to be resolved. They must overcome those problems with ingenuity and successfully deal with new story twists.

Whether you write for television or motion pictures, you can use the same principles to analyze the effectiveness of the premise. As an example, let's examine sample loglines for television, then motion picture premises.

Television Loglines

In a television series, a premise must be so clear that it can be told in a *logline*. The logline is one or two sentences that describe the story. It looks like a *TV Guide* blurb of any episode for that series. Try to get it as close to the real thing as possible, with the characters driven by motivations and conflicts appropriate for the series. It must sound like the kind of story area that fits into the franchise of the series. The *franchise* is where the story conflict springs from. For example, in "Murder She Wrote," Angela Lansbury's character thinks and acts like a mystery writer.

In a *character-driven* series, the premise is focused on lead characters and relationships, much like "Murphy Brown," "Roseanne," "Northern Exposure," "Seinfeld," "Coach," and the syndicated hit "Cheers." In a *story-driven* show, the premise is centered on action driven by the circumstances faced by the leads. Think of "NYPD Blue," "Law & Order," and "Star Trek: Deep Space Nine."

When writing an episode, focus on the key leads—with all the right actions, reactions, and story twists appropriate for the series. Your logline tells an *A story*, which is the main storyline featuring the lead characters, and a *B story*, if there is one, which outlines a subplot for other leads. In one-hour shows, there may be time to tell a *C story*, which is a subplot involving other characters in the show.

If you are uncertain about the show's structure, you can analyze the loglines from your *TV Guide* or local newspaper. Those are good resources for analyzing the story areas that have already been produced. Also, try to videotape as many episodes as you can so you can analyze the story and act structure from produced episodes.

Analyzing Loglines from Successful Series

These are sample loglines from successful drama and comedy series, with strongly developed characters and conflicts. I've analyzed these loglines to identify the driving force of each story.

NORTHERN EXPOSURE

*A STORY: A former KGB employee arrives with a dossier
revealing that Maurice unknowingly leaked information.
B STORY: Maggie is affected by another flyer's death. C STORY:
A health inspector investigates Holling's restaurant and threatens to close it down.*

Here the A story poses a direct threat to Maurice's sense of honor and
patriotism. That's the driving force of the story. As an ex-NASA (National
Aeronautics and Space Administration) astronaut, he considers himself a
bona fide American hero. At the open, his serenity is thrown into turmoil
by the inciting action—a former KGB agent blackmails him with evidence
that he sold out his country thirty years ago. He had an affair with a
woman, revealing more than she should know about NASA and the CIA.
Maurice feels like he betrayed his country, and he must now deal with
the consequences of that transgression.

The B story is set up around Maggie's reaction to the death of another
flyer. She goes on a quest to find a better way of life, trying to react calmly
to events around her. She ends up giving herself an ulcer. Joel advises her
to give up being extra nice, since it goes against the grain of her personality.

In the C story, Holling's status quo is threatened by the appearance of
a young, handsome health inspector who seems to be taken with Shelley.
The inspector gives the restaurant fourteen days to comply with the
changes or it will be shut down. That's a perfect example of a built-in
"timebomb," or driving force, for the story to unfold.

The driving forces for each of the stories are set up by the actions of
an outside character who affects the leads, but who has appropriately
departed by the episode's resolution.

*A STORY: The romantic mood of Maggie's pizza dinner to cele-
brate Mike's recovery is doused by Mike's announcement that
he must leave Cicely. B STORY: Shelley's redecorating takes its
toll on Holling. C STORY: Maurice brings north the family
home he grew up in, along with melancholy memories of his
childhood.*

The driving force of the A story is Maggie's romantic susceptibility,
motivated by her inner fear of bringing death to her boyfriends. When
Mike recovers from a long illness, she decides to have a romantic dinner

to celebrate. But Mike throws a twist in the plans by letting her know he needs to leave to take on new challenges.

In the B story, Holling's macho-sensitive character is tested beyond endurance when Shelley redecorates their bedroom in pink—including a pink canopied bed with fluffy pillows and a pink wallpapered bathroom. Holling seeks Joel's advice. He wants to make his wife happy, but feels "stopped up" in every aspect of his life as a result of the changes.

The C story exploits the susceptible side of Maurice's character. As a wealthy landowner, he brings the house he grew up in to Cicely. The mementos and memories fog his thoughts with nostalgia, giving us insight into some of his most private moments.

> *A STORY: Spring fever hits Cicely. The town believes Maggie has healing powers after she saves Dave's life. B STORY: Joel tells Shelley she's expecting a baby. C STORY: Maurice and Chris buy a prize pig.*

This episode plays on the peculiarities of the lead characters when spring fever hits the town of Cicely, Alaska. In the A story, the driving force is set up for Maggie's "transformation" when she saves Dave from being hit on the head by a roof extension. Then she gets a thank you note from Mike for saving his life. She finds herself miraculously free from an onslaught of mosquitoes which plagues the town—and which hits Joel in particular. She takes on mythic proportions and is asked to help heal the townspeople. As a result, Maggie's character faces a *motivated* metamorphosis. She's always perceived herself as a negative person with an endless stream of dead boyfriends. Suddenly, she's affecting people in a positive way. It's the new Maggie.

In the B story, spring fever hits Holling hard. He feels the urge to plant seeds in the earth, and almost works himself to death in the process. Joel advises him to take care of a stress-induced muscle spasm, to lie down and relax. He feels crushed. Shelley comforts him by letting him know he planted one heck of a seed that will grow—she's pregnant. At first Holling reveals his own susceptibility, fearful that the kid might be like his own family, a bunch of "sleazoids." But Shelley reassures him their girl can be anything she wants when she grows up.

In the C story, Maurice and Chris buy a prize pig. They expect it to find truffles in time for a Mosquito Festival. But the pig is depressed, and Maurice will give it a few days to succeed—or it will be part of the meal. That serves as a "timebomb," or driving force, for Chris. Maggie suggests that Chris read stories to the pig, which he does. And the pig succeeds in finding the truffles—just in time.

LAW & ORDER

A STORY: An entire police precinct comes under fire when Briscoe and Logan investigate the death of a homosexual police officer who was killed in a drug bust.

The universe of the show is New York realism and the episode deals head on with it. The premise is story driven, playing effectively off the headlines. The driving force of the story is set in motion when a police car dispatcher relays a call for emergency backup: a police officer's been shot. But that backup never arrives. The cop dies waiting for it. The twist occurs when Briscoe and Logan uncover the fact that the cop was homosexual and that the motivation was hatred toward gays in uniform. Our DA (District Attorney) forcefully uncovers evidence that the cops on the force harassed homosexual police officers. When the cops are investigated, tension builds in the city.

The defense lawyer is a strong antagonist. He plays on underlying social fears of gays in uniform, and the cops are eventually acquitted. At the tag, Briscoe and Logan try desperately to undo the damage, but the emotions of the jury overshadow the evidence.

A STORY: Briscoe and Logan's investigation of insulin overdose deaths at a diabetes treatment center reveals a bizarre suspect—the hospital's computer system.

This is another story-driven episode, consistent with the series' intention to have stories as current as news headlines. It deals with a complex case of human glitches in a high-tech computer system.

COACH

A STORY: Hayden attempts to recruit the country's top high school player.

The driving force is set in motion when Hayden finds out about the availability of a top high school player. The Coach is motivated to do anything he can to succeed. That's the nature of his character as created by Barry Kemp. It is the Coach's fatal flaw—and his susceptibility. His actions will inevitably result in relationship clashes with his wife Christine and daughter Kelly.

A STORY: Luther battles the cereal killers that took away his favorite breakfast food. B STORY: Hayden nearly dies laughing when Howard gets a new secretary—his wife.

In the A story, the driving force for Luther is finding out that his favorite cereal is in jeopardy. He stockpiles it in the storage room of the Coach's office, setting up inevitable comedy sight gags.

The B story deals with Hayden's strained relationship with Howard—and his wife. He thinks he has the last laugh when he realizes that the new secretary is Howard's wife. The logline is consistent with the series' intention to deal with character relationships, as well as exposing the comic susceptibility in each of the leads.

ROSEANNE

A STORY: Roseanne's dental problems bring Dan to the realization that he needs a steady job to take care of his family.

The driving force of the story is Roseanne needing expensive dental work. She clashes with Dan over the fact that he can't take care of her. He feels defensive and susceptible in the crisis. To be a "real" man, he's got to take care of his family at all costs, even in the worst of economic times.

A STORY: Darlene thinks it's high time her parents trust her, but Roseanne and Dan may soon regret letting her attend a rock concert with neighbor Molly.

The A story is driven by Darlene's teenage pursuit of independence. She deftly makes her parents feel guilty because they don't trust her to go to a rock concert with Molly. Roseanne and Dan argue with each other and with Darlene. Finally, against their better judgment, they permit her to go—and their worst fears are realized. Darlene comes back early in the morning, trying to cover for Molly who stayed out with a guy, smoking dope. In the tag, Roseanne takes charge and nails Molly.

SEINFELD

A STORY: Jerry and George must think of an idea for a TV series before meeting with network bigs.

A classic setup for the series, which spoofs everyday life. Here the driving force is the need for Jerry and George to come up with an idea for a meeting with the network. They toss out myriad zany ideas, filling themselves with angst, before deciding to pitch a show about "nothing"— and sell it to the network.

A STORY: The gang borrows George's father's car to get an engagement present for a friend. They park in a handicapped space, and as a result a woman in a wheelchair is injured.
B STORY: Kramer falls for the woman.

In the A story, the leads are driven by the need to find a gift quickly for a friend. The only parking spot available is in a handicapped zone. They convince themselves it will be okay and leave George's father's car while they go shopping. The worst of all maudlin incidents happens—a woman in a wheelchair needs the space when her battery pack goes bad. An angry crowd in the parking lot pounds George's father's car to pieces. At the tag, George's father is arrested for parking in a handicapped zone.

The B story plays out the unlikely but traditional account of Kramer falling for the woman.

HOME IMPROVEMENT

A STORY: Jill takes matters into her own hands after Tim begins ignoring household repairs to tinker with his hot rod.

A classic premise for the series. Tim is involved with the macho joy of working on his hot rod and leaves chores at home unattended. That is the driving force for Jill to tackle the problems head on, building comic tensions in the process.

A STORY: Tim confronts Jill about her checking account.
B STORY: Brad becomes careless when he babysits Jennifer's goldfish.

A typical A story. Tim wants Jill to handle money the way he would, as a man. That builds predictable comic conflicts in the relationship, and she counters appropriately.

The B story is about Brad, who is very much like Tim, and there is a mishap with Jennifer's goldfish. The audience will be waiting to see how they handle it with Jennifer.

MURPHY BROWN

A STORY: A Junior High School journalist Hacks Murphy's computer and has stolen a memo that she wrote to her management that criticizes her colleagues.

The A story is driven by Murphy's obsessiveness, and it threatens the tenuous relationship she has with her fellow workers. The story spoofs a real event, about a "Today" show newscaster who wrote a private memo critical of his colleagues, which became headline fodder across the nation. The historical context does not date this logline because it fits so convincingly with the character of Murphy Brown. The jokes play off her own susceptibility.

A STORY: A very pregnant Murphy reluctantly agrees to turn over her duties to a replacement newscaster who is dynamite looking, highly competent, and a threat to her job. B STORY: Murphy discovers her temporary replacement is an alchoholic and must confront her before a newscast.

Here the story moves out of the ordinary episodes, since the universe is dealing with a time frame that is brief—the pregnancy of Murphy. But it addresses a concern the producers may have had: specifically, how to depict Murphy during the late stages of her pregnancy.

In the A story, Murphy gets more and more irritable with her colleagues, and is physically unable to do her work. The driving force is her own demand for control of every aspect of her life, which is spinning away. She is especially susceptible to her replacement when she discovers that the woman is both beautiful and capable.

In the B story, Murphy must confront her own demons by facing an alcoholic professional who is refusing to admit that she is an alcoholic. The B story deals with the realities of alcoholism through comedy conflicts inherent in the characters, staying clear of potential preachiness.

Motion Picture Premises

In features, the premise can be told in carefully crafted sentences, suggesting how characters deal with the driving forces of the story. Screenwriters have to create emotional edges that spark their leads into action. SCHINDLER'S LIST, for example, is about a German industrialist who saved more than 1,300 Jews from Nazi death camps. Characters are deeply textured psychologically and pushed into action in critically acclaimed films like PHILADELPHIA, THE PIANO, SLEEPLESS IN SEATTLE, DAVE, THE FUGITIVE, IN THE NAME OF THE FATHER, THE CRYING GAME, UNFORGIVEN, THE REMAINS OF THE DAY, and THE JOY LUCK CLUB.

High Concepts

A film has a much better shot at being developed if it can be sold as a *high concept*. In a high concept, the premise can be told in a sentence or two, with a unique twist for casting and marketing appeal. For example, SPLASH is a high-concept fantasy: *"What happens if a kid falls in love with a mermaid?"*

In a review of summer releases, film critic Richard Corliss compiled an interesting list of high concepts. Here are a few of the titles and high concepts from that list.[2] Note how the one-liners are witty, original, and get straight to the bottom line of marketing appeal.

JURASSIC PARK: *"Modern dinosaurs snack on theme park visitors"*

SLIVER: *"Voyeur-killer. BASIC INSTINCT, only baser"*

LAST ACTION HERO: *"$60-million remake of PURPLE ROSE OF CAIRO"*

THE FIRM: *"Lawyer Tom Cruise fights in-house conspiracy"*

ROOKIE OF THE YEAR: *"12-year-old pitcher has 100-mph fast ball"*

HOCUS POCUS: *"1692 witch returns to Salem, Mass. for Halloween"*

CONEHEADS: *"Saturday Night at the movies, again"*

SO I MARRIED AN AX MURDERER: *"BASIC INSTINCT for (intentional) laughs"*

Studio readers want the high concept to be appealing to audiences. They've got to see castability, directorial possibilities, production values, and a story that can be sold with a unique hook.

Analyzing Premises from Successful Motion Pictures

These are premises from a few successful motion pictures. To show how the psychological edges of the characters push the action, I have tried to analyze the driving forces for the leads. Try to do the same when you look at films. You can find sample synopses of current films in the trade papers, in motion picture catalogues, or in movie guides. If you have an electronic interactive personal service such as America Online or Prodigy Services Company, you can call up relevant information under any appropriate resource, including *The Magill Movie Guide*.

JURASSIC PARK

Two paleontologists, two kids, a hippie mathematician, and an old billionaire developer get trapped in a high-tech theme park 120 miles off Costa Rica with a horde of hungry prehistoric dinosaurs.

This is a classic survival story written by Michael Crichton in his book and screenplay. He set up an extraordinary universe for the story. In this meeting of man and dinosaurs for the first time in 65 million years, whatever can go wrong will go wrong.

The driving force is set in motion when billionaire developer John Hammond (Sir Richard Attenborough) egotistically invites a select group to be the first to tour the park—before it's ready to open. The complications take off when the guests arrive, including Dr. Alan Grant (Sam Neill), his colleague and love interest Ellie Sattler (Laura Dern), and two insufferable pre-teen kids. They are all awestruck at what they see.

But the first twist occurs when a character motivated by greed interferes with the plans. A computer hack, Dennis Nedry (Wayne Knight), knocks out the security system so he can steal valuable vials of mosquito blood. The second twist occurs when an unexpected storm approaches and the "non-aggressively bred" dinosaurs become hungry and violent. As the crisis unfolds, each of the characters—including the two kids—has to survive in the enemy territory of the stampeding dinosaurs. At the climax, the kids, of course, survive on their own virtues.

When his book, *Jurassic Park*, was first submitted to producers, Michael Crichton's agency, CAA (Creative Artists Agency), bypassed the usual auction process. They submitted it to six studios and a few top film-makers, including Steven Spielberg, with a firm price tag of $2 million for the book. According to *Variety*, $500,000 would go toward a first-draft screenplay written by Michael Crichton. Every studio agreed to the terms, but Crichton chose to develop the script with Steven Spielberg.[3] He knew that Spielberg was a master of storytelling and special effects—an essential element in making the film's dinosaurs "real."

When the film opened, amidst a global marketing blitz by MCA/Universal (which is where Steven Spielberg was headquartered), the film shattered all box office records. In its opening weekend, JURASSIC PARK pulled in more than $48-$50 million in ticket sales, making it the biggest opening weekend in box office history. In 1993, the film grossed $338,929,640, more than any other film.

THE CRYING GAME

A romantic thriller set in Northern Ireland. A sensitive IRA terrorist, Fergus, befriends a British hostage he's been ordered to execute. After the soldier is killed, Fergus flees to London and becomes intimately involved with the soldier's femme fatale lover Dil. Fergus discovers Dil's secret—he is really a transvestite. Fergus must deal with that relationship, forcing him to question his political alliances and his life choices.

The script by Neil Jordan was nominated by the Motion Picture Academy for Best Original Screenplay and for Best Screenplay Written Directly for the Screen by the Writers Guild of America (1993). But the premise was actually considered too political and too "unappealing" for audiences. It was perceived as an art film with little prospect for box office appeal. When it was first scripted, no studio or independent producer wanted anything to do with THE CRYING GAME.

As revealed in an article in *Variety*, Neil Jordan originally wrote the script in 1983, calling it THE SOLDIER'S WIFE. The story was about an IRA member who winds up romantically involved with the wife of a soldier he held hostage. Since it was so heavily political and character driven, no one wanted to finance it. As Neil Jordan recalled, the story was "unformed and incomplete." Eventually he added the twist of a transvestite lover and the story took off.[4]

But the major studios still turned it down. An early version of the film was screened at Cannes, and the studios felt it would not make a profit. Financially troubled Miramax put up $1.5 million, and screened it at film festivals in New York, Toronto, and Telluride. At the screening, audiences were urged by Neil Jordan and Miramax not to reveal the plot twist secret.

That was the marketing ploy that worked. The marketing pitch was meant to play down the story's political elements, and play up the film's premise as "the movie everyone is talking about, but no one is giving away the secrets." They sold it as an action thriller with a big secret. It debuted domestically in November 1992, and earned nearly $40 million in domestic box office gross by March 1993.[5]

That hype usually surrounds films like PSYCHO, and reminds me of the marketing genius of filmmaker William Castle (ROSEMARY'S BABY). I was his associate on the television series based on ROSEMARY'S BABY ("Ghost Story" and "Circle of Fear"). In his heyday, horror film producer William Castle had audiences sign releases that they would not hold the studio liable if they saw the film and had a heart attack. They lined up around the block to see what the fuss was all about.

HOME ALONE

Geeky eight-year-old Kevin is accidentally left home alone by his family, who flew to Paris for Christmas. At first enjoying this unanticipated treat by indulging in junk food and videos, he eventually finds that he must deal with harsh reality—two burglars prowling the emptied house during the holiday season.[6]

In this screenplay by John Hughes, the driving force of the story occurs when Kevin (Macauley Culkin) is left alone and has to deal with his own insecurities—and two burglars. At the beginning of the film we see how vulnerable and susceptible he is in the tumultuous family, which sets him up as an appealing character. When he's left alone in the house, he actually enjoys the freedom to do what he pleases. He's forced to overcome his fear of furnaces, and then must deal with the major driving force—two burglars, Harry (Joe Pesci) and Marv (Daniel Stern). He's compelled to save his home from the intruders. He sets up clever diversion tactics and booby traps. Those actions set up sight gags for the burglars, who have little dialogue but provide funny moments for the audience. By the resolution, Kevin has made a motivated transformation, but wishes for his family back in time for Christmas. Since it is a holiday movie and a fantasy genre, that's exactly what happens.

The film was relatively inexpensive to produce, costing $18 million, and earned nearly three times that at the box office. The character was so well liked and the premise so successful that it was a natural for a sequel, HOME ALONE II—LOST IN NEW YORK. In that premise, Kevin takes the wrong plane to New York, and must fend for himself while his family vacations in Florida. He sets himself up in a fancy suite at the Plaza and deals head on with the two bandits, who also arrive in New York.

BASIC INSTINCT

A psychological cat-and-mouse game being played by a bisexual writer (Catherine) and a San Francisco homicide detective (Nick) who is investigating the ice-pick murder of her male lover. Since a rock singer was also killed with an ice pick in the prime suspect's current best seller, finding the murderer takes on complications before the story is resolved.[7]

In the screenplay by Joe Eszterhas, the story's driving force is Nick's passion for the sexual bait thrown by dangerous and sensual Catherine. He's after the murderer. She is revealed through story twists to be a bisexual ice-pick murderer. Nick's life is on the line, but he craves her.

The script for BASIC INSTINCT earned Eszterhas an enormous screenwriting fee of $3 million. The characters were highly castable, appealing to box office mega-stars Michael Douglas (Nick) and Sharon Stone (Catherine). The film drew protests from gay and lesbian groups who objected to the depiction of a bisexual murderer in the lead role. Still, it grossed more than $350 million globally.

Joe Eszterhas, writer of SLIVER, FLASHDANCE, and JAGGED EDGE, has sold several story ideas that could earn him more than $10 million over the next two years, including a $3.4 million script about mobster John Gotti. Interviewed in *Time*, Eszterhas is depicted as a feisty screenwriter who fights vigorously to keep the controversial elements and intense atmosphere in his scripts: "I've always believed in fighting for my work . . . I've taken great pride in being a writer, and I demanded a certain kind of treatment. When I haven't been treated that way, I've either fought back very hard or I've walked."[8]

MY COUSIN VINNY

Vinny, a Brooklyn attorney who just passed the bar exam, is asked to defend his cousin Bill and his college friend, Stan, who are being tried in a small town in Alabama for a murder they didn't commit. With his sexy girlfriend, Mona Lisa, he sets the local court system on its ear with his unorthodox methods.[9]

This is a high-concept comedy by Dale Launer: *"What happens when a Brooklyn lawyer who just passed the bar goes to Alabama to defend his cousin on murder charges?"* The driving force of the story is set up by the arrest of Bill (Ralph Macchio) and Stan (Mitchell Whitfeld), who accidentally shoplift a can of tuna and mistakenly confess to a murder charge. They call Vinny (Joe Pesci) to help. Vinny arrives in his pink Eldorado with his sexy girlfriend Mona Lito Lisa (Marisa Tomei). In the script,

Vinny and Mona are despised by everybody else in town, including the judge (Fred Gwynne) who cites Vinny for contempt at every turn. Vinny and Mona Lisa are driven to help at all costs, and prove themselves to be intelligent and imposing combatants. At the resolution, they win the case and free Bill and Stan.

UNFORGIVEN

William Munny, a retired outlaw who is now a farmer, takes up his gun again and rides with old pal Ned Logan and youthful Schofield Kid because he needs the reward money. The bounty hunters face brutal law enforcement opposition from Sheriff Little Bill Daggett.[10]

This is a western, but with classy dimension and castable characters. The script, by David Webb Peoples, was nominated by the Motion Picture Academy for Best Original Screenplay and by the Writers Guild of America for Best Screenplay Written Directly for the Screen (1993).

At the outset, we are introduced to Munny (Clint Eastwood), a legendary ex-gunfighter who admits he's been "lucky when it comes to killing people." We get to know him as a widower who barely makes a living as a pig farmer to support himself and his two kids. That's the susceptibility that makes him likeable for the audience.

The driving force of the story is set up when the hothead young gunslinger Schofield (Jaimz Woolvett) lures Will to join him on a bounty hunt. He needs the money and the motivation is set up for one last ride. Will pulls in his old partner Ned (Morgan Freeman), and they all set off for the bounty hunt in Wyoming.

The story creates a powerful antagonist in the character of the sheriff (Gene Hackman), who is viscerally opposed to bounty hunters in his county. So the characters of Will and the sheriff are driven, by their natures, to a bloody showdown in the climax.

As you can see, in successful premises the lead characters are integrally related to the plotting, credibly motivated, and dimensionally conceived.

Adaptations

With an increased marketplace for features and longform TV based on a novel or play, the process of adapting literary works has become an important skill for many writers. In a novel, an author can spend a great deal of time on character development, exposition, the free association of time and place. In a motion picture script, that same story must be told in a 120-minute structure. That means streamlining the plot and characters from the book.

A screenwriter must be an artistic surgeon, with a very fine and sensitive touch, knowing what must go and what must stay. Ideally, the adaptation should remain faithful to the original work, conveying the same feeling, atmosphere, plot, and characterization—even though scenes, characters, and conflicts have been modified. The final project must be producible and castable.

To give you a sense of the scope of the job, consider these character-driven feature scripts adapted from another medium, and nominated for Best Screenplay awards by the Writers Guild of America. In 1993, the Writers Guild certified 117 original screenplays eligible for nomination, and 85 in the adaptation category.[11]

SCHINDLER'S LIST by Steven Zaillian

THE FUGITIVE by Jeb Stuart and David Twohy from a story by Twohy

IN THE NAME OF THE FATHER by Terry George and Jim Sheridan

THE JOY LUCK CLUB by Amy Tan and Ronald Bass

THE REMAINS OF THE DAY by Ruth Prawer Jhabvala

The previous year saw these nominees in the adaptation category.

GLENGARRY GLEN ROSS by David Mamet, based on his play

ENCHANTED APRIL by Peter Barnes, based on the novel by Elizabeth von Arnim

HOWARDS END by Ruth Prawer Jhabvala, based on the novel by E. M. Forster

THE PLAYER by Michael Tolkin, based on his book

SCENT OF A WOMAN by Bo Goldman, suggested by a character from *Profuma di Donna* by Ruggero Maccari and Dino Risi and the novel *Il Buio e Il Miele* by Giovanni Arpino

The scripts are based on successful, high-quality novels and plays, with strong character development and casting appeal. As for new writers adapting published works, it will be no more than an exercise in futility if *acquisition rights* for television and film are not obtained in advance. Producers, major studios, production companies, networks, HBO, Showtime, and cable TV are in a constant competitive bidding war for new material and they have enormous financial resources behind them. Chances are very slim that they'll miss a newly published piece, and even slimmer that a newcomer will outbid them.

In the face of that discouraging reality, a determined writer might still dig up an old paperback or newspaper headline that has outstanding casting and marketing potential. If you do find a project that seems suited for adaptation, investigate the legal situation thoroughly. Contact an attorney to clear the names, events, and titles. Contact the publisher, or the attorney for the estate, to be certain that the rights are available. If you're lucky, you might get the rights by offering them participation in profits.

The actual form of adapted works is the same as for any well-written screenplay. It conveys the appropriate atmosphere, characterization, and dramatic integrity of the published novel or story. Do a treatment first to get a handle on the dramatic structure for the script.

Longform Television

In longform television film, where exploitation reigns, some quality character-driven projects can occasionally surface. Michael Weisbarth, co-executive producer of the Emmy-winning miniseries "LONESOME DOVE," told me that his project had a difficult birth at the network. Based on a Larry McMurtry novel, the script promised quality, atmosphere, and complex characters. However, no western had been on the air in some time, and the network did not think it would get an audience. The script, like every script in Hollywood, was put through multiple revisions. Weisbarth is a creative producer with integrity and vision, and the final shooting script closely matched the atmosphere in the book, focusing on complex character development. As a result, the script was eminently castable and made a uniquely literate miniseries that found an audience.

In the early days of primetime programming, television movies and miniseries were high-prestige items. Based on books or original scripts, they featured top writers, producers, actors, and directors. But as costs have escalated, and as audiences have fled from the network landscape, much has changed. Television movies and miniseries are extremely expensive to develop and produce and have little opportunity to win back their costs. The typical cost for a longform script in 1994 was $25,000-$100,000. The production budget could exceed $3.6 million. The networks provide only a small portion of the production costs. A license fee is negotiated, but it is much less than the production budget. Consequently, producers must find other resources for "deficit financing."[12]

As a result, development executives find themselves in a frantic race to outbid each other for high-visibility, exploitive projects based on fact. During "sweeps" weeks, their appeal to sordid interests is unflappable. The topic has to be relevant, sexy, and exploitive for marketing appeal.

Think about the headlines surrounding Amy Fisher, the "Long Island Lolita," who tried to kill the wife of her alleged lover, Joey Buttafuoco. Three of the major networks put together deals to produce films from slightly different angles. And they got high ratings. Variety correctly identified the fiasco as a "form of cultural humiliation."[13]

Yet despite the promise of restraint, the acquisition chase became unshackled. The networks battled for the rights to two different longform films about the Menendez brothers, accused of murdering their wealthy parents. Then they brawled over acquisition rights for television films based on the attack on Nancy Kerrigan, Olympic ice skating medalist winner, by her rival, Tonya Harding. As reported in Variety, ABC's leading bid for a story on Nancy Kerrigan came from Steve Tisch, in association with Disney.[14] It included an ABC movie, a primetime special, an association for Nancy Kerrigan with Disney theme parks, and a Disney book deal. The movie fee, negotiated by William Morris, exceeded one million. In the meantime, Fox developed the story from the perspective of the plot to injure Nancy Kerrigan. The producers, Citadel Productions (partly owned by HBO), used court documents as their public domain resource.

Exploitive Premises

Think about what this kind of assignment means for writers. They need to find the right story angle for the characters featured, undertake extensive research from public records, tie the story elements together, and deal with ethical issues. They also face unrealistic deadlines imposed by the networks on producers.

"IN THE LINE OF DUTY: AMBUSH IN WACO" was produced by Kenneth Kaufman, who specializes in television movies about law enforcement officers. The film was about David Koresh and four agents from the Bureau of Alcohol, Tobacco, and Firearms who were shot by members of the Branch Davidian cult. The producer conceded facing enormous pressure to get the film completed in time. He was also overwhelmed by the extensive amount of research. The writers investigated public records, consultants from law enforcement, and people from the cult.[15]

John McMahon, producer of "WITHOUT WARNING: TERROR IN THE TOWERS" specializes in psychological mystery films for the USA cable network. His project dealt with people trapped in the World Trade Center bombing. The producer was determined to develop the premise as a heroic story, rather than focusing on the disaster: "We put together enough to dramatize the story in quite an uplifting way. That was the whole point. We weren't planning to do a story about a disaster and dead and injured people . . . The core of the movie was heroic acts in one of the worst terrorist attacks on U.S. soil ever."[16] One of the most challenging problems he faced was meeting the accelerated time frame mandated by the networks.

Another longform producer, Brian Pike, producer of "TRIUMPH OVER DISASTER" relates the same problems. The premise centered on a TV weatherman who calmed Miami during the storm that ravaged Florida: "This is microwave movie making. I've never done anything this fast in my life."[17] Pike received the assignment from Warren Littlefield, NBC Entertainment president. At first, he refused, saying he did not want to exploit someone else's tragedy. Then he decided to handle the story in a way that would focus on heroes, people who calmed Miami in the face of disaster.

Brian Pike is a respected veteran of television drama, who spent almost a decade developing dramatic programs for NBC. He has a particularly relevant perspective about ethics and creativity for writers and producers of longform drama: "Real life events have always been a mainstay of television . . . What is new is this frenetic rush to the screen . . . To me, drama is about the introspection of character, and when you are rushing to the screen, there is no time for that. You are limited to recreating the events. A writer and a producer do not have the time to wrestle with ethics and morality. My fear is that we are going to breed a generation of writers who are efficient regurgitaters. There is something very creative in this process, but that's not drama—that's a new form."[18]

As a direct result of violence depicted in sweeps weeks, industry executives from networks and cable companies met with Senator Paul Simon (D-Ill) at a hearing of the Judiciary Subcommittee on the Constitution. At that session, Warren Littlefield, NBC Entertainment president, apologized for the network's response to competition for viewers and advertising. He said he regretted airing "MURDER IN THE HEARTLAND," based on the killing spree of Charles Starkweather. That TV film inspired a copycat killing in Canada. "We thought it was a good idea at the time. But it got poor ratings and was an economic disaster."[19] George Vradenburg, executive VP of Fox Broadcasting, argued that his network put violence in the proper social perspective. Shows like "America's Most Wanted" and "Cops" are dedicated to the prevention of violent crimes. He pointed out that "America's Most Wanted" has directly led to the apprehension of hundreds of felons.

In an effort to solve the problem of gratuitous violence, an unprecedented meeting of executives from broadcasting, cable, and motion pictures was held in Los Angeles.

The ethical issue is frustrating for writers—who disdain censorship in any form. In a cover story on the moral climate of screenwriting, *The Journal of the Writers Guild of America* interviewed professionals about their perceptions of violence in films. Oscar winner Ron Bass (RAIN MAN, co-writer of THE JOY LUCK CLUB) doesn't think violent films result in violent acts, but has this conviction about the artistic integrity of his own work: "Film frames issues in a way that impacts on large numbers of people. It frequently happens that we're talking about notes in a situation, and I'll say, is this what we really want our film to say? Is that insensitive to these values? or to women?"[20] He recounts only one argument with Amy Tan (THE JOY LUCK CLUB) concerning a sex scene in the nightclub. She thought it was gratuitous, he felt it was critical for the audience to understand how completely this woman was taken by the male character.

Thriller writer Dan Waters (DEMOLITION MAN, HEATHERS, BATMAN RETURNS) places the writing process in this context: "I'm at a certain point in the chain, and I'd hate to be thinking, while I'm writing, about what the effect on society is going to be. If you try to ask me to think about social responsibility, it creates bad art."[21] Justifying violent films as art is film writer Tim Metcalf (KALIFORNIA): "I think that great violent movies do exist . . . And they have the same good effect on people that you would get from seeing a Rembrandt hanging on the wall. Maybe they have a bad effect on the wrong people, but an insane person can misuse a chainsaw."[22]

In a free society, we've got the freedom to write anything we want, and it is appropriate for the public to have a multitude of choices. The industry is economically driven, and responds to box office hits and misses. The dilemma is that some producers have gone to extremes.

For screenwriters, "gratuitous" violence can be evaluated this way. Ask yourself if the violent action is necessary for heightened dramatic story telling. Does it tell us about the drives of characters? Does it move the story forward? The violence in UNFORGIVEN sets up justifiable actions and reactions for the characters to push the story forward. It is consistent with the character development and established conflicts, and is integral to the credibility of the film.

Writing for Interactive Programs and New Technologies

If you are interested in writing for interactive programs, the marketplace is at the cutting edge, and deserves serious attention. But it is difficult to give straightforward advice, because the technology is still emerging and the development process includes so many different players.

New technologies and interactive programs have aptly been dubbed "Silicon Valley's Version of Development Hell."[23] As pointed out in *Variety*, there is no single accepted formula for developing and producing interactive projects. The script for Media Vision's interactive multi-media game, "Road Scholar," was over 1,000 pages. Electronic Arts' science fiction project, "Shock Wave," was over 500 pages. The design document for Rocket Science Games' "Loadstar" was over 500 pages. This is how Steve Barrett, VP of Rocket Science, describes the development process for new interactive projects: "It usually starts with a place and characters . . . but the game player's action can take interactive stories in several different directions."[24]

One thing developers of interactive games agree on is that it is more collaborative than screenwriting, particularly with respect to the technical elements. With the advent of CD-ROM, a lot more material is being written, and companies want to know who will be helping writers execute the idea.

In interactive games and new technologies, writers must create a *design document*. That document is the equivalent of a film script. It's filled with intricate creative and technical elements. This is how it is described by Strauss Zelnick, president of Crystal Dynamics, former president and CEO of 20th Century Fox: "It might have elements of a script, elements of a novel, computer elements, mathematical elements, and even financial elements . . . All of these areas are just as important."[25]

Another informed perspective is offered by Michael Backes, co-founder of Rocket Science Games and co-screenwriter of "Rising Sun": "Up to now, the environment has been more important than the narrative . . . There's no equivalent to that in the movie world. The development process is much more intense in the game world at the beginning . . . To some degree, the story is driven by the users. An author's opinion about the choices made in the game is less important. What is more important is making sure the environment is rich enough."[26]

The fact is writers who design new programs work with many collaborators to get the project developed. This is how *Variety* interprets the strategy: "Typically, once a pitch is approved, it is turned into a treatment, which usually outlines the game elements in addition to production values and production costs. From there, the project goes to script stage, with numerous people involved."[27] Among the people involved are the game designer, production designer, conception designer, and producer.

The writer's role has expanded, and designers are now eligible for membership in the Writers Guild of America. They sought eligibility through initiatives of the Creative Media and Technologies Committee and the Guild's Department of Industry Alliance. David Vowell, a member of that committee, underscores the rationale: "Companies call them designers . . . but after reading the job description in company contracts, I call them writers. The Designer shall write documents defining the story line . . . write detailed descriptions of all interactive elements . . . write text character sheets on all characters . . . The writer shall also write all text and dialogue."[28]

That same creative process is delineated by Roger Holzberg, writer-designer for Knowledge Adventure, and a feature screenwriter: "For me the process of writing is exactly the same as the process of designing. It's facing a blank page or screen and coming up with creative vision. Writers shouldn't be afraid of considering themselves designers as well."[29]

Michele Em, a writer-producer, wrote her first interactive script for the best-selling CD-ROM hit, "Return to Zork" and an interactive screenplay for Disney, "Pirates of the Carribean." In a cover story for the *Journal of the Writer's Guild of America West*, on writing for the interactive market, she offers these insights:

> Writing interactively is a seat-of-the-pants operation. The design document serves as the blueprint, and is complex and invaluable. It is a cross between a production manager's breakdown and a step outline, and it takes a lot of imagination and technical ability to generate a good one . . . I caution you against jumping right in and announcing that you can do it all. This is a complicated business. An interactive script differs in a number of ways from a linear narrative script. The parameters are different from film or television. Depending on your target platform (CD-ROM, Sega Saturn, Genesis, floppy disk, on-line, to name a few), the limitations of playback are going to affect your dialogue. Sometimes your dialogue is going to be in text form for one platform and spoken for another.[30]

Just like the screenwriter, the creative designer does the concept and theme, and helps shape the final product.

ENDNOTES

1. William Goldman, *Adventures in the Screen Trade* (New York: Warner Books, 1983), 112.
2. Richard Corliss, "Rating the Hot Weather Hopefuls," *Time*, May 24, 1993, 73-74.

3. Peter Bart, "Mythic Megapix," *Variety*, June 21, 1993, 6.

4. "Crying All the Way to the Bank," *Variety*, March 22, 1993, 68.

5. "Art House Heavyweights," *Variety*, March 22, 1993, 68.

6. Synopsis in *The Magill Movie Guide*, 1993.

7. Ibid.

8. Jeffrey Ressner, "Gonzo Screenwriter," *Time,* May 31, 1993, 64.

9. Synopsis from *The Magill Movie Guide*, 1993.

10. Ibid.

11. "WGA Nominations Swing into Action, Comedies," *The Hollywood Reporter*, Feb 9, 1994, 19.

12. For a discussion of the impact of deficit financing, see Richard Lindheim and Richard Blum, *Inside Television Producing* (Boston: Focal Press, 1991), 24-29.

13. "Skategate Puts Webs on a Slippery Slope," *Variety*, Feb 7-13, 1994, 1.

14. Ibid., 65.

15. Patricia Brennan, "TV Drama Recipe," *Washington Post TV Week*, May 23-29, 1993, 7.

16. Ibid.

17. Ibid.

18. Ibid., 45.

19. "TV Networks Promise Lawmakers a Harder Line Against Violence," *The Washington Post*, May 23, 1993, A-5.

20. Catherine Seipp, "One From the Heart: Do Writers Affect the Moral Climate?", *The Journal of the Writers Guild of America West*, December/January 1994, 19.

21. Ibid.

22. Ibid.

23. Andy Marx, "Interactive Development: The New Hell," *Variety*, Feb. 28-March 6, 1994, 1, 78-79.

24. Ibid., 78.

25. Ibid.

26. Ibid.

27. Ibid.

28. Buzz Dixon, "poTAY to, po TAH to," *Journal of Writers Guild of America West*, December-January 1994, 43.

29. Ibid.

30. Michele Em, "The Ever-Changing Story: Writing for the Interactive Market," *Journal of Writers Guild of America West*, June 1994, 16.

3

How to Create
Marketable Series Concepts

Defining Concepts, Series Presentations, Bibles, Loglines

Industry jargon is rife with terminology for concepts, loglines, series presentations, and bibles. The terms are often used interchangeably and can be confusing. In this chapter we'll focus on concepts for original television series. The *concept* is the blueprint for the arena/setting, characters, and conflicts. It is the skeletal premise for the show. It serves as the foundation for the more detailed presentation.

A fully developed concept is called a *series presentation*. It is the entire description of the show, with fully fleshed-out stories and characters. In its most detailed form, it is called a *bible*. That is a thoroughly fleshed-out treatment of characters, dramatic narrative, and multi-part storylines. As we've seen in the previous chapter, a *logline* is the premise for a television episode, which can be encapsulated in a *TV Guide* marketing blurb.

How Series Concepts Are Developed

Developing new series has been described as television's oldest crap shoot. In the heyday of network programming, the logic, if it could be called that, was to bombard the network with thousands of ideas, and somehow one or two would make it to pilot.

When network executives were out for the largest possible audiences, it was logical to ask why they didn't break away from trends rather than imitate them. In the early days of network dominance, a classic theory was proposed by program executive Paul Klein. It was called *L.O.P.*—

"Least Objectionable Programming." The idea was simple. If a show didn't offend anyone, it would appeal to the widest possible audience. If ABC came out with a show about a group of singing termites—and if that show went through the roof of ratings' homes—NBC and CBS would have similar shows in development faster than you could call an exterminator.

But as audiences defected to competitors like Fox, Cable, HBO, Showtime, and pay TV, networks had to pay more attention to smaller, low-budget demographic targets, as well as specific weaknesses in time periods.

A program development executive receives thousands of submissions each year—in verbal pitches, in written concepts, in fully detailed presentations. He or she is responsible for bringing new ideas into the network or cable company. Once the show actually gets on the air, another department takes over—current programming. That department is concerned with time slots, competition, demographic appeal, lead-in and lead-out programs, and other factors that will affect the ratings performance.

At the networks, job security is about as stable as the changing decimals on the overnight ratings. So, understandably, some executives view innovative program concepts as a threat rather than a challenge. Jobs are literally dependent upon ideas that are greeted with enthusiasm by senior management, advertisers, and the whimsical public. If the show is inexpensive and modeled after a highly successful show, the personal risk is minimized. The executive can always blame the unpredictable tastes of the viewing public.

Does this mean you have to create the same kind of formula programs you see every night? In one sense, yes. In another sense, no. Let me explain. Television is an imitative medium. It thrives on successes and spits out a slew of spin-offs in an effort to reach the same target audiences. We've all experienced the competitive glut of sitcoms, reality-based shows, police drama, and law shows.

That doesn't mean that new ideas or innovative concepts won't make it to the screen. Each television season brings many examples of shows that break new ground. Consider "Seinfeld," "Northern Exposure," "Law & Order," "NYPD Blue," and earlier hits like "Cheers," "All in the Family," "Star Trek," and "Miami Vice." The fact is, once the ground is broken, the *imitation syndrome* runs rampant, and we quickly forget that one show was the forerunner of the current trend.

After analyzing the program development deals, this is how *Variety* summed up the trends for 1993: "Reality based programming, action hours, and the ghetto as a radical chic locale are all part of the pilot landscape. In addition, nearly every net is casting about for a hit sitcom. The phrase 'next season's "Home Improvement" ' is perhaps the most tiresome phrase that tumbles off the tongue of studio execs."[1]

In developing a new concept, it is important to think about the specific target audience it can appeal to—program executives will try to fill those demographic voids. For example, in 1993, NBC broke from its long-standing hold on adults 18–49 by signing development deals with comic John Larroquette, former star of "Night Court." CBS had a strong lineup of "female-skewed" shows, including a second comedy from "Murphy Brown" producers Diane English and Shukovsky Entertainment. One-hour action adventure shows had more appeal than softer drama series. ABC built up its action lineup for men with Steven Bochco's "NYPD Blue," and Tom Fontana's "Philadelphia Heat." Fox did a complete turnaround from its reliance on younger demographics to develop cop shows, fantasy shows, and westerns like "The Adventures of Briscoe County, Jr." and "Darkman."

These are some series concepts developed for the networks in that season. Note how they can be pitched as one-liners.[2]

> "The John Larroquette Show": *"Night Court" star as a guy who hits bottom and works in a bus depot*

> "Viper": *near-future action show that stars Chrysler's State of the Art sports car*

> "South Central": *inner-city family comedy from Ralph Farquahar ("Drexel's Class") and Michael Weithorn ("Family Ties")*

> "Knight Rider": *two-hour pilot about a woman scientist trapped in cyberspace*

> "Philadelphia Heat": *"Hill Street Blues" in a firehouse*

Creating Marketable Television Concepts

To give you a sense of how marketable concepts are developed, here are some strategies that Richard Lindheim and I detailed in *Primetime: Network Television Programming*.[3] They have been revised here to incorporate some of the latest series trends. Television professionals acknowledge that ideas are as free as the breeze. It is the successful execution of ideas that counts.

What Makes an Effective Series Concept?

These seem to be the key elements for effective series concepts: the desirability of the inherent idea, the ability to sustain the concept over many episodes, and internal conflict among series characters.

The Desirability of the Inherent Idea

The first question usually asked of any new project is, "Why will people watch this show?" In network and cable programming, each series
must carve itself a sufficient audience to survive. Networks especially
demand large audiences, numbering tens of millions, to achieve competitive ratings. New series must be inherently desirable and appealing to
draw those potential viewers

Any idea for a series must demonstrate desirability. Specifically, this
means a concept should answer affirmatively at least one of the following
questions.

(1) Is the basic storytelling arena interesting?

Is the idea set in a desirable and exotic locale (Florida, Hawaii, San
Francisco, the Caribbean)? Does it feature interesting occupations (deep
sea diver, astronaut, race car driver, mystery writer, policeman, trial attorney, TV journalist, TV comic, bar owner)? Does it have the ability to use
unusual and fascinating machinery or technology (special cars, weapons,
high-tech equipment)? Does it lend itself to an interesting visual
approach?

(2) Does the concept represent some form of wish fulfillment?

In our turbulent society, there are few places where people can turn
to satisfy the frustrations of everyday life. Many long-running television
series trade upon this frustration by showing a more comforting world, or
focusing on characters we would like to believe exist. We can fantasize
about the lifestyle of characters like those in "The Fresh Prince of Bel Air,"
"Northern Exposure," "Baywatch," or the classic "Love Boat."

(3) Is the concept relatable?

Does the idea feature characters and circumstances we can accept as
real? Television series provide us with a sense of verisimilitude, or the
appearance of reality. Under these conditions we could accept Seinfeld
as a standup comic with zany next-door neighbors, "Law & Order" as an
inside look at real justice in New York, "M*A*S*H" as a realistic war
comedy. We could accept "Home Improvement," "Roseanne," and "The
Bill Cosby Show" as a mirror of life in the nineties.

The Ability to Sustain the Concept over Many Episodes

One of the prime causes of failure in television series is the inability to sustain the premise over the three to five years necessary for financial success. Too often a network will commission a pilot that seems innovative only to discover later that it lacks the elements necessary to sustain itself over time.

Frequently network programmers will be attracted to a pilot story that is a *premise pilot*. A premise pilot story is one which shows how the characters get together. It sets the stage for the rest of the series. Unfortunately, it may be a poor indicator of what the series will be. Network development executives want assurances that the expensive pilot they commission will represent the series to come. At NBC and ABC, a rule of thumb was that the first half of the pilot establish the premise, but the remainder represent a "typical" episode. CBS almost always rejected premise pilots in favor of *midcut pilots*. That story is written as if it were being produced for the middle of the series.

Internal Conflict among Series Characters

An often overlooked but essential ingredient of both drama and comedy series is *internal conflict*. Murphy Brown is an emotional powerhouse who will clash with anyone in her way. Tensions between Maggie and Joel are rife in "Northern Exposure." Quincy was the bane of his superiors' existence. Archie and Meathead clashed on "All in the Family," as did Hawkeye and Frank Burns on "M*A*S*H."

The necessity for internal conflict fulfills important dramatic needs. Conflict is the simplest way for characters to express their opposing feelings and attitudes. If all the continuing characters love one another, all they can do is smile and support each other. That can be boring and saccharine. It fails to provide dramatic tension, and fails to provide viewers with insights into the inner life of lead characters.

As discussed in Chapter Four, the strongest series concepts tend to feature individuals who are trapped in a group or family story pattern. Those leads are forced to interact with each other by circumstance. It creates ongoing internal conflicts for characters featured in "Seinfeld," "Murphy Brown," "The John Larroquette Show," "Love and War," "Cheers," "Law & Order," "NYPD Blue," "Northern Exposure," and "M*A*S*H."

Sample Concepts from Successful Series

Let's analyze the series concept for "Coach." The series was created by writer-executive producer Barry Kemp.[4]

THE CONCEPT FOR "COACH"

Coach Hayden Fox (Craig T. Nelson) heads the athletic department at Minnesota State University. In his
early forties with a perennially losing football team,
he recognizes, but is not willing to admit, that the
forward progression of his career has ended. His
only hope is to meld the disparate team into an
effective unit. His only help in this task are the
assistant coaches, Luther (Jerry Van Dyke) and
Dauber (Bill Fagerbakke). Dauber is also a member
of the team and holds the record for being a student
at the University for the most number of years.

Coach Fox has been divorced for many years, and
has had little if any contact with his daughter Kelly
(Clare Carey). Recently, he has developed a relationship with Minneapolis newscaster Christine (Shelley
Fabares).

In the pilot story Coach Fox learns that his daughter
is entering Minnesota State as a freshman. He feels
uncomfortable as a father, but desperately wants to
re-establish a relationship with her. At the same
time, he feels awkward about exposing Kelly to his
emerging relationship with Christine.

The concept for "Coach" sets up unique character drives, strong
potential dramatic conflicts for each of the lead characters, and is set
within the setting/arena of a midwest campus. The Coach is faced with
the angst of midlife crisis, needing to succeed at all costs. He is going
against his own grain to build nurturing relationships with Christine and
Kelly. His girlfriend and daughter become pivotal additions to the potential conflicts in future episodes.

Let's analyze another sample concept, "Law & Order." This series was
created by writer and executive producer Dick Wolf.[5]

THE CONCEPT FOR "LAW & ORDER"

The pilot story for "Law & Order" is told through
the eyes of the two police officers assigned to the
case and two prosecuting attorneys who follow the

case to its conclusion. The police officers are older detective sergeant Max Greevey (George Dzundza) and younger detective Mike Logan (Chris Noth). The prosecuting attorneys are assistant district attorney Ben Stone (Michael Moriarty) and his assistant district attorney Paul Robinette (Richard Brooks).

Deliberately, there are no scenes without one of the principal characters present. The audience learns information only when it is revealed to the principal characters. In the pilot story, Greevey and Logan arrive at a crime scene, where a politically connected individual has been robbed and murdered. Tracking the perpetrators, they learn that the victim had been shot before the robbery. District attorneys Stone and Robinette are assigned to the case. Working with the prosecutors, they uncover a trail of cover-up and police corruption at the highest levels. The four leading characters, working together, trap the mob leader responsible for the killing, along with his illicit political cohorts. The final scene features assistant district attorney Stone delivering his opening remarks at the trial.

In "Law & Order" the stories are as current as the daily news headlines. Dick Wolf felt his bible was the New York newspapers. He had always conceived the series as taking place in New York City, and felt that the setting/arena of the "Big Apple" was essential to the ambiance of the series.

Unlike "Coach," this concept is totally story driven. Dick Wolf wanted the series to seem fresh against the flood of conventional character-oriented series. He chose what writers call a *closed story* structure for the show. A *closed story* is the classic mystery structure of whodunits. The only information the viewer receives is information obtained by the principal characters. In an *open story*, the viewer is provided with information that the principal characters do not have. In some shows, like "Columbo," the audience quickly learns the identity of the murderer. The crux of the open mystery story is to see how one side triumphs over the other.

How to Write Original Series Presentations

A written series presentation details these elements: arena/setting, characters, pilot story, and sample storylines.

The Arena/Setting

The first section of a written concept provides a description of the basic arena for the series.

Locations are often key elements in setting a TV series. Hawaii has been found to be charming and desirable. Florida is a hot spot. San Francisco has proven to be a favorite for a number of successful shows. New York is interesting, though expensive. New Orleans is a colorful favorite. Washington, D.C. is an interesting political backdrop. Other locales seem less appealing, probably due to production limitations. Chicago is attractive, but it is difficult to film there during the winter. Water (and underwater) shows are highly attractive (like "Seaquest") but very complex to execute on television budgets and schedules.

This is a sample of the arena/setting for a series called "Beltway Bandits," created by Frank Tavares and me.

BELTWAY BANDITS

Washington, D.C. Capital of the free world. Center of government for the richest nation on Earth. Surrounding this powerful city are dozens of suburbs—communities that house the tens of thousands who daily fight the heavy traffic on their way to offices in the federal metropolis—communities connected by hundreds of miles of local highways and expressways, and the infamous Washington Beltway.
The Beltway circles the waist of the city, looping in and out of Maryland and Virginia suburbs. Small companies, many of them high-tech consulting firms, are located in towns close to Beltway exits. They avoid the high expense and congestion of the city while easily accessing the corporations and government agencies in Washington.

With perseverance, luck, and occasional connections, the consulting firms that surround the city—the "Beltway Bandits"—compete for corporate and federal contracts to provide services and advice in every conceivable field.

Mark Cole, Tony Miller, and Renee Carlson are partners in one such suburban enterprise. Taking the bull by the horns, they've called their undertaking "Beltway Bandits, Inc.," figuring their creative posture will attract more clients than it will repulse. And so far, it's been working.

The Characters

Program development executives have learned that continuing lead characters are the key element to any successful series. Concepts contain detailed descriptions of lead characters, often including a biography that is rarely referred to in the pilot or series. Such detailed biographies provide valuable insight, especially for casting.

In preparing a concept it is not unusual for a writer or producer to contact talent agents to determine whether available known actors might be interested in the still-evolving concept. If the response is positive, the leading character may be molded after that particular actor.

In almost all circumstances a prototype or model for the leading character is identified. These are usually well-established film stars or personalities, who would never actually work in a series. Their names provide convenient images. A leading character may be described as an "Eddie Murphy type" or a "new Kathleen Turner."

This is an example of how characters are described in the series presentation for "Beltway Bandits."

THE CHARACTERS

MARK COLE, in his late thirties, is a small, well-built man who works hard to thwart the symptoms of approaching middle age. A James Spader type, he has a background in computer science and electrical engineering, and spent twelve long years working for the Department of Energy. He is level-headed and conservative, always one to carefully think things through before making decisions. His mid-life crisis was jump-started when his wife changed careers and filed for divorce just when he thought he was happily married. The divorce action has been dragging on much longer than anticipated and in the interim he's been sharing an apartment with his old high school buddy, best friend, and business partner, TONY MILLER.

TONY MILLER, also in his late thirties, is rugged and athletic. Unlike Mark, he's a risk taker, always ready to try something new. A Tom Hanks lookalike, he has had a varied and adventurous career as a writer and investigative journalist. He's been an important source of support for Mark—and a source of angst, leading the intractable Mark into uncharted territory.

RENEE CARLSON, in her late twenties, is appealing, magnetic, a Sharon Stone lookalike. Her appearance belies years of intense training as an agent for a branch of the National Security Council, referred to only as "The Agency." Although still subject to call by the Agency, she is able to work as a free agent with Mark and Tony. Her covert experience and discipline are invaluable assets for the team. She loves the work they do, but Washington is not where she wants to be. Born and raised in the Southwest, Renee is a desert artist at heart and cherishes the time she is able to steal in the quiet studio abode she inherited from her father in Nevada. Her frequent travel between her Washington townhouse and desert home is a source of humor and frustration for Mark and Tony, who argue about the injustice of Renee having four times their closet space.

The temperaments and talents of the three Beltway Bandits are different, but their friendship is cemented in a shared experience—one that began as a result of a freelance writing assignment that Tony undertook with Mark along as a lark. It was through this adventure that the two men met Renee in a dangerous exploit that permanently changed all of their lives.

The Pilot Story

A concept almost always contains a brief description of the proposed premise story that begins the series. It sets the characters in place, and provides the jumping-off point for the series. If the concept is accepted, it will be expanded to a detailed story outline, and subsequently to a full-fledged pilot script.

This is the pilot story for the series "Beltway Bandits." It's written in a typical story treatment structure.

BELTWAY BANDITS
PILOT STORY

Mark Cole is a twelve-year veteran of the Department of Energy (DOE) in Washington. Recently separated, he's temporarily living with his buddy Tony Miller, a freelance journalist. The two plan a weekend adventure in Las Vegas to lift their spirits. Tony has a writing assignment near there, and Mark tricks the DOE computer—and his chain-smoking supervisor, Stanley—into assigning him a field survey of a Nevada solar energy project a few miles away.

They soon find themselves at a small motel bar in Elton, Nevada, populated by rowdy locals, some of whom work for Hazardous Salvage, Inc. (HSI), the company Tony will be visiting in the morning. HSI is a unique operation that salvages munitions debris from a government target range. One of the locals, an attractive young woman named Renee, befriends Mark and Tony, encouraging them.

Mark's visit to the Elton project is anything but routine. He discovers that the energy project camouflages missile silos. He and Tony are questioned, then detained. The two attempt an escape, but are recaptured, and are considered enemy agents.

Mark and Tony are moved to a "secure" location. This time, a helmeted guard helps them escape, barely making it past a hail of bullets and pursuing military vehicles. The guard turns out to be Renee, who is working for an offshoot of the National Security Council. She reveals that the missiles hide even deeper secrets—virtual-reality laser weapons developed to destroy anything in orbit. The obsessive project leader, Colonel Ferguson, is convinced that nuclear warheads from the former Soviet Union will be sold to third-world terrorists. He plans to use the virtual-reality lasers and missiles in a first strike against Israel. That will force Israel into instant retaliation against former Soviet Union hidden missile sites.

The colonel has secured all communications, and there is no way to call for outside support. Renee has to rely on Tony to reach the HSI crew for help. She forces Mark to return to the project site with her, where she directs him to the missile silo as she heads to stop the colonel.

Renee is captured, but Mark and the trained HSI specialists attempt to disarm the missile. Time is too short. The missile fires. Mark and the crew race back into the complex, overpowering the colonel and rescuing Renee. She quickly elicits Mark's help and, using experimental virtual-reality lasers, they manage to divert the missile seconds before it hits.

The National Security Council moves quickly to cover up the story. No one will ever know what almost happened. Mark and Tony must remain quiet.

The two friends return home. Tony digs into another project, but Mark can't face the thought of returning to his depressing DOE office. He wants something different. He quits his job and proffers goodbyes to his bureaucratic boss. The events of the previous weeks have transformed him. He wants to be with Renee, the woman who changed his life. He offers to join her in Nevada, but she still has a job to do and puts a stop to those plans. It's better if he just stays in Washington with Tony, but perhaps there's some way they'll be able to work together again.

In the tag, Renee convinces her agency to provide Mark and Tony with seed money to start their own consulting business. That's the *least* they can do for the makeshift heroes. The bigwigs concur. They'll provide startup funds, provided they can tap into the boys' "expertise"—through Renee—whenever they want. Renee smiles.

"Beltway Bandits, Inc." is born, with promises of continued high adventure.

Sample Future Stories

The inevitable question raised by all concerned is how the series will sustain itself throughout the seasons. What kinds of stories can be told the second year? The viability of a concept is measured by its ability to sustain itself over many episodes without having to repeat storylines.

It is important to demonstrate the many avenues from which stories can be derived. About five or six new story ideas are usually included in the concept, each showing the uniqueness of the characters in conflict, without duplicating ideas.

These are sample future episodes from "Beltway Bandits."

<u>FUTURE STORIES</u>

1. Mark is hounded by calls from his ex-wife, then receives a call from Renee. She wants to see him right away. He's ecstatic. But the news is not good. She's going undercover, can't tell him more, she'll be in touch. She kisses Mark goodbye. This is serious. When he doesn't hear from her as planned, he convinces Tony to help track her down. The National Security Agency refuses to help. Finally, they acknowledge that she hasn't communicated with them, either. After many near misses, the boys finally find her—the quarry of a Mideast hit man. They swing into action to help her, and they just barely succeed. Renee—and the agency—are most grateful.

2. Mark is working at his computer in the small office of "Beltway Bandits, Inc." when the screen temporarily blanks out. It's not as benign as it seems. A computer virus threatens every interconnected computer in the Washington, D.C. area—including high-security mainframes at the Pentagon and National Security Council. Through journalistic probing, Tony uncovers a lonely computer hacker trying to undermine the bureaucracy he was once a part of. They convince him to disrupt and destroy the program he has worked on for the past five years.

3. Business is not very good, and the boys need some capital to make the bills. One large company calls, wanting them to set up a satellite communica-

tions link for international business ventures. In a plot reminiscent of "Sorry Wrong Number," Mark accidentally uncovers an investment conspiracy to gain control of the well-known company. Trying to find out more, he, Tony, and Renee discover that a murder is planned during an international flight on a corporate jet. Through their computer facility, investigative ploys, and quick action, Mark, Tony, and Renee prevent the crime.

4. Mark's ex-boss Stanley Ebert is furious. He's convinced that Mark is still plugging into Department of Energy computers. There are missing DOE files, and others that have been tampered with. Ebert threatens Mark with retaliation. He'll close down their business. Beltway Bandits are stealing the Beltway blind. The more Mark protests, the more it seems he's guilty. With the help of his former secretary, and a somber Tony, evidence is finally uncovered to point to the real culprit, a former agency executive now running for state office in the Midwest. He agrees to return the documents only on the condition that no one knows he took them.

5. While doing routine research at the Pentagon, Renee discovers that three people have mysteriously died in their offices within a two-day period. Although officials try to keep it quiet, news travels fast, and employees fear for their own health. Renee drafts Mark and Tony, who help her unravel a complicated mystery involving contamination from a biological warfare project gone awry. The contamination is contained, but all involved know how lucky they have been, and how easily it could happen again.

The Art of Pitching Ideas

In *Primetime*, Richard Lindheim and I described how to pitch ideas to the networks.[6] I've incorporated that discussion here, since the procedure varies little from network to network.

The process begins with a phone call to schedule the pitch meeting. Since network development executives are invariably busy, it may take a week or two for the actual meeting. The phone call acts as a screening process for network development executives. Individuals without representation will often be rebuffed or referred to a subordinate. Networks are wary of discussing projects with people who are not properly represented (the fear of lawsuits prevails).

Just before the meeting, all the participants assemble outside the office of the network development vice-president. The roster of individuals varies, but usually includes the creator of the concept to be pitched, the writer (if the creator is not a writer), and the creator's legal representation. If the creator works independently, this will usually be an agent. If the individual has a contract with a studio or production organization, this will be a studio development executive. The network will usually be represented by three people—the head of development, his or her assistant, and a junior member of the department who will sit silently with a writing pad to record notes about the project.

The meeting always begins informally. The development executive tries to make the nervous creative people feel at ease. There is a short period of casual conversation and jokes, while coffee and nonalcoholic drinks are served for those wishing it. Finally, the development executive tactfully brings the conversation to the business at hand.

Usually the first person to speak is the agent or studio representative, who introduces the project in a general way, expresses confidence in the creative team and the concept, often indicating time periods on the network schedule where this show might be ideally placed.

Then the spotlight is focused on the creator, who proceeds with the verbal "pitch." First, the basic concept is described, with arguments supporting the idea's merit and uniqueness. The creator explains how this project is different from present and past shows on television. In addition, he or she describes how the concept allows many different types of stories to be told from week to week.

Now the principal characters are described in detail. Their biographies (which may never appear on screen) are revealed, along with their attitudes and character quirks. Often the prototype actor or actress will be mentioned. Only the primary characters are presented in detail. The subsidiary ones may be referred to briefly or not at all. Often they are dismissed with a comment like "and of course there are several other characters who will interact with our leads."

After presenting the basic idea and characters, the individual pitching the idea usually pauses. This is the time for the network executives to respond. This response can take several forms.

1. The network executive in charge may declare disinterest in the idea or inform the group that something similar is already in the works. If so, that is the conclusion of the meeting.

2. The network executive may ask questions. In this situation, the response is critical. If a developer is asked to discuss some of the potential stories for the series, adequate preparation can spell the difference between acceptance and rejection.

3. The development executives will smile and thank the people for coming in and presenting the project. While projects are sometimes approved in the meeting, the network programmers usually maintain a placid countenance and end the meeting without stating a conclusion.

Following unwritten but established procedure, the development executives will mull over the proposal and subsequently meet to reach a consensus. One of them will then phone the project's representative (studio/production company or agent) and inform him or her of the decision. This accept/reject call usually occurs within 72 hours of the pitch session.

Personal Ingredients for Successful Pitching

There are a number of key ingredients necessary for a successful presentation of a television concept. Among them: honest enthusiasm, abundance of detail, humor, conviction, adaptability.

Honest Enthusiasm

It would seem superfluous to state that the presenter should have enthusiasm about the project. This is expected. It is crucial, however, that this enthusiasm be real and not overstated. Network executives are constantly bombarded with sales pitches for "new, wonderful series." If the presenter lapses into hyperbole, his credibility and that of the project will both suffer. The key element is realistic enthusiasm.

Abundance of Detail

While some projects succeed because of slick salesmanship, the success record of such concepts is poor. A well-thought-out concept is rich in detail, covering most exigencies. The network programmers listen carefully for flaws in the concept and to ascertain that it has been carefully conceived.

Humor

What separates contemporary television and film from the past is humor. Examine the best of today's entertainment offerings and you will discover a mixture of intense conflict and comedy, sometimes almost overlapping. Every contemporary concept, no matter how dramatic, should have humor, and levity in the presentation of any project is important as well. Network executives interpret the intensity and style of the pitch as a faithful indicator of the creator's stylistic intent for the program.

Conviction

This should not be confused with enthusiasm. The determination of the creator to have this project accepted and on the air is vital to the presentation. People who are firm in their beliefs command respect. Conviction may not guarantee acceptance, but lack of conviction will certainly encourage rejection.

It should be noted that it is preferable for a creator to present only one idea per meeting. Since network meetings can be difficult to arrange and have to be scheduled far in advance, there is the tendency to consolidate and pitch several ideas per meeting. This presents some problems. The network may interpret the bombardment of ideas as lack of conviction concerning any one concept. It also puts the executives in an uncomfortable position, choosing one idea over the others. Often they will take refuge in simply rejecting them all.

Adaptability

In the meeting, a network development executive often has suggestions about modifying the concept in some way. Obviously, to reject such advice with an unsuitable comment like "That's stupid," or "It won't work," or "I don't think so" is the quickest way to have the project rejected. The minimal response should be "That's interesting. Let me think about that."

An open mind is crucial in such situations. It does not take much psychological training to understand that accepting an executive's modification gives that person a stake in the project and increases its chances of acceptance. Moreover, development people are often concerned about the flexibility of the creative people. Since television is a collaborative effort, it is easier to work with someone who is thoughtful and accepting of ideas than someone who takes any comment as criticism and a personal assault.

During the development process, some hard-nosed creators find themselves feigning amiability. Those with reputations for being extremely difficult often solicit network "input" at the formative stages of a project. If the show succeeds, they are the ones who receive the critical and remunerative rewards. They can safely turn from Dr. Jekyll to Mr. Hyde after the series has been ordered.

ENDNOTES

1. John Brodie, "Pilots' Code: Pitch to the Niche," *Variety*, February 15, 1993, 104.
2. "Development Dance Cards," *Variety*, February 15, 1993, 104.
3. See Richard A. Blum and Richard Lindheim, *Primetime, Network Television Programming* (Boston: Focal Press), 63-66.
4. Lindheim and Blum, *Inside Television Producing*. For concept, see 57. For a discussion of the development process for "Coach," see 57-64.
5. Ibid. For concept, see 125. For a discussion of the development process of "Law & Order," see 125-150.
6. Blum and Lindheim, *Primetime*, 72-75.

PART TWO

STORY
DEVELOPMENT

4

How to Develop the Story

Genres and Plot Patterns

Once you have an idea, it might be helpful to categorize the plot according to genre and situation. An early analysis can help you keep a better handle on the focus of the story. If a story was meant to be dramatic but comic elements come into play, the plot might be enriched by that interweaving of genres. However, if comedy dominates, or a subplot becomes a main plot, it is a different story that is in the making.

In television, the industry defines genres according to the show's production format. These are the traditional genres writers get paid for: Comedy, Drama, Variety, Daytime, Serials, Children's, Documentary.

In motion pictures, genres tend to be more broadly defined. They reflect the writer's dramatic style and seem to expand with each new release: Drama, Comedy, Suspense/Horror, Action Thriller, Gangster/Detective, Love Stories, Mixed Genres.

Plot Patterns

In the process of writing the story, certain plot patterns become identifiable. One generally is dominant, while others serve as background or subplots in the evolution of the script. It's helpful to keep track of your main plot and subplots this way. But remember, this is just a general conceptual tool meant to be explored. Your script may involve several overlapping patterns, or none of them.

Decades ago, a critic named Georges Polti identified thirty-six dramatic plot situations that seemed to be at the heart of all dramatic stories.

Lewis Herman reduced that number to nine in his book (*A Practical Manual of Screenplay Writing*). More recently, I modified those patterns in an earlier version of this book, and in *Primetime: Network Television Programming*, where Richard Lindheim and I added plot patterns to identify generic television stories.

In this book, I've modified that list further, to encompass plot patterns for both television and motion pictures.

Love and Romance

Fantasy

Vengeance

Jeopardy and Survival

Search and Quest

Group and Family Ties

Return

Success and Achievement

The list is not exhaustive, but it does outline the potential for dramatic conflicts faced by lead characters in television and feature scripts.

Love and Romance

This kind of story deals primarily with romantic conflicts faced by lead characters and how they overcome those obstacles. In a traditional love pattern, boy and girl meet, lose each other, must win each other back. The story usually centers on a character's desire to maintain a loving relationship in the face of serious threats. The story may draw on elements of the classic love triangle, in which an outsider enters into the romantic competition.

In television, the series "Mad About You" highlights comic disruptions of an unsettled romantic relationship. "Northern Exposure" deals with Maggie who wants to fall in love, but is desperately afraid of the consequences. She believes she is responsible for the deaths of her former lovers. Love is also the complicating factor in shows like "Love and War," "Beverly Hills, 90210," "Melrose Place," and virtually all daytime and primetime soaps.

In features, like LOVE AFFAIR and ONLY YOU, the love pattern is a predominant one that helps sustain audience involvement in the lives of the lead characters. SLEEPLESS IN SEATTLE focuses on how two lovers destined for each other will eventually meet, and fall in love, from opposite sides of the country. The film GROUNDHOG DAY puts the lead character, a self-centered weatherman, in a time warp, fated to wake up on the same day for the rest of his life. Initially, he takes advantage of every woman around him, then tries to have a romantic relationship with his producer. She is the opposite of him—perky, humble, kind. After some comic bumbling, they finally wind up loving each other.

Fantasy

In this pattern, characters confront their own weaknesses and are permitted to act out their own fantasies on some level. In variations of the Cinderella tale, lead characters become more "whole" as a result of their fantasy experience. Some of the television shows in this genre are "The Fresh Prince of Bel Air," "Dave's World," "Baywatch," "Models, Inc.," and the classic fantasy series forerunners, "Heaven Can Wait" and "Love Boat." The shows provide viewers with an outlet for their own lighter fantasies.

In features, THE LION KING, FORREST GUMP, and ANGELS IN THE OUTFIELD are perfect examples of the fantasy pattern. HOME ALONE is also a good example, in which an eight-year-old is accidentally left alone and must overcome his own insecurities and successfully defend his house against bad guys. In ROOKIE OF THE YEAR, a twelve-year-old pitcher has a 100-mph fast ball. An earlier film FIELD OF DREAMS deals with the same kind of baseball fantasy from an adult perspective.

Vengeance

Stories in the vengeance mode deal with lead characters who personally seek revenge for some wrongdoing. Characters in this type of story want to solve crimes that are unsolved, get an eye for an eye, or simply "right" some earlier injustice. This type of story pattern is prominent in virtually every mystery, suspense, or action adventure series, including shows like "Murder She Wrote," "Law & Order," "NYPD Blue," "X-Files," and "Commish."

In features, the plot pattern is one of the most successful at the box office. Think of the powerful revenge and vengeance motives for lead characters in films like THE TERMINATOR, ROBOCOP, CAPE FEAR, LAST ACTION HERO, ROCKY, and THE KARATE KID.

Jeopardy and Survival

The jeopardy pattern is usually centered on a life-and-death situation, testing the survival instincts and prowess of the leading characters. In this story pattern, characters confront extremely difficult odds (e.g., earthquake, avalanche, hijacking, terrorists, obsessed antagonists). They use every mental and physical trick to overcome extraordinary obstacles. In some situations, those obstacles are compounded by a "timebomb" situation, i.e., something must be done before time runs out and disaster occurs.

Television movies rely heavily on survival story patterns, as do reality-based shows like "Rescue 911," "America's Most Wanted," and "Cops." Dramatic series like "MacGyver," "Seaquest DSV," and "Lois and Clark" also rely on this element, as did "Mission: Impossible."

Motion pictures have had smash successes with jeopardy films like JURASSIC PARK, in which people must survive in a theme park filled with dinosaurs. Also think of the incredible survival skills needed by lead characters in action films like THE SPECIALIST, CLIFFHANGER, and THE TERMINATOR.

Search and Quest

The search or quest pattern is centered on the notion of a person trying to find something of great importance. The quest might be external or internal. In an external quest, the character can be searching for a missing witness, clues to buried treasure, or missing information. The search stands on its own as a story, but can also be tied to larger story patterns, such as vengeance or romance.

The external search provides a more action-packed framework for stories, while the inner quest is more difficult to convey on screen. In an inner quest, the search might encompass a character's drive to "find" him or herself or deal with traumatic personal crises. In television, the wonderfully quirky characters in "Northern Exposure" and "Picket Fences" deal with inner quests each week.

In features, an external search is at the heart of the premises for STAR TREK: GENERATIONS, STARGATE, INTERVIEW WITH THE VAMPIRE, ROMANCING THE STONE, and WITNESS. The dramatic film LORENZO'S OIL deals with a couple's frantic search to find a cure for their son's rare hereditary disease. An inner search is at work in films like QUIZ SHOW, BULLETS OVER BROADWAY, and HUSBANDS AND WIVES, in which a relationship that breaks up has enormous impact on the couple's closest friends.

Group and Family Ties

This pattern involves a group of characters who normally would have nothing to do with each other, but because of circumstances are tied together in the story. Due to the arena/setting, they are forced into inter-relationships that become the thrust of the story.

This story pattern is a classic setup for character conflicts in television series. It can work anywhere: a hospital ("E.R."), a radio talk show ("Frasier"), a Boston bar ("Cheers"), a New York apartment ("Seinfeld"), a small Alaska town ("Northern Exposure"), a TV newsroom ("Murphy Brown"), a Midwest college ("Coach"), a TV repair show ("Home Improvement"), an apartment complex ("Melrose Place"), an airport ("Wings"), a police station ("NYPD Blue"), an attorney's office ("L.A. Law"), a house ("Roseanne," "Empty Nest"), a taxi dispatch center ("Taxi"), an army camp ("M*A*S*H"), even outer space ("Star Trek: Deep Space Nine").

In features, think of dramatic stories about characters bound together by their shared environment, like THE SHAWSHANK REDEMPTION, set in prison. The film ENCHANTED APRIL is about four British women who rent an Italian villa. They are incompatible strangers at the beginning, who develop deep friendships by the resolution. GLENGARRY GLEN ROSS is about a group of angry Chicago real estate salesmen, who face the shared prospect of losing their jobs. HOWARDS END, adapted from E.M. Forster's novel, is about three different families whose lives revolve around a country estate.

Return

Within one of the larger story patterns, a character may have to confront the sudden reappearance of someone or something from the past. This story element forces the character to readjust the comfortable status quo. For example, the lead character may suddenly be faced with the return of an ex-husband, high school sweetheart, wandering father, missing child, long-lost lover, or long-forgotten criminal record. This pattern may serve nicely as the driving force for individual characters in a series, but it is not generally the overriding motif for a series.

The pilot episode for "Coach" deals with the Coach's reaction to having his daughter come to the same campus. An episode of "Northern Exposure" focuses on Maurice, who is confronted by a former KGB agent who proves he was a traitor decades before.

DEAD PRESIDENTS is a film about three young men who, after serving in Vietnam, try to regain their old values as they return to their old neighborhood. In the feature PASSION FISH, a paralyzed star of daytime TV is reclusive, and returns to her home in Louisiana. At home, she strikes up an unexpected friendship with her nurse. They share poignant stories, and each has an impact on the other's life. In the comedy HOCUS POCUS, a witch from 1692 returns to Salem, Massachusetts for Halloween.

Success and Achievement

Success is another story pattern that stands on its own, but also fits comfortably into the fabric of other story types. In the success pattern, the lead character needs to achieve something *at all costs*. The goal may be self-serving (money, romance, promotion). But the character is consumed by the drive to succeed.

In "Coach," Hayden is driven to succeed, which complicates his relationships. In "Murphy Brown," Murphy is set up to be a successful and independent woman professional—to the detriment of anyone who gets in the way. "Seinfeld" is based on the ironic premise of a standup TV comic who needs to achieve as a standup TV comic on television.

In features, the need to succeed is the force behind leading characters in QUIZ SHOW, A FEW GOOD MEN, THE FIRM, BATMAN RETURNS, THE LION KING, and WALL STREET.

Plot patterns are not mutually exclusive, and any number of subplots can emerge within a given story. Still, this type of plot identification provides you with a clearer overview of the dominant story elements, and the concurrent identification of background material. Once the dominant pattern is identified, there's a smaller chance of being sidetracked by intriguing subplots or minor characters.

Software for Idea Development

Computer software programs have been developed to help construct stories and characters. Fierce debates have raged about the potential for these programs to propagate formulaic plots and characters. The arguments peaked when "DRAMATICA"™ was introduced by Screenplay Systems. It predicts what can happen in a story, based on nine or ten questions.

An informative article in *Variety* analyzed the differences between idea development software on the market.[1] "COLLABORATOR II"™ is based on Aristotle's six elements of drama and Lajos Egris' dramatic theories. It poses hundreds of questions about story and character development, but does not construct a story. It is one of the more successful programs in that regard. "PLOTS UNLIMITED"™ has a database of more than thirteen thousand plots. Writers mix and match, deriving story elements from columns a, b, and c. It has thousands of potential story ideas, which can provoke a dire sense of formulaic stories and characters.

Some writers find that no single program is right, but Joey Arch, co-writer of SLEEPLESS IN SEATTLE, used two different programs, "COLLABORATOR II"™ and "STORYLINE."™ This is his assessment: "They help you organize your thinking. But they don't help you write a movie. They are wonderful, but they can also be a distraction. It takes away the drudgery work. It's like playing a videogame."[2]

Using idea software is a personal thing. It may help organize work, cut time on story and character choices, build creative juices. Or it may be frustrating to use and stop you cold.

How to Begin: Choosing the Story Area and Lead Characters

A story idea can be derived from any personal experience, relationship, observation, music, film, or article that intrigued you, any source that sparked your imagination. But the *story area* must be capable of standing on its own as the spine of the story, vital to the motivations of your lead characters.

The story area needs a *hook*—a unique premise that will set it apart and grip the audience. If the hook is strong, the story will have marketing appeal and a much better chance of eventually reaching the screen.

Here are a few workable story areas.

- "FIERY METEOR NEARLY HITS U.S."
- "WOMAN HAS FATAL ATTRACTION FOR JUSTICE DEPARTMENT OFFICIAL WHO IS TRYING HER FATHER FOR WAR CRIMES"
- "U.S. WORRIED ABOUT SECRET NUCLEAR MISSILE SITES IN FORMER SOVIET UNION"
- "CAMPERS LOST IN UNSEASONABLE BLIZZARD"

Each offers intriguing potential for functioning as the story's spine. However, the story areas are much too broad in their present form. They need to have lead characters and a point of view.

The pivotal step is to choose a susceptible lead character and identify the conflict that he or she has to overcome. That process ensures a clear point of view for the story.

For example, the first story area deals with a near catastrophe—a meteor slamming into the U.S. That story could be told from any number of vantage points. This might be one approach:

> *"An aging scientist discovers that a fiery meteor is about to hit the U.S.—but no one believes him."*

Now the story has a lead character who is vulnerable. It's told from the perspective of an aging scientist. It also has a built-in dramatic conflict with a "timebomb" situation. The scientist must find a way to convince others, and to act, before the meteor strikes. As the story develops, other characters and subplots might be incorporated, but the basic premise is fairly well defined at the outset, and the hook can be told in a logline.

Let's look at the next story area ("WOMAN HAS FATAL ATTRACTION FOR JUSTICE DEPARTMENT OFFICIAL WHO IS TRYING HER FATHER FOR WAR CRIMES"). This one was based on a true story, with dramatic license. Finding the spine of the story, though, posed some creative challenges. In the feature script SONJA'S MEN Allan Gerson and I struggled to find the right perspective. Gerson was the first Jewish prosecutor for the Justice Department's Office of Special Investigation, which was set up to investigate and deport Nazi war criminals in the U.S. He is also the son of Holocaust survivors. In this story, a woman who is the daughter of a Nazi collaborator falls in love with the prosecutor. For dramatic purposes, we needed to set their passion against his drive to prosecute Nazi collaborators and her drive to save her father at all costs. That became the film's driving force for the lead characters. The step outline for SONJA'S MEN appears later in this chapter.

The next story area ("U.S. WORRIED ABOUT SECRET NUCLEAR MISSILE SITES IN FORMER SOVIET UNION") plays off this high-concept hook: *"What would happen if the U.S. accidentally unleashed a secret missile to demolish nuclear missile silos in the former Soviet Union?"* That's the idea Frank Tavares and I had behind the screenplay THE ELTON PROJECT. The spine of the story is centered on two pals, one a newly divorced bureaucrat from the Department of Energy, the other a journalist doing research on hazardous waste. They head to Las Vegas and encounter a secret Department of Energy missile defense plant in Elton, Nevada. They are the driving force for the project to be activated. The missiles have hidden codes connecting them to bases in the former Soviet Union. The leads hook up with a woman CIA agent who halts the flying missiles with virtual-reality weapons.

Finally, look at the last story area ("CAMPERS LOST IN UNSEA-SONABLE BLIZZARD"), and try to define the best dramatic angle. You might choose the point of view of one camper or a number of them. Or you might want to tell the story from the point of view of the rescuers. The basic conflict and plot pattern centers on a survival situation, but who is in jeopardy? And how great is the sense of urgency for escape and survival? Those decisions dictate the direction and visual approach of the story. Later in this chapter we'll see how they were developed for a TV film, "THE WIND CHILL FACTOR," which Dan Wilcox and I wrote.

How to Advance the Story Effectively

In order to move from the narrative treatment into script, there is an ongoing need to set proper story sequences in order. I've found that the use of *dramatic action points* is an effective way to select and arrange key incidents in the story so that the dramatic drive of the story is clear. I call them "dramatic action points" in deference to Irwin Blacker's analysis of how to strengthen stories with Aristotelian playwriting theory. There are roughly 26-35 major action points in a 120-minute film, which translates to four or five pages for each sequence in the script. Those are, of course, very general figures, but they do provide some guidance in assessing the time count for an eventual script.

Dramatic action points are referred to by some writers as *dramatic beats*. They are the basic dramatic units and events that advance the story. Once these beats are identified, they can be placed in different contexts—much like the restructuring of a puzzle—to strengthen the plot structure. They can be used to orchestrate the pacing and balance in the story.

How do you know which sequence begins the story? It helps to identify an *inciting incident* or a point of attack for your lead character. Why is this day, this moment, this situation critical to his or her life? Then you can build the most effective combination of scenes to unravel the story. But which scenes go where? Which characters are needed at what points? Which scenes build the conflict? Which scenes are extraneous?

Aristotle talked about the importance of the proper arrangement of incidents in a plot to have the greatest impact on the audience. Twentieth-century writers agree. Eric Bentley (*The Playwright as Thinker*) contended that a carefully arranged sequence of actions is essential for achieving maximum effect. He called it a "rearrangement" of incidents as opposed to a simple chronological arrangement. In short, *dramatic action* rather than literal action.

The use of dramatic action points—or dramatic beats—is an ongoing process in the story development phase. As an example of how it might work, let's look at one of the premises mentioned earlier:

"CAMPERS LOST IN UNSEASONABLE BLIZZARD"

We might try to outline these points for the opening sequences:

1. A family is en route to the Berkshires for a camping weekend.
2. They arrive and find the campgrounds in disarray, but decide to stay.
3. They get snowed in.

Even in this sketchy form, it becomes apparent that the inciting incident, or point of attack, is not strong. There is no suggestion of conflict or character. The action points can be revised accordingly:

1. A couple's marriage is shaky. The husband works too hard and they need a vacation.
2. They head up to the Berkshires for a camping weekend. He brought along work anyway and they argue.
3. They arrive at the campground, which is in disarray. It's late at night, and they decide to stay.
4. It snows.

But even here there are some problems. The points are too choppy, and are not really comprised of individual dramatic sequences. The action needs to be clarified and the characters need more definition. It might be possible to merge the first two action points for the sake of pacing and add other people to the story—their children, other campers, perhaps even a pet that is lost in the storm.

This is what the revised outline might look like:

1. BARRY, SHARON, and KIDS ride to the campsite. We learn they have marriage problems.
2. They arrive at the campgrounds and find it in disarray. It's late, they're tired, they decide to stay.
3. Setting up camp, we meet other campers, and follow up the marriage conflict.
4. It snows as they sleep.
5. An expensive trailer reaches camp, finds no power. The irate owner blames Barry.
6. In morning, Barry's kids play in the snow. Their dog gets swept away in the river.

And so on. Dramatic action points provide a very bare but specific blueprint for the structure of the story.

The Treatment and Step Outline

The story must be written in a form called the *treatment,* which is the narrative version, or the *step outline,* which is a detailed outline of proposed action sequences for the script. Both forms are acceptable. They make it easier to move directly into script form. Examples of each are provided below.

The purpose of the treatment is to work out story problems and to get feedback from people you trust to strengthen plot and character development. It has to have a beginning, middle, and end, character conflicts, act builds, story twists, comedy moments, high points of crises, and the story's resolution.

In episodic television, treatments are about 5 to 10 pages in length, giving an accurate picture of the setup, characters, conflicts, universe of the story, tone of the show, act breaks, and plenty of laughs if you're doing comedy. You can sprinkle in dialogue to show where the jokes play.

In features, the treatment is about 5 to 30 pages. The shorter, the better. You can depict the genre, dramatic setup, character development, crisis, and story progression.

As an example of a narrative treatment, this is the opening act from "THE WIND CHILL FACTOR." It demonstrates how the action points translate into the treatment. The following act is derived from those action points.

<u>THE WIND CHILL FACTOR</u>

April. A bright spring day.

We follow BARRY and SHARON RUTLEDGE and their SON and DAUGHTER riding in a new but small camper from New York City to the Berkshire Mountains. Throughout the trip, we hear innocuous commentary from the radio about a cold front moving in from Canada. But the noise is lost in the sounds of the children at play and the dog barking.

The marriage is rocky. BARRY is a lawyer who works too hard and is constantly afraid he won't be advanced. This family weekend was arranged to save the marriage, but BARRY has brought along a legal brief anyway.

Action
point
2
They reach the Berkshires just at dusk, and follow the signs to the campground. They drive down a steep dirt road into a valley nestled among the mountains. But when they arrive, they find the campgrounds in disarray. A sign that reads "OFFICE" points to some prefabricated walls lying unassembled on the ground. Another car is parked nearby—a VW. The young couple inside, STEPHEN and MARIAN, commiserate with the RUTLEDGEs; they, too, made reservations, but the campground obviously went bankrupt before it could open.

They're all undecided about what to do. They should find another campground. But it's getting dark and there's a storm brewing. Besides, this place can shelter them—the campsites are cleared, there are picnic tables, fireplaces, there's a centrally located water pipe, and there are two outhouses, one male, one female. The two couples decide to stay until morning, when the storm will be over.

Action
point
3
BARRY struggles through the unfamiliar tasks of setting up a campsite, and he is forced to finish in the rain. Thunder and lightning follow him as he returns to the camper, drenched to the bone. The KIDS think it's outrageously funny.

Another car arrives, drawn by the light from the lanterns. It's a group of FRIENDS, two boys and a girl, who set up a rudimentary tent in a nearby campsite.

Inside the RUTLEDGE camper, after dinner, the family goes to bed, accompanied by the sound of rain on the roof. SHARON bickers with BARRY, who refuses to go to bed without reading over his brief. Angry, SHARON gets into bed. BARRY reads. The sound of the rain peters out. BARRY offers his wife some minimal consolation—at least it's stopped raining.

Action
point
4
But in a WIDE SHOT of the campground, we see that it's begun snowing.

During the night, a sleek, flashy, expensive-looking silver trailer arrives in the snow, driven by CHARLES EVANS, who is camping with his wife, MAGGIE, and their teenage daughter, BETH. The family is dismayed to see the condition of the campground, and an irate CHARLES follows the only visible light—BARRY's—to register his complaint.

Action point # 5

BARRY is surprised to see it snowing, but he suggests that CHARLES do what everyone else has done: camp here for the night. After all, how long can a snowstorm last in April?

CHARLES tries to connect his electrical system to the power outlet at the campsite, but finds that the power has not been turned on. He's furious; now he has no heat. And, like everyone else, he has no cold-weather clothing. Disgruntled, he bundles his family into the silver trailer for the night. Gradually, the campground lights go out, first in the EVANS camper, then in BARRY's.

Action point # 6

In the morning, it is still snowing heavily. The RUT-LEDGE KIDS, eager to build a springtime snowman, find make-shift winter clothing—dishrags for their ears, pinned-up blankets for sweaters, plastic bags for galoshes. And they rush out into the snow, with their dog, to play.

This is all derived from Action point #6

When SHARON calls them to breakfast, the dog (a city dog, used to a leash) bolts and races along the edge of a small river. The pup loses its footing in the snow, falls into the water, and is swept downstream.

The KIDS race along the riverbank, following their pet, plodding through the snow, calling to him. STEPHEN spots them, races over, and restrains them from following the dog. He tries to explain that they can't save their pet. It couldn't see the footing in

the snow; neither can they. But the children are
unheeding; they scream and cry as they watch their
pet sweep out of sight...

Sample Step Outline for a Motion Picture

This is a step outline from SONJA'S MEN that I wrote with Allan Gerson about his experiences as a prosecutor with the Justice Department's Office of Special Investigations. The screenplay is based on fact and deals with many different issues, so we had to be sure that the script didn't become too broad. It is a screenplay dealing with the prosecution of Nazi collaborators for war crimes. The research involved emotionally compelling depositions and trial transcripts. Yet we couldn't have the script deal exclusively with the issue of responsibilities for war crimes, or it would seem thematic, rather than dramatic.

After much deliberation, we decided that the focus of the story is about how characters deal with personal betrayals. Deception takes many different forms. Aaron deceives Sonja, she deceives him. Sonja's father deceives her, and he is deceived by the government. Aaron feels betrayed by the government, and the government feels he betrayed them.

Because it was a character-driven screenplay, we built the film around a three-act structure. We placed a story twist at the end of Act I (beat #16), where Aaron discovers that his lover's name is the same as that of the Nazi collaborator he's investigating, Tyrowicz. The second story twist occurs at the end of Act II (beat #23), when Aaron discovers that his supervisor was the one who leaked information about Aaron's parents lying on their visas. In a later twist, we learn it was Sonja, who leaked the information to save her own father.

In the step outline, we uncovered a problem in the perception of Aaron's character at the setup (beat #2). He appears unsure about the reason he wants to join the Justice Department. It was suggested by a producer that Aaron's character would be more susceptible if he was driven and passionate about the reason for the change. So, in the script we made that change. Aaron is driven to right the wrongs inflicted on his parents and family during the Holocaust. That drive conflicts with his supervisor's intention, which is to get as many political wins as possible. And it conflicts dramatically with Sonja's intentions—to save her father. That change made Aaron a more likeable and identifiable character.

We had another problem at the resolution (beat #34), where Aaron returns to his old job. Given the change in his character arc, it wasn't likely that he'd go back. He needed more at stake, so we set it up in the script that he couldn't return, and instead had to deal with more intense dramatic consequences.

SONJA'S MEN
BY
ALLAN GERSON AND RICHARD BLUM

STEP OUTLINE

1. Tidal basin. Jogging early morning, we meet
Aaron, running toward his office. The atmosphere of
Washington, D.C. is vivid.

2. Law office. His current boss, Jim, congratulates
him. Aaron's still not sure why he's decided to take
the new position with Justice. Something is compelling him, maybe just the need for a change of
pace.

3. Georgetown restaurant. His friend Charlie toasts
him. He notices a lovely woman nearby, arranging
photos in a portfolio. This is Sonja. Aaron initiates
small talk, asks for her card. She's prepping for a
show, has a studio in Dupont Circle.

4. Dupont Circle studio. Aaron is taken by the
sophisticated photos in her exhibit, all on the
Ukraine. He notes another portfolio, and she, embar-
rassed, explains that those are boudoir photos. That's
how she can make a living. Her father would wring
her neck if he found out what she was doing. The
photos in the Ukraine were enough. He kisses her.
What was that about, she asks? He's not sure. His
parents would kill him for kissing a shiksa. He sees
a self portrait, a small photo of her. He can have it
if he wants.

5. His parents' house. This is strained. They don't
know why he's moving to another job. Why he is so
restless. He thought they'd be proud of him. We're
always proud of you, mom answers vaguely.

6. Director's office—OSI. Parker is a no-nonsense
superior who wants wins. He briefs his new staff on
the status of two cases, Osidatch, who was chief of
police, and Tyrowicz, who was the S.S. liaison. Charlie will set up two depositions in California.

7. From his office, Aaron calls Sonja, tells her he'll be out in L.A. for a deposition, will call when he gets back. She tells him she's on her way to California. She has a show in LA County and will be seeing her dad. She'd love to see Aaron when he's free. She gives him her number in La Jolla.

8. Flight to LA. Aaron reads the files, absorbed by the photos of young men from another era. Then looks at his photo of Sonja. On the back, she's jotted something we can't see.

9. LAX. Charlie meets Aaron in a rented red thunderbird. They've got interviews that night and in the morning.

10. Ida Kempner, an older woman, identifies both Osidatch and Tyrowicz. She feels comfortable with Aaron, who speaks Yiddish. She recounts how she was forced to save herself by jumping from a train heading to a "work" camp.

11. Tyrowicz is interviewed in his home, overlooking a rose garden. He is a Nazi collaborator who is a greasy bastard. He admits knowing Osidatch, but refuses to answer straightforward questions about his own work with SS headquarters.

12. Marriott Hotel—night. Aaron is asleep, fitfully, reliving the nightmare-flashback of Ida being thrown from the train. He wakes up, very disturbed. Sees Sonja's picture and calls her. They'll meet tomorrow.

13. La Jolla. Beautiful settings. They discuss how much she missed her dad. She used to live in DC when her husband used to work with NASA, but since he died, there's nothing holding her to DC. Now she considers California home, much closer to her family and friends. They wine, dine, and make love.

14. Parker's office. The debriefing. Parker tells Aaron they have enough to go after Osidatch and

Tyrowicz, but warns him not to get moral in the
prosecution's brief. This is immigration fraud, not
historical justice. To see how it will be handled, go
to the Supreme Court hearing next week. Another
Nazi collaborator, Federenko, is appealing his extradi-
tion. Aaron is uneasy about this.

15. U.S. Supreme Court...marble steps...full nine
judges' trial of Federenko. He's been sentenced to be
extradited, but appealed on grounds that what he did
was involuntary. Justice Stephens demands to know
whether the prosecution's argument is about historic
justice or about illegal aliens? Parker's comeback:
"aliens." Aaron has a major disagreement with
Parker—he didn't say one word about Jews or Nazis
in his argument. Parker warns Aaron to stick with
the legal strategy in dealing with Osidatch and
Tyrowicz or he's gone.

16. New Orleans, Mississippi river boat. Aaron's feeling tense from the animosity with Parker. Sonja
asks him what's wrong, he can trust her. He talks
evasively, but emotionally, about people's responsibility for the past. Sonja's taking photos and reveals
how worried she is about her father. Some people
from the Immigration Naturalization Service started
asking him what he did during the war. They've
accused him of being a Nazi. My dad's no angel, but
he could never have done those things. Aaron tries
to be non-committal—advises that he should get a
good attorney. Then he asks her last name. She's
just known as Sonja T. "Tyrowicz," she announces
proudly.

17. Parker's assistant finds the bills for the L.A.
trip. On the car rental extension, Sonja's charge card
was marked on the bill. Parker also found an open
letter sent to Aaron's old law firm; it was forwarded
here, marked "S. Tyrowicz" on the return. She's the
only daughter of Tyrowicz. Parker orders a complete
FBI and INS investigation of Aaron.

18. Parker's office. A bombshell is about to drop.
Parker knows Aaron's been screwing the daughter of

a Nazi collaborator. He also hits Aaron with a new charge—Aaron's parents lied on their immigration visas. Background checks revealed they used false names on an application—just like Osidatch and Tyrowicz. If the Ukrainians find out, it could prejudice the case against Tyrowicz. Parker doesn't know if Aaron can stay on the job.

19. He talks to Sonja, to share some of the burden of lies uncovered. She asks why he didn't tell her about being with the OSI. He tells her he was afraid it would push her away. Now he needs to put things in perspective. He doesn't believe his parents could have lied all these years about their name. He's got to visit and take care of them. Sonja defends her own father, guilty of the same thing—lying on an immigration form in the past. This is a rough moment for her, deeply concerned about her father. They both realize they're prisoners of their parents' past, and intricately bound up in their survival and way of life today.

20. Aaron's parents. They're frail and worried. Painfully, they recount the truth. They used another family's visa to escape the brutality of Ukrainian forces. They were close enough in physical features to get away with it, but their names were different. They adopted that family's name in the U.S. Aaron is astounded that they never told him about it. He sees how upset they are, and promises to protect them. Everything will be okay.

21. A Ukrainian reporter calls Aaron. He got the information from a "well-placed" source. Tomorrow's headlines will demand that Aaron's parents go on trial, just like Tyrowicz. Both lied on their visas, both should go on trial. They want the same treatment for the Jews and Ukrainians.

22. Parker's office. Parker informs Aaron that he's got to place him on leave. He's been besieged with calls to take him off the case. He'll put him on leave until this blows over. Aaron is outraged; he needs to clear his parents' name.

23. Aaron tries to track down the source of the news leak with Charlie's help. Aaron knows the leak could have been implemented by Sonja in a desperate bid to save her father. Charlie comes up with evidence that it was Parker himself who leaked the information, because he wanted to bring proceedings against Aaron's parents. It would mean a promotion in his home district.

24. Preparing for the Tyrowicz trial, it's apparent that they need depositions from Moscow, Israel, and other sensitive sources. Aaron is the only one who speaks Russian and Yiddish, and can get difficult witnesses to testify. Charlie convinces his boss to bring back Aaron as the prosecutor. The witnesses feel comfortable with him.

25. A deal is struck. Parker will see that the charges against his parents are dropped, if Aaron strictly adheres to the immigration strategy as prosecutor. Get Tyrowicz extradited to the Soviet Union because he lied on his visa. He'll be executed in Russia. Needless to say, Aaron must also stay away from Sonja.

26. He lets his parents know that the charges will be dropped. They're happy, but this has taken its toll emotionally and physically on them.

27. He meets Sonja discreetly in LA, lets her know he's going to prosecute her father. She tells him she'll be staying with her father throughout the deportation process. She asks why he ever wanted to be with the OSI. He tries to explain: to bring a semblance of responsibility for what happened in the past. And they can't be in communication after this.

28. Sonja and her father in Del Mar Beach. They talk about the lies of the past. He claims there was no choice. If he didn't carry out his responsibilities, he would have been killed. It was a different time and place.

29. In California Superior Court, the trial begins. Aaron introduces Soviet and Israeli depositions. We hear revelations from witness after witness that Tyrowicz was guilty of war crimes. He was chief SS liaison, working closely with Osidatch. The Ukrainians are outraged, claim the Russians are sending wrong information about him. Judge bangs the gavel. Sonja watches the proceedings solemnly.

30. Trial wraps up. Aaron proves that Tyrowicz was guilty of lying on his immigration visa. He would not have been allowed to become a citizen if the material facts were known. Judge's decision: deport Tyrowicz to the Soviet Union. Parker's team has been effective.

31. Kennedy Airport. Sonja is with her father as INS agents escort him toward a waiting Soviet Aeroflot.

32. Aaron hands in his resignation.

33. He calls Sonja; there is no answer.

34. Washington, DC. Aaron takes early morning jog before returning to his old job.

Roll Credits:

CHARGES AGAINST AARON'S PARENTS WERE DROPPED.

SONJA'S FATHER WAS EXTRADITED TO THE SOVIET UNION WHERE HE WAS EXECUTED.

ENDNOTES

1. Andy Marx, "Screenwriters Getting Computer-Age Assist," *Variety*, September 20, 1993, 8.
2. Ibid.

5

Dramatic Elements and Act Structure

Dramatic Elements in a Story

A useful artistic resource for film writers is the inclusion of dramatic elements established by Greek playwrights to heighten the effectiveness of a script: inciting action, complication, crisis, climax, reversal, denouement.

Inciting Action

This is an initiating event at the beginning of the story that forces your lead characters to move into action. It's the point of attack.

Complication

A *complication* occurs when your character tries to deal with a conflict and faces unforeseen obstacles.

Crisis

The *crisis* is a dramatic conflict that builds story momentum as your character faces enormous odds against achieving his or her goal.

Climax

The *climax* peaks the story as your character confronts the most fateful consequences of the rising action.

Reversal

A turning point twists the story in a new direction at the end of the act. It usually occurs at the ends of Act One and Act Two.

Denouement

This is the resolution to the story. It happens at the end of Act Three.

Classical Three-Act Structure

Television and screenwriters can use a dramatic structure that parallels effective playwriting strategy. Classical playwrights used three acts to build actions and complications for the characters.

Act One sets up the inciting action, characters, and conflict. At the end of the act, a turning point twists the story in a new direction.

Act Two develops the complication and builds the dramatic crisis. At the end of the act, a turning point twists the story in a new direction.

Act Three builds the story's crisis to a climax. At the end of the act, the crisis is resolved in the denouement.

Act Structure in Television

In television, act structure is defined by the story length, so it can be confusing for writers to think about the right act structure to build the story. The act breaks in television are set up to accommodate commercial breaks, and each act should have enough story twists to keep an audience interested in seeing how the story unfolds. It might be helpful to think about a three-act structure as the building blocks to reach the beginning, middle, and end.

Half-Hour Series

A half-hour show runs about 24 minutes when produced—to allow for commercials. It can have a *teaser* of 30 to 60 seconds. Act One is about 10–12 minutes; Act Two is about 10-12 minutes. A *tag* or *wraparound* closes out the action in less than a minute.

A half-hour show can be written in two or three acts, with each act about the same length. Be sure to get copies of episodic scripts—or taped episodes—so you can define exactly how that show's episodes are structured.

As an example, the 30-minute pilot script for "Coach" has two acts, with a teaser to quickly establish the premise. This is the breakdown of the pilot episode for "Coach."[1]

COACH

TEASER, 3 PAGES
ACT ONE (2 SCENES), 21 PAGES
ACT TWO (3 SCENES), 22 PAGES

In contrast, "Murphy Brown" is written in a classical three-act structure. This is a typical breakdown of that series:

MURPHY BROWN

ACT ONE (2 SCENES), 13 PAGES
ACT TWO (2 SCENES), 17 PAGES
ACT THREE (3 SCENES), 18 PAGES

One-Hour Series

All sixty-minute scripts are broken down into four acts. All are approximately equal length, totalling about 60 pages.

Longform Television Films

Television films are broken down into seven acts. All are about equal length, totalling 90 pages for an hour and a half, or 110-120 pages for a two-hour film.

Act Structure in Motion Pictures

A theatrical motion picture screenplay is constructed as if it followed a classical three-act structure, but there is no act designation in the written script.

Among screenwriters and teachers, this is the generally accepted act structure.

Act I sets up the action in about 1-15 pages. It starts with an inciting action, builds the conflict, and unravels the first plot point or story point that turns the story in a new direction.

Act II can be about 45-60 pages. It develops the story with rising action to heighten the conflicts. It unravels the second plot point or story point, which twists the story in a new direction.

Act III is about 25-30 pages. This act is paced quicker. The conflict builds to a climax. Then the story is resolved in the denouement.

The development of an act rests on the established principles of story plotting and scene construction—hook the audience early, and build the action and conflict at a steady pace. The entire story has to be told within the parameters of a given number of acts and a limited number of script pages.

Plotting Audience Interest in Your Story

As a former studio executive and producer, I know how studios depend on audience testing techniques to measure the appeal of story and character elements in television and film. Many television programs and feature films go through the process of audience testing to provide studios and networks with some idea of the script's effectiveness. By means of electronic testing, a graph is generated and instantaneous viewer response is recorded. Producers can literally see how every joke, line, car chase, action sequence, or romantic intrigue holds audience interest.

Conceptual devices for story development can help sharpen a script's impact and appeal. An audience's interest curve is especially helpful in conceptualizing the story needs for each act. You can block out the major crisis point in each act and build the story conflict accordingly. With the interest curve in mind, you can examine the function of each act and determine its effectiveness in the total plot structure. You can see whether an act sustains or builds audience interest, and whether it makes effective use of dramatic beats or action points throughout the show.

Figure 5-1 is an example of how a 60-minute script, with four acts, might be set up.

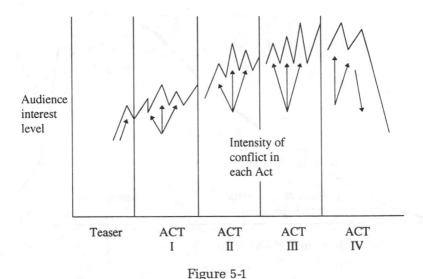

Figure 5-1

As with many shows, it begins with a short teaser, which hooks audience interest in a minute or so. The script builds the rising action and complications throughout each act, peaks to a climax at the end of Act III, and resolves the intensity of conflicts in Act IV, where the denouement falls. The end of an act usually peaks audience interest—to hold viewers throughout the commercial—and reflects a natural break in the storyline.

You can apply that same principle to the plotting of any film story, creatively guiding audience interest levels. For example, a two-hour television film might be charted as shown in Figure 5-2.

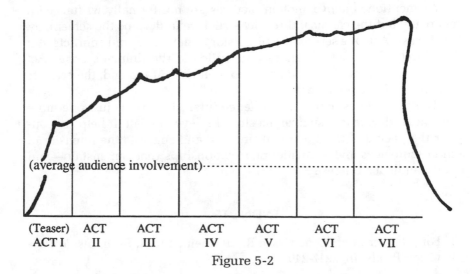

Figure 5-2

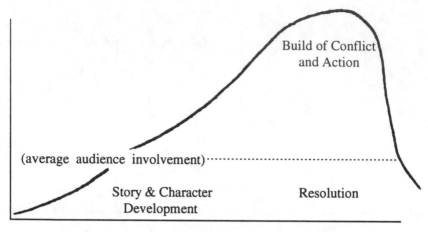

(No Act Breaks in Feature Films)

Figure 5-3

If you read from left to right, you can see that the short teaser was very effective as a hook, and that each act break was designed to maximize audience interest up until the commercial breaks. Interest picks up, with a snowballing effect throughout the entire show, and sustains until the end of Act VII.

For motion pictures, the chart might look a little different. A screenwriter has more time to develop characters and can build a slower pace that increases throughout the film. The result is a classic three-act structure and a skewed bell-shaped curve, as shown in Figure 5-3.

As mentioned above, motion pictures are not formally written with act breaks, but the classical three-act structure underpins the screenplay. In this case, Act One sets up the film's story, characters, and conflicts. Act Two develops the complications and builds to the dramatic crisis. Act Three builds the conflict and action to a climax. At the end, the crisis is resolved in the denouement.

The plot interest curve, or audience interest curve, is just one more conceptual device to visualize the story in development. It helps to consider the pacing of the story as it unfolds, and suggests the intensity of action sequences and dramatic interrelationships that can sustain—and build—audience interest.

ENDNOTE

1. For pilot script of "Coach," see R. Lindheim and R. Blum, *Inside Television Producing*, 217-249.

PART THREE

CREATING REALISTIC
CHARACTERS AND DIALOGUE

6

How to Create Credible and Castable Characters

As emphasized throughout this book, *characters are the driving force of your story*. Your hero must be someone the audience cares about—identifiable, susceptible, and vulnerable. That makes him or her appealing and castable.

To push the edges of conflict as far as possible, it helps if a protagonist faces powerfully motivated antagonists. The leads in THE FUGITIVE and UNFORGIVEN face extraordinary opponents, who are motivated to kill them at all costs.

If you create lead characters who are *proactive*, they are even more appealing to actors and audiences. In other words, they take positive action to get themselves out of a crisis, rather than sitting back passively.

Characters must resonate like real people, with a consistent pattern of behavior and dialogue and a complete, holistic, psycho/socio/physical being. The development of unique characters is indispensable to a compelling story and script. In the heat of sexual liaisons, encounters with aliens, car chases, or preparation for a trial, characters must be consistent in things they do, say, and think.

Creating Credible Characters

Knowing the character's 'inner life' is a crucial part of story development and scripting. You might not be able to define inner realities at the conceptual stage, but in the process of development, the character's personality emerges. It helps to know who the character is, how the character thinks, reacts, interrelates, behaves in any given situation. When characters are first created, detailed biographies can serve as springboards for story development. But the script must unveil that development through astute dramatic exposition.

One technique that helps identify realistic characterization is tied to the way actors interpret and analyze their roles. This approach is "the Method," taught by proponents of Stanislavski's acting system. Constantin Stanislavksi was artistic director of the Moscow Art Theatre in Russia, and his techniques provided actors with tools for realistic character development. He brought his techniques to America in the early 20th century.

Those techniques were modified, criticized, attacked, and misunderstood over the years, but they played a prominent role in the way actors, directors, and writers approached a script. In the U.S., the system was adapted by Lee Strasberg, Stella Adler, and others at the Group Theatre in New York in the 1930s. Later, at the Actors' Studio, Lee Strasberg put his emphasis on exploring inner techniques and psychoanalytic realism. That "psychoanalytic realism" became the cornerstone for Method training. It was also at the heart of artistic controversy in the 1950s and 1960s.

Stella Adler, who studied with Stanislavski, came to a different conclusion. Like Stanislavski, she had the greatest respect for playwrights and scripts. She taught that actors must derive their understanding of characters from analyzing given circumstances in the script.[1]

Using Acting Techniques: "The Method Writer"

I've found that television and screenwriters can benefit from the tools used by Method actors. Just a word of caution. Don't tell anybody you're using "the Method," or you'll get funny looks. Like you escaped through a time warp from Greenwich Village in the 1960s. But the fact is, no technique has more relevance for screenwriters, since every word you write is meant to be cast and performed in bigger-than-life closeups. In addition, variations of the Method remain the staple for acting training in television, film, and theatre today.

An actor trained in the Method approaches his or her character with a disciplined sense of creativity and spontaneity. In this sense, "disciplined" means using tools to create a sense of inner life for the characters in every scene of the script, from beginning to end.

As a "Method writer," you can flesh out the text and subtext in every scene. You can explore the motivations of characters, the consistency of attitudes, the justifiable actions and reactions in the plot structure. As the writer, you get to play every part, and if a behavioral problem is discovered, there's still time to fix it in a rewrite.

Here are some of the tools you can use to sharpen the realism and credibility of your characters: super objective, throughline of action, intentions, motivations, sense of urgency, state of being, moment-to-moment realities.

1. What Is the Super Objective?

The *super objective* is the main reason the character has been created. Each character, no matter how briefly he or she appears on screen, has a major objective to accomplish. This differentiates each character from the next.

2. What Is the Throughline of Action for Each Character?

The *throughline of action* is a conceptual thread that shows how each character fits into your main objective. Each character serves a very specific function in relation to the plot development and the realization of the super objective. Each scene should bring you closer to those goals.

3. What Is the Character's Intention?

The *intention* is the character's physical action in each scene. Intentions can change from scene to scene, and even within a scene—*if properly motivated*. Intentions are usually expressed as physical objectives. The character wants to do something, e.g., find a killer, experience a new theme park, fight a conspiracy, clear a cousin of murder, trip up burglars at home.

4. What Is the Character's Motivation?

The *motivation* explains *why* a character needs to achieve a specific intention. The analytical edge provides a more dimensional understanding of the character, and imprints a uniqueness on everything he or she does and says. It helps to convey the emotional subtext of each character.

If a character wants out of her marriage, there might be any number of emotional factors contributing to that decision. She may be frustrated, unfulfilled, afraid, attracted by someone else. The motivation imprints a uniqueness on her character, and provides a psychological framework for action and reaction throughout the treatment and script.

In BASIC INSTINCT, Nick, a homicide detective, knows the ins and outs of criminal minds, and is eager to close this case. But he's motivated by a steamy attraction he feels for Catherine. He knows she could be the murderer, but places himself in jeopardy because he's sexually enmeshed by her. Catherine is motivated by the complex psychological cat-and-mouse game she plays, her power over men (and women), her need to hide her secrets.

In JURASSIC PARK, John Hammond, billionaire developer, is motivated by egotism when he invites a select group to tour the park before it's ready to open. Dennis, a computer hack, is motivated by greed when he knocks out the security system to steal valuable vials. And when the dinosaurs run amok, all the characters—including the kids—are motivated by another basic instinct—survival.

In UNFORGIVEN, Munny, the bounty hunter, is motivated by the need to earn money to support himself and his kids. He's a widower who barely ekes out a living as a pig farmer.

5. What Is the Character's Sense of Urgency?

The sense of urgency is tied into the concept of intentions and motivations. It tells viewers how badly the character needs to achieve some goal or fulfill an intention. A rule of thumb: *the greater the sense of urgency, the greater the dramatic conflict.* If a character desperately wants to achieve a goal, and some obstacle is thrown in the way, the dramatic tension heightens in direct proportion to that emotional intensity.

In BASIC INSTINCT, Nick needs to find out who's responsible for the ice pick murders before she strikes again. It may be the woman he's sleeping with.

In JURASSIC PARK, the characters are fighting for survival at all costs—using their wits against predatory dinosaurs.

In MY COUSIN VINNY, an attorney who just passed the bar needs to save his cousin and friend wrongly accused of murder. If he fails, they'll go to prison for life.

There is always something important at stake.

6. What Is the Character's State of Being?

The *state of being* is a character's total psychological and physical frame of reference in a scene. A writer creates more realistic dimensions by incorporating given circumstances into the character's thoughts, behavior, and attitudes.

Let's create a scene with these given circumstances as an example. Joel is frantic to see Maggie. He runs over to her place, and finds it empty. It's been raining; it's late at night. What behavioral reality needs to be conveyed? Joel is wet, cold, out of breath, concerned, anguished. We can convey it all without a line of dialogue. The stage directions might suggest this: "Joel slams open the door, glances anxiously around the room, sees no one. Breathing hard, he wipes the rain from his face." And so the stage directions can paint reality through description, keeping alive all the elements in the circumstances of the scene.

7. Are the Moment-to-Moment Realities Established in the Scene?

These are the character's reactions to everything she or he experiences in the scene. These realities take into account all the circumstances of the scene, including the imprint of other characters, the imposition of the physical environment, and the psychological realities of each moment in the scene.

The *moment-to-moment reality* is a character's reaction to each and every dramatic unit, giving time to build attitudes and make internal adjustments. Let's set Tony up as a supervisor in a defense plant that's scheduled to close due to the recession. His orders are to reduce his staff, including Mona, his executive VP. When she learns about it, she may argue, storm out in anger. But Tony remains resolute. Only after the conflict is over does he take a beat (a *beat* is a dramatic moment in which the character makes internal transitions in thought or attitude). He picks up the phone and tells the president he'll quit if he has to do anything like that again. That action, in the privacy of his office, makes him a more sympathetic character in the eyes of the audience.

Such private moments are important for establishing the true inner nature of characters. The audience can see how genuinely concerned they are, how brutal, how comic, how gentle, how disturbed. It helps to build in a sense of vulnerability or susceptibility for each character. That makes them more identifiable and provides a more interesting dimension to their behavior.

Suppose we're in Seinfeld's apartment when a power failure hits New York. When the lights go out, Jerry would never think that the whole city is powerless. He would have to build logically to that moment of discovery. First, he might try the light switch or test the bulbs. Then he might discover that the light is out in Kramer's apartment. They both search for a flashlight, check the circuit breaker. And that's where they discover that the whole apartment building has gone dark. Jerry still has no idea of the scope of the blackout. He and Kramer go out into the street and find that the whole block is out. Then, through a neighbor, he learns the momentous reality—the whole city is dark.

Meanwhile, what are his moment-to-moment attitudes? This depends on Jerry's state of being, intention in the scene when it opened, motivations, and sense of urgency. If he was getting ready for an appearance on the "Tonight Show with Jay Leno," the power loss is frustrating. And he would go through each moment credibly to build that frustration. At first, he would simply be annoyed. That motivates him to correct the situation by finding a light bulb. However, the power is out in the other room. His reaction? Greater annoyance. He can't complete his intention. Now he learns that the whole apartment building is dark. His attitude? Frustration! He'll never have time to get ready for the "Tonight Show" appearance. When he learns that the whole city is dark, his attitude is coupled with anxiety and curiosity.

Each moment can be played out credibly, and each reaction conveyed effectively to the viewer. With the proper builds and reactions, we can avoid inconsistent or manipulated action that forces an incident or telegraphs the story. A viewer may know that the lights went out in New York, but there is no way for the character to know it until the actual moment of discovery.

That same technique can be used for building tensions in a scene. Suppose we create an obsessed escaped convict in the house of police siren Lynn. The viewers may know the danger, but she doesn't. That orchestrates the pacing of the drama. Once the audience knows the danger, we can take our time bringing Lynn to that confrontation scene—and heighten suspense. The obsessed convict takes a weapon and glides silently into a closet. Lynn may come into the room, take off her police uniform, and head to the closet—then spot a newspaper on the table. She tosses her uniform on the chair, glances anxiously at the paper's headlines about the escaped convict. Instinctively, she locks her front door. Now Lynn picks up her uniform, moves to the closet—and the phone rings. She answers. It's Molly, a partner who wants to know if she's all right. She reassures her partner, then hangs up. Now she heads to the closet. This time she opens it, and—nothing. She gets a hanger for her uniform and turns to go. Then, suddenly, a hand reaches out, and grabs her!

We can play all those realities in the plot to heighten the eventual confrontation. Hold the audience, surprise them, play out all the moment-to-moment tensions. But now the story needs a twist to help Lynn escape. Perhaps she breaks away through some ingenious action or special skill as a police siren. If she has some special skill, it's important to plant it earlier in the story, so it won't appear to be contrived. A story plant provides a logical and proper buildup for action on the screen.

"What if—?" Technique

A good suspense story is usually brimming with unusual turning points for characters—twists and turns in the plot, "red herrings," the unexpected. If a character gets into a hopeless situation, and the audience is totally caught up in the action, it is anticlimactic for the police to burst in and save him or her. The audience has seen it a hundred times before. The action becomes predictable and clichéd.

Think of the visual and dramatic turning points faced by lead characters in films like THE FUGITIVE, CLIFFHANGER, JURASSIC PARK, ROBOCOP, THE FIRM, PHILADELPHIA, BASIC INSTINCT, LAST ACTION HERO, UNFORGIVEN, ROMANCING THE STONE. The leads have to overcome enormous odds and then face even greater story twists.

One of the most useful devices for finding innovative twists is the *"What if—"* technique. As the story develops, ask a steady stream of *"What if—"* questions, until you find a number of different possibilities. *"What if this happens? What would my character do?"* Try to go beyond the first, immediate response. Give yourself a number of alternatives. Try any combination of thoughts that are consistent with the credibility of the piece.

The more you ask, *"What if—,"* the greater the possibility of keeping the characters alive, appealing, and castable. The flip side was aptly illustrated by a cartoon I remember seeing. A frustrated writer sits by a computer, pages strewn over the room. The caption went something like this: "Oh, to hell with it! 'Suddenly a lot of shots rang out, and everyone fell dead. The End.' "

Character Arcs

And that brings us to the subject of a *character arc*. Over a span of time, *motivated changes* occur in your characters, forcing them to act and react in ways that are driven by dramatic events. As a result, your character changes by the end of the film, but in a way that is consistent with who he or she was at the beginning.

In motion pictures, a character arc should seem natural and self-fulfilling. For example, at the beginning of THE CRYING GAME, Fergus befriends a British hostage he's been ordered to execute—which sets him up as a sensitive character. The driving force occurs when his hostage is accidentally killed. Fergus is proactive—he flees to London, and initiates a search to find his hostage's girlfriend. Fergus finds Dil, becomes romantically and sexually entangled with her, only to discover she is a he. It forces him to change his political alliances and his life choices. In the climax, he sacrifices himself in jail for the sake of Dil. That character arc is credible because Fergus is initially shown to us as a "sensitive" character.

In HOME ALONE, we meet Kevin, an eight-year-old, who is vulnerable and susceptible to the barbs and mishaps of his chaotic family. When he's left alone, he enjoys the new freedom, successfully overcomes his fear of furnaces, and then is ready to deal with two burglars. He is proactive—initiating booby traps. At the climax, he has more confidence and an understanding of himself and his family. It is a character arc that is fully motivated by the events that transformed him.

In television, character arcs refer to something different. They are the planned evolution of the characters and relationships in a series. That evolution is usually determined by a *show* runner (writer-producer) after a series has been on the air and the relationships are still changing. Some characters may be targeted for romance, breakup, promotion, or unemployment.

Sexual tension that bubbles between two leads is a wonderful way to maintain audience interest in a series. Think of the romantic undercurrents between Joel and Maggie in "Northern Exposure," Paul and Jamie in "Mad About You," the Coach and Christine in "Coach," Sam and Rebecca in "Cheers."

If the romantic tension is successful, that's one of the reasons audiences tune in. It is a daunting leap to have the character arcs resolved with an affair, marriage, breakup, or living together. But those elements do add freshness to series characters and have appeal for big audiences (especially during sweeps weeks). Nonetheless, the audience expects characters to have the same kind of tensions after the big event.

Character arcs allow actors to grow in ways that are credible for the character and conflicts already established.

ENDNOTE

1. For more on the Method, see Richard A. Blum, *Working Actors: The Craft of Television, Film, and Stage Acting*, Focal Press, 1989; R. Blum, *American Film Acting: The Stanislavski Heritage*, UMI Research Press, Ann Arbor, MI, 1984; Stella Adler, *The Technique of Acting*, Bantam Books, 1988; David Garfield, *A Player's Place: The Story of the Actors' Studio*, New York, Macmillan, 1980.

7

How to Create Realistic Dialogue for Comedy and Drama

Dialogue is an integral part of scripting, and is intricately bound up with character development. Inner values and motivations are communicated by the uniqueness of dialogue. What a character says—or doesn't say—tells us about that character's state of being.

Ideally, dialogue should be motivated by the circumstances in the scene, and should be consistent with the character development already established. Just as the writer has an "inner eye" for visualization, you've also got to have an "inner ear" for dialogue that makes the character come to life, adding a dimension of spontaneity and realism to the roles.

Dialogue for TV Comedy

In television, the style of dialogue matches the character as we've come to know him or her. In comedy, television producers are particularly finicky about the familiarity of characters to set up the gags to work properly. Let's look at some examples.

In "Coach," the audience knows that Coach Hayden Fox is a macho character who tries to succeed no matter what. His susceptibility lies in his desperate attempt to succeed in relationships. In this scene from the pilot, written by Barry Kemp, the Coach and Christine are trying to have a romantic dinner, but Hayden untaps surprising paternal feelings he has for his daughter who has just come to campus.

<u>SCENE D</u>

(HAYDEN, CHRISTINE)

<u>INT. HAYDEN'S CABIN—LATER THAT NIGHT</u>

<u>SFX: FIRE IN FIREPLACE</u>

HAYDEN AND CHRISTINE SIT AT THE CANDLE LIT
TABLE, HAVING DINNER AND A BOTTLE OF RED
WINE. BEHIND THEM, THE REMNANTS OF A FIRE
CRACKLES IN THE FIREPLACE. EVERYTHING THEY
USED TO MAKE DINNER IS STILL SITTING OUT IN
THE KITCHEN, BUT IT DOESN'T LOOK SO BAD IN
THE ROMANTIC GLOW OF FIRELIGHT. HOWEVER, IT'S
OBVIOUS BY HAYDEN'S DEMEANOR THAT HE IS NOT
REALLY INTO THE ROMANCE OF THE EVENING,
ALTHOUGH THAT'S NOT ANY FAULT OF CHRISTINE'S.
SHE'S MAKING AN EFFORT.

                    CHRISTINE

        (INDICATING HIS PLATE) Didn't you

        like it or were you just not hungry?

                    HAYDEN

        (REALIZING) No, it was good. I

        was...just trying not to get too full,

        that's all.

                    CHRISTINE

        Somehow I don't feel like I have your

        full attention tonight.

HAYDEN

(SHRUGGING THIS OFF) It's the game
Saturday. I'm always this way before
the season starts, you know that.

CHRISTINE

You want to talk about it?

HAYDEN

What about our rule? I thought we
decided we have so little time together
we wouldn't waste it discussing...

CHRISTINE

...things that really matter to us?
(OFF HAYDEN'S SMIRK) Well, if we're
going to get to the business we both
came for, I think we'd better clear up
the other stuff first.

A BEAT.

HAYDEN

(CONFESSING) I was thinking about my
daughter.

CHRISTINE

(UNEASILY) I thought you said you were thinking about the game.

HAYDEN

I lied. You still want to hear this?

CHRISTINE

(SQUEAMISHLY) This is really personal, isn't it? Okay, go ahead. Just go slow. We're both new at this, remember.

HAYDEN

(WITH A SIGH) I was just wondering what kind of guy I am sometimes, that's all. I could've made Kelly stay this afternoon if I'd really wanted to, but the truth is there was a part of me that wanted to be here tonight with you and not with her.

CHRISTINE

I'm having a hard time telling you that was a terrible thing.

HAYDEN

It's not terrible, it's just selfish. My whole life I've told myself I was doing the noble thing by not being more a part of Kelly's life. The truth is, I just didn't want to take the time. I don't know why time scares me, but it does. I wonder if I got into coaching because I really like it, or because four years is about all the time I'm capable of committing to any one human being.

CHRISTINE

(PUSHING AWAY FROM THE TABLE)

O-kay, that's going deep enough.

HAYDEN

(QUICKLY TAKING HER HAND) I'm not talking about you.

SHE STOPS. HE LOOKS AT HER A MOMENT, HOLDING HER HAND.

HAYDEN (CONT'D)

Can I say something really honest?

CHRISTINE

(UNEASILY) Yes. If you really have to.

HAYDEN

I wish I'd made Kelly stay today. I
know that's a lousy thing to say to
you, but—

CHRISTINE

Hayden, you don't have to be sorry for
feeling something for your daughter. I'm
not jealous.

HAYDEN

No?

CHRISTINE

No. In fact...(SUDDENLY SURPRISED)
...how's this for honest? All those
times I've told you I found you sexy?
Like when you're stalking the sidelines
during a game, or when you're working
in the den real intensely coming up
with some brilliant new play?

HAYDEN

Yeah?

CHRISTINE

You're not nearly as sexy as you are

right now.

HAYDEN

(SURPRISED) Yeah?

CHRISTINE

Yeah. (A BEAT) And now I have to

leave you.

HAYDEN

(CONFUSED) Why??

CHRISTINE

Because you have to call your daughter.

The wrong person's hearing these

things.

SHE RISES FOR HER COAT AND BAG.

HAYDEN

(ALSO RISING) But you don't have to

leave. You can wait. I'll call my daugh-

(MORE)

HAYDEN (CONT'D)

ter while you're cleaning up the

kitchen. Or heck, I'll clean up the

kitchen and you can just drink wine.

CHRISTINE

(GATHERING UP HER THINGS; AMUSED)

Not tonight, Hayden.

HAYDEN

But I don't think you realize how much

better I feel now.

SMILING, SHE WALKS OVER TO HIM AND GIVES HIM
A VERY LONG AND TENDER KISS.

CHRISTINE

I'll see you next time I'm in town.

SHE GRABS A SET OF HIS KEYS AND STARTS OUT.

HAYDEN

Christine, wait...

CHRISTINE

I'm taking your car. I'll park it dis-

creetly on the side street near the

hotel so no one will see it. You can

ride your bike in tomorrow.

HAYDEN

My bike?

CHRISTINE

It'll be good for you. I have a feeling you're going to have a lot of pent-up energy to burn.

HAYDEN

Come on, don't do this to me...

CHRISTINE

(AS SHE HEADS OUT) Call your daughter, Hayden.

HAYDEN

Christine!...

CHRISTINE

(AS SHE CROSSES THROUGH THE PORCH) And clean your kitchen. (STOPPING AND TURNING BACK) God, I want you.

SHE TURNS AND EXITS FROM THE PORCH. HAYDEN IS LEFT ALONE.

HAYDEN

(TO HIMSELF) This isn't fair...

AS HE CLOSES THE DOOR, WE...

DISSOLVE TO:

The dialogue shows the susceptibility of both characters. It forces them into a crisis that's resolved in a comic twist. With the best of intentions, she leaves him stranded and frustrated.

The same comic potential is true of all characters who reveal their vulnerability. In this scene from "Murphy Brown," an exasperated Murphy confronts her replacement, who is everything Murphy relates to—attractive, independent, and an alcoholic in hiding. Murphy confronts Hillary five minutes before air time.

HILLARY

Okay, okay. So I had a little to drink.

I just needed to relax. I'll be fine by

showtime.

MURPHY

You've got fifteen minutes.

HILLARY

Oh god.

HILLARY LOOKS AROUND THE ROOM IN A PANIC.

MURPHY

Looking for the bottle, aren't you? Boy, this takes me back. "I can't go on the air without a drink." "I can't get to sleep without a drink." And my personal favorite—"I can't go out for a drink without a drink."

HILLARY

You know, this holier-than-thou attitude. I've had about all I can take. So if you don't mind, take a hike. I have a broadcast to do.

HILLARY GETS UP WITH SOME DIFFICULTY, KNOCK-
ING THE CONTENTS OF A COFFEE CUP ONTO HER
NOTE CARDS.

HILLARY (CONT'D)

Oh dammit. (TRYING TO BLOT WITH KLEENEX) You see what you made me do.

MURPHY

...Hillary, you can't go on the air now.

                        HILLARY

        Oh, you'd like that, wouldn't you, huh.

        You'd like that a lot.

                        MURPHY

        (SOMETHING SNAPS) What the hell am

        I doing? Why do I even care?—I don't

        need to go through this again. I'm out

        of here.

SHE STARTS TO EXIT, THEN STOPS BEFORE SHE
GETS OUT THE DOOR.

                        MURPHY (CONT"D)

        I just want to say one thing. I know

        you, Hillary. I know all the work and

        the pushing and every single thing you

        gave up to get here. Years of missing

        people's birthdays and spending Satur-

        day nights by yourself in some airport.

        All that sacrifice, just to get a chance

        like this . . .

HILLARY LOOKS UP AT HER.

                    MURPHY (CONT'D)

...And in one hour, you're blowing it.

Good for you.

MURPHY TURNS TO GO.

                    HILLARY

Murphy, wait.

MURPHY STOPS.

                    HILLARY (CONT'D)

...Okay, I got myself into a little trou-

ble tonight. But you know how it is.

This business—it's so hard. Especially

for a woman. And the pressure of live

television—

                    MURPHY

Sorry, Hillary, put the blame where you

want. But in the end, it's just you in

the mirror. If you're ever going to beat

this thing, you have to admit you need

help.

                    HILLARY

I think I just need a vacation. I

haven't taken any time off in three

years. Maybe a little rest or—

                    MURPHY

I don't have the energy for this. I

can't even tie my own shoes. I can't

see my own shoes.

                    MURPHY (CONT'D)

(THEN) Look, Hillary, I can get you

through this. But you have to admit

you need help or I'm not putting

myself through another eighty-proof

wringer. What's it going to be?

                    HILLARY

I know you're right, Murphy. I need to

be a better person.

                    MURPHY

That's not what I said. Listen to me.

You need help. Say it.

HILLARY

I understand. Counseling is probably the way to go. I tried it once, but the therapist was such an idiot, it didn't—

MURPHY

Hillary! I—need—help. Say it.

HILLARY

I—I wanted to be great tonight. Oh god. How did I let this happen?

MURPHY

Say it.

THERE'S A LONG PAUSE. THIS IS SO DIFFICULT. THEN FINALLY—

HILLARY

(QUIETLY) I need help.

MURPHY

Alright. (SMILING) Alright. This is good. The first step. There are eleven more after this, but we can talk about that later...How do you feel?

                    HILLARY

Drained. Sick...and very relieved.

                    MURPHY

Congratulations. (THEN, TAKING

CHARGE) Okay, I'm a little out of prac-

tice, but here's what we do. We come up

with a good excuse for why you can't

do the show, I sit in for you this week,

and you do the show next week. (ON A

ROLL) The key is the excuse has to be

believable. My personal favorite: food

poisoning. Quick, dramatic, and nobody

wants the details. God, it's amazing how

it all comes back to you.

                    HILLARY

Murphy, I don't know how to thank

you.

                    MURPHY

Oh, that's easy. You'll let me make a

reservation for you at Betty Ford. I'll

                    (MORE)

MURPHY (CONT'D)

ask for my old room. I carved a couple

of raunchy limericks in the middle desk

drawer you might enjoy. Now I'll need

your notes. I've got to get to the set.

MURPHY PICKS UP THE COFFEE-STAINED NOTE
CARDS.

MURPHY (CONT'D)

Who am I interviewing again?

HILLARY

The Secretary of Defense...what's his

name.

MURPHY

Aw God...it's on the tip of my tongue.

HILLARY

...begins with a "c"...

MURPHY

...I've known the man for years...

HILLARY

Richard something...

AS THE TWO THINKING-IMPAIRED WOMEN TRY TO
HIT ON THE NAME, WE—

FADE OUT.

END OF SHOW

The script, "On the Rocks," written by Ron Lux and Eugene Stein, handles the complications effectively. The dialogue could have gone to extremes, and pushed a message about the Betty Ford clinic. If that had happened, the comedy would have been lost. But the dialogue sounds real for Murphy. She's exasperated, annoyed, and takes charge.

Television critic Richard Zoglin did an interesting analysis of the comedy in "Seinfeld" and "Cheers." He felt the laugh points in "Cheers" have become so familiar they could almost write themselves. The jokes center on the characters' vulnerabilities—Woody's naiveté, Carla's surliness, Cliff's "out to lunch" mailman monologues, and Sam's womanizing. This is a scene he used to prove the point. In it, Frasier is upset by a good-bye letter from Lillith.[1]

FRASIER
(Reading goodbye letter from Lillith)
"Dear Frasier, Life in the Eco Pod is
wonderful. Gogie and I are happier
than we've ever been. Please start
divorce proceedings. Our marriage is..."
(He is overcome)

WOODY
(dumbly)
Made in heaven..?

FRASIER
"...our marriage is over."

CLIFF
That really burns my hide that Lillith
sent him that mailgram.

FRASIER
Well, thank you, Cliff.

CLIFF
All of a sudden the first class stamp
isn't good any more?

The jokes play around the dialogue of intimate and embarrassing moments happening at the bar—a classic group and family pattern show.

In contrast, Zoglin dissects the Seinfeld characters, who play off the intimacies and susceptibilities of a group of neurotic friends who really seem to care about each other. As he points out, the series, created by Jerry Seinfeld and Larry David, is an outgrowth of standup comedy, but dialogue spins off trivial observations. Here, George complains about his vulnerability now that he has a job as a comedy writer.[2]

GEORGE
Can you believe my luck? The first
time in my life that I have a good
answer to the question, "What do you
do?" And I have a girlfriend. I mean,
you don't need a girlfriend when you
can answer that question. That's what
you say to get girlfriends. Once you
can get girlfriends, you don't want a
girlfriend, you just want more girlfriends.

JERRY
(deadpan)
You're going to make a very good
father someday.

The characters play off the paradoxes of everyday life, with transcendent comic effect.

Dialogue for TV Drama

Drama plays strong if the leads sound like the characters of the show. For example, in the series "Law & Order," Stone likes to be poker-faced and in command. In this scene from the pilot, written by Dick Wolf, Stone is about to force a deal with a mobster, Scalisi, and his attorney. Stone adroitly exploits the vulnerability of his antagonists in his office.

ACT FOUR

FADE IN

INT. STONE'S OFFICE-DAY
He waves his hand in dismissal.

                    STONE
          We'll get back to you...

                    COSMATOS
          I haven't even made an offer.

                    STONE
          Trust me...you wouldn't like the
          counter.

Scalisi glares at his lawyer, then turns to Stone.

                    SCALISI
          I can tell you things...

Stone turns his poker face to Scalisi.

                    STONE
          What? You going to tell me all about
          Parking Tickets?
                    (shaking his head)
          Yours is already punched, pal...we
          know all about Carnegie Collections.

Scalisi is rocked by Stone's announcement.

                    SCALISI
          I've got a lot of names.

Stone shakes his head and points to the door.

                  STONE
See you in court.

                  SCALISI
       (getting upset)
Hey! I'm not talking G-4s here...these
are your basic elected officials and a
deputy Police Commissioner.

                  STONE
       (to Cosmatos)
Don't have him make me call security.

Cosmatos takes his client's elbow.

               COSMATOS
Come on, Tony.

                  SCALISI
       (facade cracking)
I ain't going down alone behind this...
       (to Stone)
What do you want?

Stone manages a tiny smile.

                  STONE
Want? I want it all. You testify. You
give names, dates, and amounts. You
flush all those true blue public officials.

                  SCALISI
That gets me a walk?

                  STONE
       (shaking his head)
Only way you walk is you tell me who
gave the order.

Silence. Scalisi looks at Stone.

                              SCALISI
          You know I can't.

                              STONE
                         (shrugging)
          No Masucci, no free ride.

Cosmatos takes off his glasses and cleans them with
his tie.

                              COSMATOS
          But the public officials could lead to a
          plea of let's say ... assault?

                              STONE
          Let's say voluntary manslaughter.

                              COSMATOS
          Let's say involuntary.

                              STONE
          Then he wears a wire.

                              SCALISI
          Are you crazy? They'll know I've been
          busted ... they'll smell it.

                              STONE
          You let me worry about that.

                              COSMATOS
          What kind of sentencing recommenda-
          tion?

                              STONE
          Depends what's on the tape.

He looks from Scalisi to Cosmatos, then looks at his
watch.

                              STONE (CONT'D)
          Tick tock, gentlemen ...

Scalisi nods miserably.

>   STONE
>   (nodding back; satisfied)
>   I'll have it typed up.

>   ROBINETTE
>   (to Stone)
>   We'd better get to the hospital...

>   CUT TO

INT. SURGEON'S SCRUB ROOM-DAY

Stone and Robinette talk to Dr. Goldberg, a cardiologist in a sweat stained operating gown.

>   GOLDBERG
>   The guy had arteries the diameter of
>   capillaries.

>   ROBINETTE
>   So with the traumatic loss of six units
>   of blood, there was a causative connec-
>   tion between the assault and the coro-
>   nary?

>   GOLDBERG
>   C'mon, guys...you don't want to ask
>   me that..."causative connection?"

>   STONE
>   Whoa, whoa...excuse me...
>   (adopting a courtroom demeanor)
>   Mr. Halsey had a regular doctor, right,
>   Dr. Goldberg?

Stone's dialogue plays like a ticking timebomb. He sets up the deal, working on his instincts. He works Scalisi through the wringer with dialogue, hitting all the raw edges to exploit the characters' vulnerabilities and fears.

Problems and Solutions in Writing Dialogue

Often, the first run at dialogue presents some problems. Lines may be choppy, staccato, unrealistic, or perhaps melodramatic. The script might be peopled with characters transposed from an English drawing room comedy ("quite grammatically correct, but evuh so bor-ing, dahling"), or with characters misplaced from an unedited version of reality-based TV ("Well . . . um . . . uh . . . y'know what I mean . . . huh?").

To help identify and overcome those problems, with some deference to David Letterman, here is a list of "The Top Ten Most Common Dialogue Problems and Solutions."

"The Top Ten Most Common Dialogue Problems and Solutions"

1. Too Head-On

This is dialogue that is much too literal and embarrassingly obvious. It sounds very contrived. For example:

CHRISTINE comes in the door and COACH smiles.

> COACH
> Christine, I'm so glad to see you. I love you so much. I've been waiting to see you for so long.

That kind of dialogue is pretty embarrassing. No subtlety at all. It would be more effective if he were too overcome to speak. Or he might grab her close and say nothing. Then, after a beat, he might say:

> COACH
> Y'know, I can't stand to see you.

And they hug.

Well, of course, actions speak louder than words, and you've built a nice counterpoint to the action. Christine knows what he means, and so does the audience. Subtlety can be achieved through understatement, "playing against" the expected material, and playing out the characters' subtexts and inner attitudes.

2. Too Choppy

This is dialogue that is staccato. Filled with one-liners. A word or two. When you thumb through the script, it looks like an early Pinter stage play rather than a cinematic project. This is an example of dialogue that's too choppy:

> DAN
>
> I'm hungry.

> ROSEANNE
>
> Me too.

> DAN
>
> Let's go out to eat.

> ROSEANNE
>
> O.k.

> DAN
>
> Is the deli o.k.?

> ROSEANNE
>
> Yes, it's o.k.

One solution to this problem is providing credible motivation for dialogue. The characters need a motivation and intention for speaking. They need a pre-established pattern of thought and behavior. Dan, for example, might be checking out the refrigerator through an earlier piece of action, then:

> DAN
>
> Hey, there's nothing in here. Wanna go out?

> ROSEANNE
>
> Mmm. I'm famished.

> DAN
>
> How does the deli sound?

ROSEANNE
Like chicken soup heaven.

And they race each other out the door.

In essence, the dialogue is the building block for moment-to-moment realities in the scene. It should spark behavioral action and reaction to be most effective.

3. Too Repetitious

Dialogue becomes repetitious when a character repeats himself or herself in a number of different ways. The character offers redundant information, or repetitive phrases.

ILENE
I had such a good time on the trip. It was one of the best trips I ever had.

ARTIE
I'm glad you enjoyed the trip.

ILENE
It was so good to be away. It was a terrific trip.

It seems as if the writer doesn't know what the character should say next, so relies on earlier dialogue—or is afraid the audience won't "get" a specific point unless a character emphasizes it. One solution is to go back into the script and clearly motivate each speech—or delete the speech altogether. This is how the dialogue above might be handled in revision:

ARTIE
You must have had some time. I never saw you so relaxed.

ILENE
It was wonderful. I'm sorry it's over.

The simple character interchange affects the whole point of the dialogue exchange. One character reacts to the other's emotional and physical state of being in the scene. As for points the viewer should "get," put some preliminary plants in the script. Then a casual line of dialogue by a character is sufficient to trigger the "Aha!" syndrome for the audience.

4. Too Long

Dialogue that is too long reads like an editorial speech or a philosophical diatribe. It creates static action in the script and often includes related problems of redundancy and preachiness. Let's examine this speech:

> JESSICA
>
> (to Anne)
>
> You didn't get the position because you're a woman, not for any other reason. If you were a man you would have been hired on the spot. Don't let them do that to you. Go back and fight for what you believe in. They wouldn't get away with that on me. I can assure you of that. I remember when I was growing up, my mother always told me to look out for sexists. You've got to stand up and let them know you're not going to take that kind of treatment.

The speech tends to dominate visual action and incorporates too many different thoughts, without essential breaks for transitions or reactions. It would be helpful to intersperse reactions and stage directions at the end of each major unit of thought. That makes the speech seem less formidable, and its impact more immediate. Here's what it might look like.

> JESSICA
>
> (to Anne)
>
> If you were a man you would have gotten it.

Anne tries not to pay attention. She's in no mood
for Jessica's tirade.

> JESSICA (CONT'D)
> Don't let them treat you that way. Go
> back and fight for what you believe in.

Anne says nothing. Jessica sees she's getting
nowhere, crosses over to her friend and speaks
softly but urgently.

> JESSICA (CONT'D)
> I was always warned about sexists like
> that. Let them know you're not going
> to take it.

A BEAT, then Anne turns to look at her friend. The
conviction is sinking in.

The idea is to integrate emotional reactions into a long speech and trim
the excesses. Long speeches are not always a problem, especially in court
dramas. But emotional reactions add much to the context. It might be possible for Jessica, for example, to blurt out the dialogue in anger and frustration. That emotional reaction might be germane to her state of being. If
so, the speech can stand on its own merits.

5. Too Similar

Sometimes characters sound the same. Their dialogue patterns are
indistinguishable from each other. Once that happens, the character's
individuality has been lost. Can you distinguish between these two?

> MONA
> Hey, did you bet on the car race?

> VINNIE
> Yeah, I did. Did you?

> MONA
> Yeah. Did ya win?

> VINNIE
> Nah, not when I needed it.

The characters sound precisely the same, and they're redundant on top of it. One way to counter the problem is to provide some psychological richness to the scene. The characters need to be re-examined in terms of motivations, intentions, and sense of urgency.

Since Mona and Vinnie are two different human beings, their inner thoughts and attitudes might be expressed in totally different dialogue structure. Here's how the scene might play.

> MONA
> (tentatively)
> You bet on the race?

VINNIE shrugs off the question.

> VINNIE
> Sure.

> MONA
> Did you win? Vinnie?

No response. Then:

> VINNIE
> Not this time. Not when I needed it.

She crosses to him and puts her arms around him, reassuringly.

The conflicts are implied. When creating dialogue, remember that your characters are unique human beings, with the ability to interact at the highest levels of subtlety and complexity.

One producer told me he covers the names of characters during the first pass at a script, to see if they're drawn dimensionally. If he can't distinguish between the blocks of dialogue, he discards the script as "characterless."

6. Too Stilted

This is dialogue that sounds as if it came from a history book, a poem, a newspaper, a grammar text, but not from a person. This is an example of stilted dialogue:

> JEFFREY
> It is my responsibility to provide you
> with my interpretation of the event. You
> are the only person that might accept
> that perspective. You must hear me out.

Unless Jeffrey has a particularly pedantic problem it would be more appropriate for him to colloquialize and get to the bottom line quickly.

> JEFFREY
> You gotta listen to me!

And that says it all. Don't be afraid to use contractions in dialogue. That's the way real people speak.

It helps to read dialogue aloud to hear the character in action. If the speech pattern is stilted, you can improvise to find a more spontaneous feel to the character's actions. At your desk, with no one else around, put the same characters into different conflicts. You'll be surprised how much you learn about them.

7. Too Preachy

This is a problem related to being "head on," "redundant," "too long," and "too stilted." The character tends to sound very formal, and espouses thematic ideas or philosophical notions. He or she becomes an ideological mouthpiece for the writer, rather than a dimensional being. This speech, for example, borders on the preachy:

> MIKE
> Do you see what happens when convicts
> run free? They belong in jail, or they
> threaten the very fiber of society. This
> sort of thing would never happen if we
> had stronger lawmakers and laws.

If a character must speak with strong convictions, it doesn't have to sound like an editorial. Mike can get the same point across by growling:

MIKE
The bastard oughta be locked away.

The exact nature of the dialogue is, of course, dependent on the unfolding action in the scene, and the consistency of the motivations and behavior of the character throughout the story and script.

8. Too Introspective

This problem deals specifically with the character who is alone, and speaks out loud. This cliché is typical:

MICHELLE
(to herself)
Oh, how I long to be with him now.

That's enough to make any writer cringe. How often does a person actually talk to herself or himself? Not very. And when we do, it's *not* in complete, logical sentences. Logic is antithetical to the emotion of the moment. The dramatic conventions of a Shakespearean soliloquy are very different from the cinematic expectations of television and film.

It makes more sense for the character to build a private moment on screen. She might glance at a picture, close her eyes, and try to regain her composure. Once again, actions speak louder than words.

9. Too Inconsistent

This means that a character is saying something that doesn't "fit" the personality already created. The dialogue is incongruous with character. In some cases, that inconsistency is due to lack of proper transitions in the scene. This is an example of erratic dialogue or attitudes that change too quickly to be believed.

JENNIFER
I wish you would both listen to me.

> JASON
>
> No! Fran and I have better things to
> do.

> JENNIFER
>
> I'm telling you this for your own good.

> JASON
>
> O.k., we'll do it.

The thought transitions are simply too quick to be credible. It might work better if the proper actions and reactions are built into the scene through suggested transitions. This is one way of handling that problem.

> JENNIFER
>
> I wish you would both listen to me.

> JASON
>
> No!

He glances up at his sister, and sees the hurt in her eyes. Then, softer, he tries to explain.

> JASON (CONT'D)
>
> Fran and I have important things to
> do.

That obviously has no impact. She tries to control the urgency in her voice.

> JENNIFER
>
> I'm telling you this for your own
> good.—

A long BEAT, then Jason turns away, heading toward the couch. He mulls it over. Finally:

> JASON
>
> O.k., we'll do it.

Jennifer breathes a sigh of relief.

Sometimes the problem of inconsistent dialogue can be helped by analyzing the character's inner drives and attitudes on a moment-to-moment basis in the scene. The solution might simply be to build more transition time, or build more character development into the script.

10. Too Unbelievable

This is a catch-all category that implies that a character doesn't sound real for any number of reasons. You can test the credibility of dialogue by speaking it aloud to judge whether or not it rings true. It should sound like a real person responding to the immediate circumstances we've just seen.

If there is a problem, try this exercise: *improvise*. Out loud, or on your computer, put the same characters into a different conflict. It should be a direct conflict of wills, each with totally opposing intentions. The two characters might thrash out the conflict in two or three pages. One may give in, one may walk out, both may compromise. The outcome is not important. However, the dialogue, motivations, and behavior must be logical and consistent. Once you know how the individual characters interact, the integrity of the characters is assured. The original dialogue can be tested against your heightened insight into motivations, intentions, and attitudes.

ENDNOTES

1. Richard Zoglin, "Passing the Sitcom Torch," *Time*, May 10, 1993, 60.
2. Ibid.

PART FOUR

SCRIPT
VISUALIZATION

8

How to Write Effective
Script Visualization

Your writing style can flourish with imagery used in scene descriptions. You can paint the universe of stories and characters with vivid descriptions of locale, and character actions and reactions. Visual descriptions greatly enhance the mood, atmosphere, pacing, and producibility of a script.

New writers tend to be concerned about the length of stage directions. Each scene requires its own analysis in the context of the production format. A general rule is: Try to keep stage directions as short as possible, but replete with the imagery necessary to keep the characters alive in the locale.

In film, you have the luxury of building richly textured scenes. Not so in episodic television.

Television Comedy

In television comedy, descriptions are considerably shorter, simply because of production pragmatics. The half-hour script concentrates primarily on the dialogue of the characters and the main stage business of the characters in the main sets.

For the most part you'll be working with characters and sets that are standard for the show. Here is an excerpt from a sample "Murphy Brown" script. It opens up in the middle of a scene (INT. BULLPEN) with all the characters present, praising Murphy's replacement. In the next scene, INT. MURPHY'S OFFICE, a jealous Murphy breaks into her own office to find her replacement, Hillary, passed out.

MURPHY

This is great. She's doing my story,

she's in my office. Why don't you just

give her the keys to my car?

MILES

Come on, Murphy. The woman is fan-

tastic. A real perfectionist. (CROSSING)

I don't want to interrupt her while

she's working. When you see her, tell

her we've already gone down to the

studio, okay, Murphy?

MURPHY

(LITTLE)...Okay.

THEY ALL GET INTO THE ELEVATOR. AS THE <u>DOORS</u>
<u>CLOSE</u>:

MURPHY (CONT'D)

(LOST)...Bye.

SHE STANDS THERE FOR A MOMENT, A KID LOST IN
A PARKING LOT. THEN SHE WALKS OVER TO HER
OFFICE AND TRIES TO SUBTLY LOOK INSIDE

THROUGH THE BLINDS. SHE SEES SOMETHING. SHE
GOES TO THE DOOR AND QUIETLY OPENS IT.

RESET TO:

INT. MURPHY'S OFFICE - CONTINUOUS ACTION
(Hillary, Murphy)

HILLARY IS NOT WORKING ON HER COPY. HER
COPY IS SPREAD OUT ON THE DESK IN FRONT OF
HER AND SHE IS SLUMPED OVER IT.

MURPHY

...Hillary?

NOTHING.

MURPHY (CONT'D)

(A LITTLE LOUDER) Hillary.

HILLARY

(STIRRING) What?...

MURPHY

Rise and shine. Up and at 'em.

SHE LIFTS HER HEAD UP — BARELY AT FIRST. SHE
LOOKS AWFUL.

HILLARY

Oh no. I must have fallen asleep. I've

been working so hard...

<pre>
                    MURPHY

    Yeah, uh-huh. Working hard. (MURPHY

    STARTS CHECKING OUT THE ROOM)

    Gee, smells lovely in here. Reminds me

    of the stockroom at the Liquor Barn.
</pre>

MURPHY SPOTS SOMETHING UNDER SOME PAPERS
ON THE DESK. SHE PICKS UP AN EMPTY BOTTLE OF
LIQUOR.

<pre>
                MURPHY (CONT'D)

    Ah, here it is. The expensive stuff.

    Well, at least you're a discriminating

    drunk.
</pre>

MURPHY DROPS THE BOTTLE IN THE TRASH.
THROUGHOUT, HILLARY IS COHERENT, BUT IS WORK-
ING VERY HARD TO SOUND SOBER. SHE IS NOT
SUCCESSFUL.

The directions are funny, quick, and consistent with Murphy. She finds Hillary passed out, Hillary lifts her head up; Hillary looks awful. When Murphy checks out the room, we know from her actions and dialogue that it smells like a brewery. It motivates her to look for the bottle of liquor, find it hidden under some papers on the desk, and drop it in the trash. The writers (Ron Lux and Eugene Stein) give us the look, smell, and feel in stage directions—even in the compressed half-hour format.

Let's look at another example. This is the visual description of Hayden's office in the pilot script for "Coach." With humor, it sets up the locale, characters, actions, and dialogue.

ACT ONE

SCENE A

(HAYDEN,
LUTHER,
DAUBER)

FADE IN:

INT. COACH'S OFFICE - DAY

LOCATED IN THE BASEMENT OF THE FIELDHOUSE,
THE OFFICE IS A COLLECTING BIN FOR EVERY POS-
SIBLE ITEM YOU CAN MAKE TO PROMOTE MIN-
NESOTA STATE FOOTBALL, INCLUDING COFFEE MUGS,
GLASSWARE, LAMPS, WASTE BASKETS, BLANKETS,
CALENDARS, KEY RINGS, SEAT CUSHIONS, CAPS,
SWEATSHIRTS, BUMPER STICKERS, LITTLE STUFFED
SCREAMING EAGLE MASCOTS, ETC. ALSO PROMINENT
ARE A BLACKBOARD, A WEIGHT SCALE, A POSTER
OF THE UPCOMING SEASON'S SCHEDULE, AND A
LARGE WALL-HANGING PROCLAIMING: "THIS IS MIN-
NESOTA STATE FOOTBALL!" AT THE MOMENT, HAY-
DEN IS SITTING BEHIND HIS DESK, FEET UP,
ENDURING AN INTERVIEW ON THE PHONE.

HAYDEN

(INTO PHONE) Well, East Texas is a

physical team — well-coached. They had

some tough luck last year winning only

two and losing nine but a break here

or there and they could just as easily

have been nine and two.

LUTHER VAN DAM SUDDENLY ENTERS. IN HIS MID
'50'S, MARRIED ONLY TO FOOTBALL, AND WITH A
WALK THAT LOOKS AS IF HE'S BEEN BLOCKED IN
THE KNEES ONE TOO MANY TIMES, LUTHER IS A
MAN LIVING FOREVER UNDER THE BELIEF THE SKY
IS FALLING, AND IT'S ABOUT TO LAND ON HIM.

At the top of the scene, note the names in parentheses: "HAYDEN,
LUTHER, DAUBER." That is a designation to explain who is in the scene.
It's typically used in half-hour shows, but not in longform or features.

In the descriptions, Barry Kemp cleverly sets up the locale (INT.
COACH'S OFFICE) as a "collecting bin for every possible item you can
make to promote Minnesota State football." We learn a lot about Hayden's
character, sitting behind the desk, feet up, "enduring" yet another interview on the phone. When Luther enters, we find out he's mid-50's, married only to football, and "with a walk that looks as if he's been blocked
in the knees one too many times"—a good comic touch.

Incidentally, the characters are described here because this is the
pilot script. Hayden was introduced when he first appeared in the teaser.
In a regular episode of a show, you wouldn't describe them at all, except
for stage actions and reactions. You would have to describe any *new* characters in the script.

Television Drama

In one-hour drama and television films, you have more time to
embellish the scenes. The locations have a built-in value for the dramatic
involvement of characters and production values. Just keep in mind that
some locales can be very costly to produce.

When Dick Wolf created "Law & Order," he wanted the show to have
a distinctly different visual atmosphere. He wanted the look and feel of
New York streets, with handheld cameras and a fast-paced, story-driven
drama. This is how he described it on the first page of the pilot script:

PRODUCTION NOTE

"Law and Order" represents a conscious shift away
from many of the conventions of one hour dramatic
series. Aside from the format change of following
one case through the criminal justice system by

telling two discrete stories with two separate sets of
stars (Police and D.A.'s), there will be a visual difference which will help set the tone of the series. It
is anticipated that the show will be shot on 16mm
Panaflex and finished on tape, the aim being to
achieve a <u>cinema verité</u>, semi-documentary look,
replete with hand held camera and naturalistic lighting. In line with this look, almost all locations, with
the exception of the requisite standing sets, will be
practical. In addition, there will be an editorial style
of "hard cutting." The series will avoid the use of
transition shots of cars driving up, exterior establishing shots of buildings, people walking into rooms,
etc. This style will also influence pace, which will, of
necessity, be quick, as we will move from story
point to story point. In addition, there will be a
locked P.O.V. — the audience will see or hear only
what the cops or D.A.'s do. The fact that each half
hour will essentially be telling the same type of
story that might be seen in an entire hour of a typical cop show necessitates a certain economy of style
which will, in turn, become the series' stylistic signature.

Despite the expense of shooting in New York, he wanted the produced scripts to look as if they were shot in the city, conveying the
urgency of an urban cop's beat.[1]

Motion Pictures

In features, you have more time to build the visual pacing of the
script. In motion pictures, scene descriptions can be long enough to establish the full flavor of the place and action, or short enough to keep the
pacing alive and the reader interested in the story flow and dialogue.

Using recognizable locales in the script gives it familiarity and
embellishes the scene. If a character is near a theme park in Orlando, tries
to find parking in Georgetown, waits under the arch of McDonald's, real
images are conjured up.

In this script sample from SONJA'S MEN, my partner (Allan Gerson)
and I wanted to set everyday actions, like puttering in the garden, against
the unexpected reality our lead character is enduring. Sonja has just

learned that her father may be guilty of war crimes, and will be put on trial to be deported. In this scene she tries to get the truth out of him, as he putters near a pomegranate tree. She watches him, noticing how frail he looks. Sonja tries to understand, but he goes back to the tree, fixing some mound of earth.


```
EXT. TYROWICZ BACKYARD - DAY

Sonja and Tyrowicz are near the large pomegranate
tree. He's preoccupied, taking care of the garden.

                    TYROWICZ
          It's all the Russians doing, Sonja.

                    SONJA
          Papa, there must be more to it. Tell me
          the truth. What did you do during the
          war?

He continues to putter in the garden.

                    TYROWICZ
          I was a clerk. I did what the Germans
          wanted. Translated orders.

                    SONJA
          Death orders?

                    TYROWICZ
          I had no choice.

SONJA AND TYROWICZ

She confronts him, gently touching his shoulders,
looking into his eyes.

                    SONJA
          You're telling me you had no choice?

He becomes enraged.
```

                    TYROWICZ
What should I have done—died? For
what? There were no jobs. The Jews
were doomed anyway. Why should I
die, too? It was a different time. You
must understand.

                    SONJA
What do you mean, a different time?

                    TYROWICZ
Life was different then. It was a different, how do you say—a different reality.

                    SONJA
But you did have a choice.

                    TYROWICZ
Yes, I chose. I chose to help the
Ukraine! And I'm proud of it! That's
your motherland, too. And you should
never forget it.

ANGLE

She moves closer to her father, wanting this settled
once and for all.

                    SONJA
Did you ever sign orders for deportation to the death camps?

                    TYROWICZ
          (vaguely)
I was a <u>translator</u> for the Germans.
I've told you this.

NEW ANGLE

Now he goes back to the garden, fixing something
near the bottom of the pomegranate tree.

> SONJA
> And you never mentioned that on your
> visa application, and that is why the
> government instituted proceedings.

He continues to putter around the tree.

> TYROWICZ
> They are so naive. If I had told the
> truth they would have sent me back to
> Russia. And you know what the Rus-
> sians would have done to me.

NEW ANGLE

She watches her father bent over, noticing how frail
he suddenly appears.

> TYROWICZ
> And now - who would believe - it is
> the Americans who are trying to send
> me back. This is America? Who could
> believe such a thing is possible.

> SONJA
> This is all very hard for me to under-
> stand, Papa.

He goes back to the tree, fixing something beneath
the earth.

> DISSOLVE TO:

INT. TYROWICZ HOUSE - NIGHT

Sonja is serving dinner to her father. They're sitting
at the dining room table.

ANGLE ON TYROWICZ

She sadly watches her father, trying to recognize
him as the same man who coddled her as a child.

The last scene is set around another common place, the dining room table. Sonja is watching her father from a domain familiar to us all. She's trying to recognize him as the man who used to coddle her as a child.

Here's another example of visualization from an action comedy, THE ELTON PROJECT. In this sequence, my partner (Frank Tavares) and I wanted to set up the ambiance of the desert, and the flavor of the local motel. To set the scene, Mark and Tony are driving a rented car to Nevada, expecting to do some quick business, then head to Vegas.

               TONY
      Looks like Kuwait before Desert Storm.

NEW ANGLE

Mark takes in the desolate world of sand and scrub brush—so far from Washington. He looks down and tries to read the map, that is hopelessly wet and sticky.

               MARK
     Oughta make these damn things water-
     proof. Somewhere out here is Elton or
     Harwood. Where are we staying?

               TONY
     Right in the middle. A crossroads motel
     called "The Olde Desert Inne." I'm not
     sure what to expect. They spell "old"
     and "inn" with an "E" at the end.

               MARK
     Oh, oh.

And they laugh.

                             CUT TO:

EXT. DESERT - DUSK

Their car speeds across the large expansive desert, alone, far, far from civilization. Our view of the car is partially obscured by the movements of a COYOTE, watching the intruders race across the land. The animal's ears are piqued, waiting for something to happen.

CUT TO:

EXT. OLDE DESERT INNE MOTEL - NIGHT

The now dusty Buick pulls into the gravel parking lot of a small motel at the crossroads. A sputtering neon sign in the front reads: OLDE DESERT INNE - A DAY OR A LIFETIME - VISIT OUR LOUNGE. A sign in the window reads: FOR SALE.

A half-dozen cars, off-road vehicles, and pickup trucks are parked at the end of the lot by a wing of the motel that houses a noisy bar. Mark and Tony get out of the car, stretch their legs, and unload their luggage from the trunk. Mark nods, glances around.

> MARK
> For this I could have stayed in Gaithersburg, Maryland.

> TONY
> Look at it as a pit stop. When we're through earning our money, we'll break speed records to Vegas.

He picks up his suitbag and attaché.

> MARK (CONT'D)
> Wonder if they got slot machines here.

And they head inside to find out.

CUT TO:

INT. OLDE DESERT INNE OFFICE - NIGHT

The motel office is small, with only a counter, a Coke machine, and a wall rack filled with sightseeing brochures. No slots. A doorway opens into a dark-ened, closed coffee shop. Another door, behind the counter, opens into the manager's living quarters. A television set is blaring somewhere beyond the door. The place will never become a Holiday Inn. Tony rings the bell on the counter.

> MARK
> (to Tony)
> A shower and a beer would do it.

Tony hits the bell again and the DESK CLERK shouts from the back.

> DESK CLERK (O.S.)
> Hold on, hold on, I heard you.

ANGLE ON DESK CLERK

The Desk Clerk comes in. He's late 30's, short hair, very muscular, wears light slacks and a worn T-shirt that proclaims "It's Better in the Bahamas." He's holding a toothpick that he puts in his mouth.

> DESK CLERK
> Yeah?

> TONY
> Name is Miller. I called yesterday.

The desk clerk reaches behind the desk, pulls out two registration forms.

> DESK CLERK
> Yeah. Two people, two nights. Got a
> nice room for you. Hundred fifty bucks.

NEW ANGLE

Mark's not sure he heard right. He pulls out his wallet and shows his government i.d.

                         MARK
             Uh, you offer government discounts?
             I'm here on official business...

Tony cringes. The desk clerk looks at the i.d. thrust
in his face.

                       DESK CLERK
             Sure, seventy-five bucks each—up front.
             Checkout twelve noon. I got a conven-
             tion comin' in.

Tony smiles at the prospect, and reaches for the
registration pad.

                         TONY
             We'll take it.

He fills out the form while Mark, thinking twice
about asking if the Olde Desert Inne takes travelers
checks, counts out the cash. The desk clerk gives
them two separate keys.

                       DESK CLERK
             Room one-twenty. Coffee shop opens at
             six in the morning. Lounge is open 'til
             one.

ANGLE ON DESK CLERK

He points them in the direction of the room, and
watches them move on. Once they're gone, he
reviews the information on the registration pad,
picks up the phone, and dials.

                                          CUT TO:

INT. MOTEL LOUNGE - NIGHT

A sign behind the bar shows its official name, "THE
BOMB SHELTER." It's a smokey place, obviously pop-
ular with the locals. Interior could have been
designed by Arnold Schwarzenegger and Sylvester

Stallone. Replicas of military weapons everywhere. Pictures from Terminator and Rambo movies fill the blank spaces on the wall. A poor man's "Planet Hollywood."

At one end of the room, the twisted casing of a dummy thousand pound bomb is held aloft by four steel cables. It's covered with painted graffiti, mostly names of the bar's patrons and a crudely drawn picture or two. Incongruously, sitting atop the sculpture, a stuffed coyote surveys the scene below. A jukebox is playing country and western music.

ANGLE ON LOCALS

Among others, sitting at the bar are three very tough-looking LOCALS. Joking loudly, each wears a T-shirt with a picture of a cartoon rat eating a bomb.

ANGLE ON MARK AND TONY

Mark and Tony find their way to a table, past one of the locals - FULLER. Fuller is big. Could be a pro football player - 6'5", 290 pounds. Fuller has everyone's attention.

> FULLER
> ...so, he spends years digging up tons
> of that shit, half of it still undetonated.
> Bounces it around in the back of his
> truck, never a scratch. Saves his
> money, retires somewhere in Oregon,
> and gets his head blown off cleanin'
> his damn shotgun.

The others break into laughter at the irony, and click their beer glasses. Boy, ain't that the way it is. Next to them, we see RENEE a very attractive lady. She's early 30's, short blonde hair, and trim. She wears jeans and a khaki workshirt.

Notice the descriptions of the desert, the Olde Desert Inne motel, and the visual descriptions of the motel lounge. We wanted to give a sense of the peculiar nature of the motel and The Bomb Shelter bar—a poor man's "Planet Hollywood."

Typical Problems in Scene Descriptions

Just as there are common problems in dialogue, so there are predictable pitfalls in scene descriptions. These are some of the more common stylistic problems.

1. Too Choppy

Some scene descriptions are written too choppily, presumably to account for each piece of stage business. Here's an example of that problem:

```
Marsha picks up the garbage. She stops to feed the
dog. She goes to the back door.
```

The writing style can be smoothed out by avoiding separate sentence units and excessive use of pronouns. The action can be described more comprehensively:

```
Marsha picks up the garbage, stops to feed the dog,
then continues on her way out the back door.
```

2. Too Confusing

A similar problem occurs when a number of different characters are in a scene, and the writer wants to keep them alive. The tendency for pronoun confusion increases with the number of characters interacting in the sequence. For example:

```
The dog barks. Artie enters. Ilene sees him and tries
to calm him. She gets him coffee from the kitchen
and he barks louder.
```

Confusing to say the least. The problems can be corrected by addressing the specific characters and compressing the action:

> As Artie enters, Ilene tries to calm the barking dog. Unsuccessful, she heads toward the kitchen and gets Artie some coffee. The dog barks louder.

3. Too Redundant

A related problem is redundancy in visual description. A number of key words might be repeated needlessly. It helps to "flag" those words. You can literally circle them to see if they intrude on the reading flow:

> Jennifer smiles and Fran smiles back. Fran crosses to the fireplace and he starts the fire and lights the wood. He pokes the fire with brass tongs and the fire begins to crackle.

The stage directions need to be smoothed out. The phrasing can be modified and polished:

> They exchange smiles as Fran crosses to the fireplace. He lights the wood, pokes the brass tongs into the flames. The fire begins to crackle.

Limiting the amount of repetition—in both words and phrases—cleans up the description and makes the script more readable. Clean and well-written scene descriptions help keep the tempo of the script alive and the rhythm flowing naturally from scene to scene.

4. Too Long

Descriptions become too long when you put in too much narrative detail. There is sometimes a fine line between having a creative, literary quality to a script, and having so much detail that it confuses the reader. Remember, this is a cinematic vehicle, meant to be produced. A book can take its time unravelling atmosphere, but you've only got a prescribed number of pages to write a script.

5. Too Expository

Be careful of scene descriptions that tell us things we can't possibly know, like the fact that Frank and Jennifer met in Washington, D.C., grew up in the same town, or married and divorced twice. The only way we can know it is if one of your characters reveals it in dialogue.

6. Too Technical

This happens when you try to direct the film, rather than write it. As a general rule, stay away from camera angles, over-the-shoulder shots, medium shots, or any other directorial call. You'll only get in the way of the director.

7. Too Expensive

This happens if you call for unnecessary locales and production requirements, including aerial shots (require expensive helicopters and cameras), snow or rain, hundreds of people who have talking parts (extras must be paid extra if they speak), scenes requiring travel to many different cities, many different locales.

8. Too Potentially Litigious

A different kind of problem arises if you want to incorporate recognizable names of real people, or stories from real life that you don't own. In our litigious society, be cautious, and obtain the necessary rights and clearances.

The same is true for the use of songs or lyrics. Unless a particular song is critical to the needs of a script, you can simply suggest a song style rather than provide someone else's lyrics. For example:

```
In the b.g. (background) we hear the strains of a
blues song, and the husky voice of a nightclub vocal-
ist. Over the song, we hear the din of the supper
club crowd, ignoring the music behind them.
```

This scene description sets atmosphere, without defining the song or the lyrics. On the other hand, some screenwriters deliberately choose a song to establish the period atmosphere of a piece. The appropriateness is determined by the needs of a specific project and your artistic style.

ENDNOTE

1. The development of the script is detailed in Lindheim and Blum, *Inside Television Producing*, 125-150.

9

Script Revisions

Writing is rewriting, as any writer who gets notes from producers, directors, agents, and friends can attest. Once you've completed the draft, you enter the bottomless abyss of revising. It is a time-consuming process that is designed to make your script more competitive and producible.

With stoic objectivity, you can build and refine the story's pacing, the visual imagery, and the credibility of the characters and dialogue.

A Checklist for Script Revision

Here is a checklist of some critical questions to help you analyze the first draft of your work.

1. Is the Script Visual?

A script should be cinematic. As you read the draft, can you actually visualize the scenes unfolding? Are the descriptions clear? If not, camera angles can be suggested, character actions amplified, locations sharply defined. As you spot problems in the draft, note them in the margins.

2. Is the Script Producible?

No matter how good the script, it won't be produced if it calls for $535 million worth of sets, period costumes, world-wide locations, hundreds of stars, thousands of extras, and impossible camera shots. The script should be realistically conceived in terms of production requirements, locations, and casting needs.

3. Is the Script Format Professional and the Content Readable?

Even the most powerful script can end up by the wayside if the format looks amateurish to a reader. If you have questions about script form, check the sample formats in this book. In addition, look at the clarity of writing in the script. Sometimes scene descriptions are too choppy, cluttered with information, or too repetitious. Smooth out the writing style for the greatest impact on the reader.

4. Is the Story Focused and Well Developed?

Here you must examine the structure of the dramatic action points. Some scenes may lag, others may be redundant. As you read the script, assess the effectiveness of the plot sequences. If the story is unclear or erratic, it's time to cut and paste. One sequence might work better at the beginning or end, which means reorganizing the entire storyline, dropping scenes, adding new ones, polishing others.

5. Is the Dramatic Conflict Strong and the Pacing Effective?

The script should hold and build audience interest throughout each act. If the conflict is cleverly set up, and the stakes are high—the sense of urgency is great—audience involvement with the characters and conflicts increases. The pacing is most effective when scenes build upon each other in a careful, logical sequence of dramatic action.

6. Is the Mood Accurately Conveyed?

Each scene should help create the atmosphere of the project. If the descriptions are not vivid enough, take time to rewrite them. Don't settle for less than the most illustrative images of the place, action, and characters.

7. Are the Characters Likeable, Identifiable, and Consistently Developed?

Be sure the characters are fully and credibly motivated. Are the interrelationships clearly drawn? If not, see if you can strengthen them through Method writer constructs, using super objectives, through-line of action, intentions, motivations, sense of urgency, and moment-to-moment realities.

8. Is the Dialogue Realistic and Sharply Defined?

If the dialogue appears to be awkward in some places, check all the pertinent problems. Characters are unique individuals, and their dialogue should reflect that individuality. If a word is off, write "b.w." (find a "better word") in the margin, or write "b.l." (find a "better line") to point out the problem. It may seem like nit-picking, but don't let those little problems slip away. If your characters make it onto the screen, those lines will make you, and probably others, cringe.

The Final Polish

Once all the points are addressed, and the major revisions are incorporated into the script, there's one more stop-check point. It's called the polish. Once more, go over the script with a fine-toothed comb. Be sure the story is focused, the characters are three-dimensional, the dialogue is refined, the action is visual, the mood is conveyed, and the pacing is effective. After all, this is the script that may eventually wind up in the archives of the Academy of Motion Picture Arts and Sciences—or at least in the hands of a reputable agent.

PART FIVE

SCRIPT FORMATS FOR TELEVISION AND MOTION PICTURES

10

Television Script Format

The more scripts you read, the more familiar you'll become with industry styles, forms, and techniques. Not long ago, scripts were available only through special holdings at professional libraries. But accessibility has become so important to new writers that some stores now publish catalogues of their current holdings. (For a list, see "Where to Find Sample Television Scripts and Screenplays" in the Bibliography.) Scripts might also be available from independent production companies and special collections at libraries and universities. If you find a script in a book, keep in mind that the form might have been edited for spacing and economy.

Sample Videotape Format

If a program is to be produced on videotape, or with multiple cameras, a spacious format is used, derived from the early days of live television. The right margin is wide enough for directors and talent to jot down their needs. The script uses less camera coverage and fewer angles than film scripts. Consequently, the page count is much longer than in film. In tape, a thirty-minute script can run anywhere from 45 to 52 pages.

The following script model provides a look at the structure of this type of format.

SAMPLE VIDEOTAPE SCRIPT FORMAT ←(*Title*)

Written By

Your Name ←(*Writer's name*)

(*You can indicate first or final draft*)

FIRST DRAFT   Agent or Lawyer's Name

                                    Address

WGAW Reg.   (phone) (*Your address, production company, agent, or business manager*)

(*This indicates the project is registered with Writers Guild of America, West*)

<u>SAMPLE VIDEOTAPE SCRIPT FORMAT</u> ← *The title goes here*

<u>ACT ONE</u>

This is how to begin a script

<u>SCENE ONE</u>

FADE IN:

This is the "slugline" or description line which identifies each new scene

<u>INT. HOTEL LOBBY - NIGHT</u>

(YOU'LL NOTICE THAT NO SCENE ACTION CAN

OCCUR UNTIL YOU'VE FADED IN. THEN YOU MUST

USE A "SLUG-LINE" OR LOCALE DESCRIPTION LINE

TO SET THE NEW SCENE'S EXTERIOR OR INTERIOR

LOCALE AND THE TIME OF DAY.   *Scene descriptions are double-spaced*

(<u>ILENE ENTERS</u>, LOOKS FOR SOMEONE. SHE SPOTS

ARTIE AND SMILES.)

(YOU'LL SEE THAT ALL THE NECESSARY INFORMA-

TION IS IN CAPS AND IS DOUBLE-SPACED. YOU

MUST DESCRIBE YOUR SHOT, THE CHARACTERS WE

SEE, AND THE STAGE ACTION OCCURRING. ALL OF

THIS IS IN PARENTHESES.) ← *scene descriptions and stage directions may or may not be in parentheses*

ARTIE

The dialogue is centered under your

character's name, and is double-spaced.

(MORE)

ARTIE (CONT'D)

The character's name is capitalized and centered above dialogue

dialogue is double-spaced

That gives the director room to work

on his or her shooting script.

ILENE

(SMILING)

Character reactions can be suggested in parentheses or written in the stage directions

It also allows the actor and producer to

see the lines at a glance.

(BE SURE TO INCLUDE ANY ACTION, BUSINESS, OR

REACTIONS YOUR CHARACTERS MAY HAVE.)

(THIS IS WHERE YOU DESCRIBE WHAT THEY DO,

AND HOW THEY REACT.)

(TRY NOT TO OVER-DIRECT THE SCENE WITH A LOT

OF CAMERA DIRECTIONS. THIS IS THE RESPONSIBIL-

ITY OF THE DIRECTOR, NOT THE WRITER. THERE IS

NO NEED TO SPECIFY TECHNICAL DESIGNATIONS

THAT ARE NOT TOTALLY NECESSARY TO THE

IMPACT AND IMAGE OF YOUR SCENE.)

ARTIE

You look wonderful. It's so good to see

you again.

(HE GIVES ILENE A PLAYFUL HUG. WHEN YOU END

YOUR SCENE, TRY TO GO OUT ON A REACTION OR

A KEY PIECE OF ACTION, AND THEN YOU CAN)

Here's how to indicate a switch to a totally different location and scene CUT TO:

ACT ONE

SCENE TWO

INT. HOTEL LOBBY - DAY ← *here's how to set up the new scene*

(SINCE THIS IS A NEW SCENE, IT WOULD APPEAR

ON NEXT PAGE.) *The new scene is described here*

(AGAIN, YOU MUST DESCRIBE THE SET AND

DESCRIBE THE CHARACTERS. BE SURE TO STATE

WHO THEY ARE, WHAT THEY LOOK LIKE, AND

WHAT THEY ARE DOING.) *A small piece of character "business" or action might go in the stage directions above or here*

ARTIE

(LIGHTING HIS CIGARETTE)

Dialogue, by the way, should be crisp

and to the point. And don't worry if it

doesn't look grammatically correct. Peo-

(MORE)

ARTIE (CONT'D)

ple just don't talk that way. They

speak colloquially, you know? So make

your characters talk like real people.

ILENE

Attitudes can be suggested here

(TRYING TO HIDE HER JEALOUSY)

And don't forget that characters react

to everything they see and hear. Spo-

ken or not. This helps build credible

motivations and identifiable behavior

patterns.

Music or sound effects are set up in a separate line of stage directions

SFX: IF YOU HAVE MUSIC OR SOUND EFFECTS, THIS

IS HOW TO WRITE THEM IN.

If a character is continuing dialogue from above, uninterrupted

ILENE (CONT'D)

I'd rather listen to the stereo, wouldn't

you?

here's how to write a reaction without cutting to a CLOSE-UP.

(ARTIE GRINS)

FADE OUT.

This is the last direction in any script

This script format has several distinct features.

1. Each new scene or act begins a new page. Pages are numbered
consecutively. When the first scene is over, the next scene begins on a

page labeled SCENE TWO. When the first act is over, the next page begins ACT TWO.

2. New scenes are capitalized and underlined, as are camera directions and special effects.

3. Everything is capitalized in the script—except dialogue. Set descriptions and character actions and reactions are capitalized, as is every piece of stage direction. The dialogue alone remains in lower case.

4. Margins on the right are three to four inches wide.

5. There are no "Continueds" on the bottom of pages for scenes that are continuing to the next page.

6. Every line is double-spaced, from the opening sequence to the final FADE OUT. That includes all dialogue, stage directions, and visualization. In contrast, episodic comedy scripts that use multi-camera tape technique, like "Roseanne," or film technique, like "Murphy Brown" or "Coach," scene descriptions are single-spaced (see examples below).

To help format scripts as you write them, certain computer software programs can help set up automatic margins and page breaks for television scripts and screenplays (see "Resources for Screenwriting Software" in the Bibliography).

Sitcom Format

Multiple Camera Video Format
Only one sitcom format is used for shows that are shot on multiple tape format, like "Roseanne." This sample was provided by Dan Wilcox.

1.

I-1

(ANDY, JOEL, RICHARD,

CHRIS, STANLEY, TILLMAN,

MRS. MOFFETT)

ACT ONE

SCENE ONE

EXT. BUCKMINSTER SCHOOL - NIGHT - WIDE SHOT
(CAMERA PUSH INTO:)

<u>INT. MRS. MOFFETT'S OFFICE - NIGHT</u>

MOFFETT

(INTO P.A.)

...And in closing, due to the theft of

the Baker's chocolate there will be no

chocolate cake until further notice. To

the culprits I say, "Beware." I know

who did it.

<u>CUT TO:</u>

<u>INT. THE BOYS' BEDROOM - NIGHT</u>
(ANDY, JOEL, RICHARD AND CHRIS LISTEN TO THE
END OF THE ANNOUNCEMENT)
(CHRIS STANDS ON A DRESSER PEERING OUT THE
TRANSOM ABOVE THE CORRIDOR DOOR)

ANDY

Good. She doesn't know who did it.

(HE TOSSES A PIECE OF CHOCOLATE TO CHRIS)

RICHARD

How come this stuff is so good and the

chocolate cake is so awful?

CHRIS

They don't use this in the cake. They

use it in the tuna casserole.

(JOEL CROSSES TO HIS BUNK)

JOEL

...Now can I get back to my story?

ANDY

Why don't you just write it up and

we'll read it in Playboy?

JOEL

So anyway, as I'm walking out, she

says to me in this husky voice, "Come

back in the morning," and as I left I

could feel her eyes boring hot holes of

passion in my back.

ANDY

Mrs. Fishbein? The nurse?

JOEL

What's wrong with that? She's really

built.

RICHARD

Maybe, but the ground breaking was

sixty years ago.

CHRIS

Mayday! Mayday! Somebody's coming.

(RICHARD HIDES THE CHOCOLATE UNDER HIS PIL-
LOW. STANLEY ENTERS, CLOSING THE DOOR BEHIND
HIM.)

STANLEY

Hello peasants.

ANDY

If you're lost, Stanley, your room is

next door.

RICHARD

If you're not lost, get lost.

STANLEY

I just had this craving for a piece of

chocolate.

5.

I-1

ANDY

What makes you think we've got choco-

late?

STANLEY

C'mon. Any time you've got Dobbs

posted as lookout, you've got some-

thing. And there's chocolate missing.

JOEL

We don't have any chocolate.

This script has several distinct features:

1. The right hand margins are almost four inches wide, so directors can mark them up.
2. New acts and scenes are centered at the top of the page.
3. Business and action are flush left, single spaced, capped and set in parentheses.
4. Dialogue is double-spaced and not capped.
5. Characters appearing in the scene are identified before the scene begins.
6. Page numbers are consecutive throughout the script.
7. There are no "Continued's" on pages to indicate continuing scenes. In this case, scenes are identified as part of the same sequence at the top right hand of the page. For example, "I-1" tells us this is "Act I, sc. 1."

<u>Multiple Camera Film Format</u>

If you're writing an episodic comedy script for a series using multi-ple-camera film techniques, like "Coach" or "Murphy Brown," stage directions are single-spaced, but descriptions are still kept to a minimum.

The scene sets up the basic information concerning place, characters, and action, and the director takes over from that point. Compared to film, there is not much latitude for embellishing mood and atmosphere.

Here is a sample of how that common script format looks. This is an opening sequence from a "Murphy Brown" script. Let's assume Scene "A" is in black, then this scene follows.

INT. FYI SET - NIGHT

(Jim, Frank, Corky, Miles, John, Murphy, Carl, FYI Set Extras, Interviewee Extra)

JIM, FRANK, AND CORKY SIT AT THE ANCHOR DESK. MURPHY'S INTERVIEW, A MIDDLE-AGED MAN, IS BEING LED TO HIS CHAIR. HE WAITS IN THE CHAIR. IT APPEARS TO BE A TYPICAL COMMERCIAL BREAK WITH ONE EXCEPTION. MURPHY IS NOWHERE TO BE SEEN. EVERYONE'S IN A SEMI-PAN-ICKED STATE EXCEPT MILES, WHO IS EERILY CALM.

                    JOHN

Look alive, people. We're coming out of

commercial in sixty seconds. Where the

hell is Murphy?

                    CORKY

(PANICKED) She's never going to make

it back from the bathroom in time. Not

with all the extra weight she's hauling

around. Miles! Why aren't you doing

anything?

MILES

(FIGHTING ANXIETY) I am doing something. I'm refusing to panic. Because
that's what Murphy wants. She's testing
me. Her whole pregnancy is about testing me. The constant racing into the
bathroom, the mood swings, the increas-
ing absent-mindedness. All she wants to
do is provoke my hysteria. Well, it's not
going to work! Not this time.

FRANK

(CHECKING WATCH) Aw man! The
woman's memory is shot. Maybe she
forgot why she went to the bathroom.
Maybe she's just sitting there waiting
for the inflight movie to start.

JIM

(PANICKING) This is all your fault,
Miles. I told you three weeks ago, "Get
the woman a port-a-potty."

ALL ANXIOUS EYES ARE ON MILES.

                    MILES

I will not panic! (CALLING) Do you
hear me, Murphy! I'm picking up a
newspaper. I'm doing a crossword puzzle. Six down! An aquatic mammal!

                    JOHN
Thirty seconds to air!

                    MILES

(GOES NUTS, SHREDS PAPER) Oh God! I
can't see the letters! I'm blind, I'm
blind! Are you happy now, Murphy!

                    CARL

(LOOKS OFFSTAGE) Here she comes!

                    JOHN
Murphy's coming!

MILES MENTALLY KICKS HIMSELF.

                    CARL

Clear a path! (CLEARS ONE) Come on,
darlin', you can make it.

MURPHY WADDLES IN, AS QUICKLY AS SHE CAN.
EVERYONE'S ENCOURAGING HER AS IF THEY'RE
WITNESSING A MARATHON FINISHER.

> MURPHY
>
> Whoever invented those hot air hand
>
> dryers is a moron!

HAIR AND MAKEUP JUMP IN. MURPHY FOLLOWS
JOHN TO HER SEAT, NODS TO HER INTERVIEW WHO
IS BEING FITTED WITH A MIKE.

> JOHN
>
> Chair assistance! Come on, Carl, I need
>
> a counter weight!

> CARL
> Flyin' in.

CARL RUNS ONTO THE PLATFORM AND HELPS JOHN
TO LOWER MURPHY INTO HER CHAIR.

> CARL (CONT'D)
>
> ...easy now, easy...

> MURPHY
>
> Aw, God. Everyday I think I can't get
>
> any bigger. And then I do.

MURPHY IS SUCCESSFULLY LOWERED INTO THE
CHAIR.

CARL

(ANNOUNCEMENT) Okay, she's in!

JOHN

She's in!

MILES

She's in!

MURPHY

Miles, just remind me. Do I have ten

or twelve minutes to interview Mr....

What's his name? (TRIES TO REMEM-

BER HIS NAME)

MILES

(LOUD WHISPER) Fremont! Charles.

Insurance fraud. Any of this ringing a

bell?!

MURPHY

(NO PROBLEM) Okay, okay, I've got it.

JOHN

Better smile, Miles, because we're going

live—In five, four, three—

MURPHY SMILES AT THE CAMERA.

                    MURPHY

    Welcome back. I'm here now with Mr.

    Charles Fremont, the president and

    chief operating officer of . . . (BLANK)

    Of uh . . .

FREMONT MAKES A MOVE TO SPEAK. MURPHY
STOPS HIM.

                MURPHY (CONT'D)

    No, no. I'll get it . . .

ON MILES' LOOK, WE:

                                    DISSOLVE TO:

The directions, dialogue, and character actions play appropriately for a
typical "Murphy Brown" episode.
    Let's examine the same format for a "Coach" episode. This is a scene
from the pilot script. The top of the page indicates that we're in Act One,
Scene "B."

                    SCENE B
                            (HAYDEN, LUTHER,
                              KELLY, A MAN)

INT. HAYDEN'S CABIN - ONE WEEK LATER - LATE
AFTERNOON

A ROUGH-HEWN HOME ON THE WATERFRONT OF ONE
OF MINNESOTA'S SMALL LAKES. IT'S A VERY MAS-
CULINE ENVIRONMENT, WITH A LARGE STONE FIRE-
PLACE DOMINATING THE UPSTAGE WALL OF THE

LIVING ROOM, FLANKED ON EITHER SIDE BY LARGE WINDOWS LOOKING OUT OVER THE LAKE VIEW. A SMALL DEN IS STAGE RIGHT WITH A WINDOW THAT LOOKS OUT TO THE FRONT SCREENED-IN PORCH. IT IS THROUGH THIS PORCH THAT PEOPLE PASS TO GET TO THE FRONT DOOR. THE OPEN KITCHEN IS STAGE LEFT, ALL KNOTTY PINE AND ACTUALLY VERY COZY. THE HOME IS FURNISHED WARMLY IN ODDS AND ENDS, BUT NOTHING IS "DECORATED." A LARGE MOUNTED FISH INDICATES ONE OF HAYDEN'S OTHER PASSIONS. EXCEPT FOR A FEW THINGS IN THE DEN, THERE ARE VERY FEW REMNANTS OF HAYDEN'S LIFE AS A COACH. RATHER, THIS PLACE IS AN ESCAPE FROM THE PRESSURES OF THE JOB. AT THE MOMENT, HAYDEN IS IN THE KITCHEN DOING DISHES. OFF-STAGE, WE CAN HEAR THE SOUND OF AN ELECTRIC SWEEPER RUNNING (LIVE). IN A MOMENT, IT SHUTS OFF. IN ANOTHER MOMENT, <u>LUTHER ENTERS</u> FROM THE DOOR LEAD-ING TO THE BEDROOMS, CARRYING THE SWEEPER.

                    LUTHER

     I think I just broke your vacuum.

                    HAYDEN

     Don't worry about it.

                    LUTHER

     I think it sucked up a comb.

                    HAYDEN

     It's okay, Luther.

LUTHER

I'll put it back on the porch.

LUTHER CARRIES THE SWEEPER TO THE PORCH.

HAYDEN

(CALLING) How do you think the place

looks?

LUTHER

(RE-ENTERING) I thought it looked okay

before we spent six hours cleaning it.

HAYDEN

I just want to make a good impression.

LUTHER

You're going to make such a good

impression she's going to end up want-

ing to stay here, you wait and see.

HAYDEN

That's out of the question. This is

going to be enough of an adjustment

without complicating matters by living

together.

SFX: OUTSIDE, A CAR HORN HONKS.

              HAYDEN (CONT'D)

Is that her?

              LUTHER

(LOOKING OUT THE WINDOW) White

Mustang?

              HAYDEN

(RIPPING OFF HIS APRON; EXCITEDLY)

That's her. I bought her that car for

her sixteenth birthday. Guess she must

have liked it, huh?

HAYDEN QUICKLY MOVES TO THE WINDOW AND
LOOKS OUT. HIS WHOLE EXPRESSION CHANGES AS
SOON AS HE SEES HER.

              HAYDEN (CONT'D)

Oh, Luther, would you look at that? (A

BEAT) My God, I can't believe she's

that grown up.

              LUTHER

You don't need me here. I'll just slip

out the back way.

HAYDEN

No, I want you to meet her.

LUTHER

Well, good, because there isn't any back

way, I just realized.

THROUGH THE SCREEN PORCH WE SEE <u>KELLY</u> CROSS
TO THE FRONT DOOR. HAYDEN SMILES AS HE OPENS
THE DOOR. SHE STOPS AS THEY STAND THERE FOR
A MOMENT, JUST LOOKING AT EACH OTHER.

HAYDEN

Well, well, well, look who's here.

KELLY

(SOMEWHAT SHYLY) Hello, Dad.

HAYDEN

Hello, sweetheart.

THERE IS AN AWKWARD MOMENT BEFORE HAYDEN
REACHES OUT AND THEY SORT OF HAVE A HUG.

HAYDEN (CONT'D)

Welcome to Minnesota. (REMEMBERING)

This is a good friend of mine, Luther

Van Dam. This is my daughter, Kelly.

LUTHER

Actually, I met you once before at a
game in Louisville. You don't remember.
You were about...(INDICATING HER
SIZE)...ten weeks old.

KELLY

(SMILING) No, I don't remember.

LUTHER

Well, listen, you two have things to
talk about. Nice to meet you, Kelly.
Hope I see you again real...somewhere.
(TO HAYDEN) See you at practice
tomorrow.

LUTHER EXITS OUT THE BACK. THERE IS A BEAT.
LUTHER RE-ENTERS AND EXITS OUT THE FRONT.

HAYDEN

Thanks, Luther. (EXPLAINING) I asked
Luther to come over and kind of help
me get the place in order. With the
season starting things are sort of in a
mess.

                        KELLY

It looks fine. (LOOKING AROUND) I like

it.

                        HAYDEN

Do you? It's pretty secluded. Of course,

that's on purpose. I can't eat lunch or

go to the bathroom when I'm in town

without someone stopping and wanting

to talk about the team. It's nice to

have a place to get away from every-

body.

HAYDEN LOOKS WISTFULLY OUT THE DOOR.

                  A VOICE (O.S.)

(Calling) Hey, Coach, how's it going'?

HAYDEN SMILES AND WAVES AND CLOSES THE
DOOR.

                       HAYDEN

Of course, they pretty much find you no

matter where you are. (AN AWKWARD

BEAT) You look wonderful, by the way.

                       (MORE)

HAYDEN (CONT'D)

You must have left a few broken hearts

behind in Ohio.

KELLY

(KINDLY) Just Mom's.

HAYDEN

(REALIZING) Yeah, right. (ANOTHER

BEAT) Well, so, where are you going to

be staying? Here, I hope.

KELLY

(CAUGHT OFF GUARD) Here?

HAYDEN

Why not? There's plenty of room.

KELLY

Actually, I wasn't sure that'd be such

a good idea. This is going to be enough

of an adjustment for the two of us

without complicating matters by living

together.

HAYDEN

Well, golly, I hadn't thought about that
but maybe you're right.

KELLY

To tell you the truth, I wasn't all that
sure you'd really want me here.

HAYDEN

Wouldn't want you here? Didn't your
mother tell you how excited I was you
were coming?

KELLY

Yeah. She also told me you sometimes
say whatever you think people want to
hear. I just didn't want to come out
and mess up your life.

A BEAT.

HAYDEN

(GENUINELY) Kelly, I may not always
have shown it, but the happiest day

(MORE)

                         HAYDEN (CONT'D)

I've ever had in my life was the day

you came into it.

SHE LOOKS UP AT HIM AND SMILES, SOMEWHAT
EMBARRASED.

                         KELLY

And now I'm back.

HE FORCES AN AWKWARD SMILE.

                         HAYDEN

   Right.

SFX: THE PHONE RINGS.

                         HAYDEN (CONT'D)

That's probably a reporter. Sorry.

(ANSWERING THE PHONE) Coach here . . .

(CAUGHT OFF GUARD) Christine. . .

HE SHOOTS A NERVOUS LOOK TOWARD KELLY.

                         HAYDEN (CONT'D)

What a surprise. Where are you calling

from? . . . (NERVOUSLY) No kidding, that

close, huh? I thought you were going

                         (MORE)

HAYDEN (CONT'D)

to be in Madison this weekend covering

the Golden Gophers ... (HE CUPS THE

PHONE) Christine's a sportscaster in

Minneapolis. We're friends.

KELLY NODS. AS HE TALKS, KELLY BEGINS TO
ROAM ABOUT THE HOUSE LOOKING AT VARIOUS
MOMENTOES OF HER FATHER'S LIFE, INCLUDING
PHOTOGRAPHS. AS SHE DOES, SHE GRADUALLY
BEGINS TO REALIZE HOW MUCH OF HIS LIFE THERE
IS, AND WHAT A LITTLE PART OF IT SHE APPAR-
ENTLY IS.

HAYDEN (CONT'D)

(INTO PHONE) What? ... Oh, I was just

talking to my daughter ... Yeah, she

just got into town a little while

ago ... Uh, four years. She's going to

be going to school here ... (HE SMILES

NERVOUSLY AT KELLY) ... Gee, I'd have

loved to, but it's her first night and

all. You understand ... (HE SMILES

ONCE MORE AT KELLY, WHO SMILES

BACK SELF-CONCIOUSLY) I knew you

would. But we'll take a raincheck,

(MORE)

                    HAYDEN (CONT'D)

okay? . . . Yeah, if anything

changes...You, too...G'bye.

HE HANDS UP AND SMILES.

                    KELLY

(SELF-CONCIOUSLY) Dad, if you want to

go out tonight you should go. I don't

expect you to change your whole life

just because I'm here.

                    HAYDEN

Changing my life is no big deal. (OFF

HER LOOK) I mean, I wasn't expecting

to do anything anyway.

                    KELLY

Do you and Christine see each other a

lot?

                    HAYDEN

You know, whenever schedules permit.

Minneapolis is only sixty miles from

here.

KELLY

Well, tonight they permit so I really

think you should go out and I should

go back to the dorm.

HAYDEN

But I was counting on being with you.

KELLY

But now you want to be with Christine,

and I understand that. I've got a mil-

lion things to do anyway. I'll see you

tomorrow.

HAYDEN

Kelly, wait . . .

Scene B opens on a new page, and the characters needed are listed at the top (HAYDEN, LUTHER, KELLY, A MAN). Because it is the pilot story, the opening scene description of the cabin is vivid, setting a detailed look at locale and characters. In a regular episode, the description of the cabin would be much shorter, since we know what the characters and set look like.

The stage directions are capped, and single spaced. Character entrances and exits are capped and underlined. Short character business is briefly noted in dialogue, and set in parentheses. Those reactions help explain what might otherwise be misinterpreted or confusing. For example, KELLY (SMILING), HAYDEN (REALIZING), KELLY (CAUGHT OFF GUARD).

Stage directions are also important for understanding motivations

and beats of the character. For example as HAYDEN talks, KELLY begins
to roam about the house, "looking at various momentoes of her father's
life, including photographs. As she does, she gradually begins to realize
how much of his life there is, and what a little part of it she apparently
is." Another example is the concluding sequence in which HAYDEN
stands at the door knowing he's blown their first night together, as we
FADE OUT. The next page begins ACT TWO.

When an act break is reached, this is how ACT TWO is set up in the
"Coach" pilot script.

ACT TWO

SCENE C

> (HAYDEN,
> CHRISTINE,
> YOUNG MAN,
> CLERK)

FADE IN:

INT. HOTEL LOBBY - THAT NIGHT

SFX: FIRE IN FIREPLACE

THE VERY SMALL LOBBY OF A TINY DOWNTOWN
HOTEL, CONSISTING PRIMARILY OF A RESERVATION
DESK, A MAGAZINE STAND, AND A SMALL SEATING
AREA. THE ONLY PEOPLE PRESENT ARE A CLERK
AND A VERY ATHLETIC-LOOKING YOUNG MAN SIT-
TING IN THE WAITING AREA. HAYDEN ENTERS,
DRESSED IN SLACKS AND A SWEATER, AND
APPROACHES THE RESERVATION COUNTER.

HAYDEN

Excuse me, would you call Christine

Armstrong's room and tell her Hayden

Fox is here?

CLERK

(BRIGHTLY) Sure, Coach.

At the open of ACT TWO, Scene C, we know HAYDEN, CHRISTINE, YOUNG MAN, and CLERK will be in the scene since their names are identified. The scene is visually set up, including sound effects of the fireplace.

Cast and Set Lists

When episodic comedy scripts are ready for production, producers usually work up cast and set lists to identify which characters are needed, and what sets will be used in each scene. (Those lists are not used if you're writing for television films or features.) Dan Wilcox, one of television's most knowledgable writer-producers, cautions against putting in your own cast and set list. It will look amateurish, as if you are trying to convince us the show is actually in production.

For the sake of production budgets, it's a good idea to limit sets to the ones regularly used in the series; otherwise producers will have to budget in a "swing" set or new locale for the episode. Dan Wilcox found that three sets are ideal—one main set and two others. He has also successfully written up to five sets for some of his productions.

This is a sample cast and set list from the "Coach" pilot.

COACH

"PILOT"

CHARACTERS

HAYDEN FOX	CRAIG T. NELSON
LUTHER VAN DAM	JERRY VAN DYKE
CHRISTINE ARMSTRONG	SHELLEY FABARES
KELLY FOX	CLARE CAREY
DAUBER DYBINSKI	BILL FAGERBAKKE
YOUNG MAN	GARY KASPER
SECRETARY	PAT CRAWFORD BROWN
CLERK	BILL SCHICK
ELOISE DUPREE	GRETA BROWN
A MAN	
LIVINGSTON DUPREE	

• • •

<u>SETS</u>

<u>TEASER</u>

INT. LIVING ROOM - NIGHT

<u>ACT ONE</u>

INT. COACH'S OFFICE - DAY

INT. HAYDEN'S CABIN - ONE WEEK LATER - LATE
AFTERNOON

<u>ACT TWO</u>

INT. HOTEL LOBBY - THAT NIGHT

INT. HAYDEN'S CABIN - LATER THAT NIGHT

INT. COACH'S OFFICE - THE FOLLOWING AFTERNOON

Since the main characters have been cast, their names are listed. Extras are listed, but not yet identified. As for the sets, notice how minimal and relevant the requirements are. The teaser takes place in a living room. Act One requires two scenes in the same location—the Coach's office. Act Two is comprised of a hotel lobby where Christine is staying, and the Coach's cabin, a primary set for the series.

Let's examine another set list, this time from "Murphy Brown."

<u>MURPHY BROWN</u>

<u>"ON THE ROCKS"</u>

<u>SETS</u>

<u>ACT ONE</u>

SCENE A - INT. FYI SET - NIGHT

SCENE B - INT. FYI SET - A LITTLE LATER

<u>ACT TWO</u>

SCENE C - INT. BULLPEN - MORNING (TWO DAYS

        LATER)

SCENE D - INT. PHIL'S - A LITTLE LATER

<u>ACT THREE</u>

SCENE E - INT. BULLPEN - A FEW DAYS LATER

SCENE E - INT. MURPHY'S OFFICE - CONTINUOUS

        ACTION

SCENE H - INT. BULLPEN - THE NEXT MORNING

SCENE H - INT. MURPHY'S OFFICE - CONTINUOUS

        ACTION

SCENE H - INT. BULLPEN - CONTINUOUS ACTION

Here, set requirements for each scene are consistent with the show's conventions. Act One has two scenes that take place in the FYI set. Act Two takes place in the Bullpen and at Phil's bar. Act Three takes place in the Bullpen and in Murphy's office. By the way, the term "continuous action" means that the scene occurs right after the preceding one.

Drama Format

If you're writing a script for an episodic drama, miniseries, or television film, *the format is the same as for a motion picture screenplay*. That format is examined in detail in the next chapter. In the meantime, this is a script sample from a one-hour dramatic pilot for "Law & Order."

<u>LAW AND ORDER</u>

<u>EVERYBODY'S FAVORITE BAGMAN</u>

<u>TEASER</u>

FADE IN

EXT. WAREHOUSE DISTRICT - NIGHT

Deserted streets. The intermittent high pitched whine of garbage trucks compacting the day's industrial waste. The background jabbering of a police radio is a continuous, unemotional chronicler of the night.

            POLICE RADIO (V.O.)
    ...340 West 26th...see the manager
    ...man with a knife...all available
    units sector eight...Code 3...shots
    fired...hit and run, Park and Astor,
    pedestrian down...

                        CUT TO

INT. PATROL CAR - NIGHT

Their P.O.V. is through the windshield, we can hear, but not see, the two patrol cops, as the car cruises the industrial area.

> POLICE RADIO
> Sector Four, nearest unit, domestic dis-
> turbance...540 West three one...3rd
> floor rear...

> DRIVER
> I want the Coupe de Ville...I'm happy
> with the velour, not even leather...
> what do I end up with? A goddamn
> Nipponese bug box...

The unit turns a corner into an alley bordering a series of loading docks. Nosed into one of them is a Mercedes 560 SEL. As the headlights wash over the car, two black seventeen year-olds, "Simonize" Jackson and Tremaine Lewis, bolt from the Benz and head down the alley.

> SHOTGUN COP (V.O.)
> Must've forgotten their keys...

His hand moves into frame and hits the lights and siren as the V8 opens up and the patrol car leaps forward.

Tremaine turns, sees the black and white hurtling down the alley and starts climbing the chain link fence that runs along one side. Simonize joins him as the cops fly past the Mercedes.

SHOTGUN COP'S POV:

Charles Halsey, an overweight fifty year-old, is sprawled half in and half out of the car, the entire front of his Vicuna coat blood stained.

> SHOTGUN COP
> Hold it...we got a vic...

CUT TO

EXT. ALLEY - NIGHT

The patrol car comes to a screeching halt. Tremaine and Simonize roll over the top of the chain link fence and drop into the courtyard of a deserted tenement. They pick themselves up and run into the gutted building. As the shotgun cop runs to Halsey the camera follows the driver as he takes off after the two perps, scaling the chain link fence, dropping into the courtyard and running to the door of the tenement. He stops, sticks his head into the hallway, comes back out and unholsters his gun. He wipes a thin film of sweat off his upper lip, and swallows off a sudden case of dry mouth. This is a cop's nightmare and the camera is right with him, showing us why—the building is dark and ominous.

                                        CUT TO

INT. TENEMENT - NIGHT - CONTINUOUS

The driver takes a deep breath, listens to the thundering silence, races through the first floor and continues out to the street, the camera with him, step for step, as leather squeaks and handcuffs jingle.

EXT. TENEMENT - NIGHT - CONTINUOUS

The driver comes out of the tenement and checks out the bombed-out looking street. It's totally deserted. Breathing hard, he holsters his weapon and puts his fists on his hips, a portrait of total frustration, as he tries to get his breathing back under control.

                                        CUT TO

INT. BODEGA - NIGHT

Detective Sergeant Max Greevey, 40's, is counting out four dollars and twenty-eight cents from a clumped up mass of small bills and change cupped in a ham sized paw. Three inches of cheap cigar are burning in the corner of his mouth. He's wearing a two hundred dollar suit and a tie a blind man wouldn't be seen in. What can't be seen is the mind, which on one level is a cornucopia of seemingly useless information, and on another is a veritable data base of police information. He's been married to his high school sweetheart for twenty years and has three daughters, nineteen, fifteen and six, all of whom can wrap him around their little fingers. He's also an NBA fanatic, and a Knicks fan, an unfortunate combination that has cost him thousands in lost bets since the team's glory days of the early seventies. Greevey's been a cop for eighteen years and has seen everything twice, but he can't stand seeing the bad guys win. He squints at Jesus, the clerk, through a swirl of cigar smoke and shakes his head in disbelief.

> GREEVEY
> Since when's a ham sandwich two seventy-five, Jesus?

> JESUS
> Since last Friday.

> GREEVEY
> Didn't know ptomaine had gone up...

The line goes right over Jesus' head.

> JESUS
> We don't use none of that...it's all home made.

There's an impatient honk from outside. We follow him out the door.

> CONTINUOUS

EXT. STREET - NIGHT

A green Plymouth Fury with no chrome's parked at the curb. Detective Mike Logan, early 30's, is a good looking Irishman with a temper to match. He's been Greevey's partner for the past two years. There's a

mutual trust and respect, but it's a professional relationship—these guys don't spend any more time with
each other than the job demands. They don't confide
their secret fears to each other, they don't socialize,
but they both know that the other would put his life
on the line if the situation required it.

Logan has a B.S. in Police Science, reads books, likes
Woody Allen's early comedies, has a Marine Corps
screaming eagle tattooed on his forearm, drinks
Bushmills, and has a mostly monogamous relationship
with a uniformed policewoman. He's never been married, but he has a five year-old daughter that he
supports and sees. He's putting a bubble gum light
on the roof of the unmarked car as Greevey comes
out of the bodega, pulls open the passenger door and
climbs in.

                    GREEVEY
        What?

                    LOGAN
        We got a 211...could turn into a homi-
        cide.

                    GREEVEY
        Vic conscious?

                    LOGAN
                (shaking his head)
        Ambulance is on the way.

Greevey takes the lid off his coffee, sips and nods
for Logan to drive.

                    GREEVEY
        Around the potholes...suit's just back
        from the cleaner.

                                        CUT TO

EXT. LOADING DOCK - NIGHT
Halsey, unconscious, is being lifted into the back of
an ambulance. Logan looks at the paramedic.

>   LOGAN
>   Odds?

>   PARAMEDIC
>   Fifty-fifty...but I'm an optimist.

Greevey looks down at the bloodless face.

>   GREEVEY
>   I've seen this guy...
>   (calling uniform over)
>   Hey, Hochmeyer.

One of the uniforms leaves the Mercedes and crosses
to the ambulance.

>   GREEVEY
>   Any I.D.?

>   HOCHMEYER
>   (shaking his head)
>   Took his wallet, but we ran the car.
>   (yells to other uniform)
>   Who owns the Benz, Eddie?

The other uniform comes over, pulling out his note-
book.

>   EDDIE
>   Registered to Charles Halsey, Kew Gar-
>   dens.

Greevey's face twists into a pissed-off frown.

>   GREEVEY
>   Oh great...that's just terrific.

> LOGAN
> You know him?

> GREEVEY
> <u>Councilman</u> Halsey? Ring a bell?

> LOGAN
> The tubesteak who's always mouthing
> off about the streets being unsafe?

> Greevey tosses away his cigar stub in annoyance
> and shakes his head in frustration.

> GREEVEY
> I <u>hate</u> media cases.

> FADE OUT

<u>END OF TEASER</u>

The script sets up the place, action, and characters. We can see the quick pacing of the scenes, and hear the rough-edged dialogue of the cops. The characters are described vividly, as are the urban locales.

Talk Show and Variety Format

Talk shows and variety shows are often taped before an audience with a full complement of video cameras for editing. In late-night shows like "David Letterman," "The Tonight Show with Jay Leno," "Saturday Night Live," scenes are referred to as *segments*. Each segment is paced carefully for timing. The script conveys the talent requirements, stage blocking, and dialogue for comedy sketches and music.

Because segments are shot in continuity, each is written as a separate unit. SEGMENT ONE appears at the top left-hand corner of the page. SEGMENT TWO follows on a new page when the previous one is over.

Here's what a sample song segment might look like for a musical segment on "The Late Show with David Letterman."

SAMPLE SONG SEGMENT: LATE SHOW WITH DAVID LETTERMAN

SEGMENT TWO: Jason B. sings

(DAVID HOLDS UP JASON'S NEW C.D. FOR THE
AUDIENCE TO SEE, GETS AUDIENCE APPLAUSE.
JASON PICKS UP HIS GUITAR, CROSSES TO THE
MAIN SET, AND PLAYS THE OPENING LICKS. PAUL
AND THE BAND BACK HIM UP.)

                    JASON

            (SINGING)

    What's the sense of talking

    If your talking ain't real talking

    And if you don't mean anything you're

    sayin'?

    What's the sense of meaning

    If your meaning is deceiving

    And your actions don't believe in what

    you're sayin'...[1]

(PAUL SMILES AT THE GREAT GUITAR WORK, CLAPS
LOUDLY AND THE AUDIENCE BREAKS INTO
APPLAUSE.)

Documentary Format

A narrative double-column format is sometimes used for documentary scripts, news-oriented programs, commercials, and other projects requiring a running narrative, like PSAs (public service announcements). This form breaks the script into two columns. The left is for *video*, the right is for *audio*. Generally, every camera direction, scene description, and stage direction is capitalized. Only the dialogue remains in lowercase letters.

End Note

1. "What's the Sense?", music and lyrics by R. Blum, Laurelton Music & Entertainment. All Rights Reserved.

11

Screenplay Format

Sample Screenplay Format

On the following pages, you'll find a film script model which is appropriate for motion picture screenplays, longform television films, and television film episodes. Film scripts run about a minute of screen time per page. A full-length screenplay is about 120–130 pages, with no act breaks. A two-hour television film is around 110–120 pages and has seven acts. A ninety-minute film is about 90 pages, with seven acts. A one-hour dramatic episode is approximately 60 pages, broken into four acts.

SAMPLE FILM SCRIPT FORMAT

The title goes here, Capitalized and underlined

Written By

Writer is named here

Your Name

You can indicate first or final draft here, sometimes adding the date of completion

FIRST DRAFT

WGAW Reg.

This means: "Registered with Writers Guild of America, West"

Agent's or Lawyer's Name

Address

(phone)

This can be your address, production company, agent, or business manager

*This is the first
written direction
in every script*

SAMPLE FILM SCRIPT FORMAT ← *The title
goes here*

FADE IN:

EXT. CITY STREET - DAY   *This is a "slugline"
which identifies each
new scene*

This is the way you start a film script, with a suc-
cinct designation in the slug line of Exterior or Interior (use EXT. or INT.), the location of the scene
(HOSPITAL PARKING LOT; MCDONALD'S RESTAURANT;
DAVID'S BEDROOM; THE HOTEL BAR; etc.), and the
time of day, i.e., DAY or NIGHT. That information is
necessary for the production unit manager to determine the set requirements, location requirements, and
lighting requirements of your show. ‖ *double-space
implies new angle* ‖

*locations,
actions, and
characters
re described
ere*

Sometimes you can simply skip a paragraph to
describe another angle in the scene, without actually
having to label it above. This is particularly true if
you are thinking of a related piece of stage action
in a master shot or wide shot. This saves you from
over-directing your script, and permits ease of reading.

ANGLE ON PARKED CAR ← *You can specify an angle
this way*

You should use specific angles when you want to
focus our attention on a specific visual item —
objects, people, POVs (Points of View). This helps
move your plot forward in a linear fashion. Note
that the above angle does not have to include any
other slug-line reference (e.g., DAY/NIGHT), because
it is still part of the same scene (EXT. CITY STREET
- DAY). You are merely calling for a different angle
within that scene.

INT. CAR - DAY ← *This indicates a different
scene and location*

If you change the physical locale of the scene, you
must provide a new slug line. You'll note that it
isn't necessary to put CUT TO from the previous
scene, because it is still part of a related visual
sequence, occurring at the same time and place.

When you describe your CHARACTERS or any information pertaining to CAMERA SHOTS, be sure to cap
that information.

Try to be as visual as you can in your description
of the CHARACTERS—who they are, what they look
like, what they're doing at the moment we see them.
Don't forget the setting in the scene. You'll have to
describe it in vivid detail, to give a rich and clear
picture of the mood, atmosphere, and dramatic
action.

> *This is how to set up dialogue*

                    JANET

  Let's move on to something else, O.K.?
  How about the shot numbering system?

> *parenthetical directions can be used to clarify an attitude or interpretation*

                    TOM
               (mock disgust)
  You mean numbering all of the camera
  shots? Forget it! That's done by the
  production secretary after the final
  shooting script is turned in. Writers
  don't have to be concerned with that.
  Directors will want to change it, anyway.

> *This is one way to indicate reactions*

JANET shrugs, starts the car, and pulls away.

EXT. STREET - DAY

> *A new location and scene*

We see the car pulling away from the curb and dis-
appearing down the street in light traffic. Notice that
it is unnecessary to provide a new slug line, because
we are now shooting outside again. If we CUT back
to JANET and TOM in their car, we would have to
designate another INT. CAR-DAY description. But we
can use another technique to keep the dialogue alive
and the visuals wide open. That's the use of VO
(VOICE OVER) or OS (OFF SCREEN).

> *here's how to indicate "voice over"*

                 JANET (VO)
  So, while you see the car pulling down
  the street, you can still hear me talking.

> TOM (VO)
> Incidentally, there is a technical differ-
> ence between the voiceover and the off-
> screen voice. The VO is generally used
> like this or sometimes by a narrator.
> The OS is used when one of the char-
> acters isn't seen in the shot but we
> know he or she is in the scene, per-
> haps on the other side of the room.

> JANET (VO)
> That's confusing. No wonder a lot of
> writers are just using VOs all the time.

HIGH ANGLE ← *a new angle in the same scene (EXT. STREET-DAY)*

From an AERIAL SHOT, we see the car blend into
the light maze of traffic on the city streets.

here is the same description

CUT TO

EXT. BEACH - DAY ← *here's the new scene*

We're in a totally different location now, so the first
thing you must do is describe it. Try to set the right
visual and emotional atmosphere with your description. If we see TOM and JANET, do they look tired
after driving all day? Are they wearing different
clothes? Are they tense? bored? anxious? happy?

CLOSEUP TOM ← *One way of indicating CLOSE-UP*

The CLOSEUP can be called in a number of ways,
e.g., CU TOM, CLOSE ON TOM, or simply: TOM. Now
you describe what the CU reveals. Perhaps it is a
look of concern.

TOM'S POV - DOWN THE BEACH ← *One way of indicating "point of view"*

In the distance, he sees the light of a bonfire. Several FIGURES are huddled nearby. Note that the
point-of-view shot clearly describes what the character sees.

here's what the charac- ter sees

JANET (OS)

Tom? What's the matter?

BACK TO SHOT ← *one way of returning to a previous shot*

This is how to indicate "off screen" dialogue

This designation simply calls the scene's prior establishing shot. You might also use ANGLE ON TOM AND JANET, which calls for a shot featuring both characters.

TOM

(tense)

Nothing's the matter.

↙ parenthetical directions under character's name should be short

The parenthetical information should be used if the attitude of the character is not clear by dialogue alone. It wouldn't be necessary for you to say TOM speaks angrily if he shouts, "Get out of here!" You might also include some relevant stage business for the character, if this can be done succinctly. For the most part, however, try to let the dialogue speak for itself. Stage directions can generally be incorporated in this space. For example: JANET glances down the beach, squints to see the bonfire OS (off screen), and looks back at TOM. A BEAT, then she packs their belongings hurriedly.

JANET

Let's go.

A "BEAT" is described here

The beat that was used above is a filmic version of the dramatic pause, or the Chekovian pause. It implies a second or two for the character to digest the information before he or she acts on it.

NEW ANGLE ← *Another way of calling a shot in the scene*

This is a legitimate angle designation, which implies a different camera angle from the previous one. You don't have to specify the shot, but you should describe the action taking place. Note, too, that if some background action is occurring, you identify it as b.g. (not spelled out); similarly, if the camera is focused on foreground action, you would say f.g. *("foreground")*

ANGLE ON THE CAR

JANET and TOM trot through the beach to their car, and hastily climb in. She starts it up, but the engine won't start. In the b.g., we can make out the FIG-URES by the bonfire, moving toward them.

←("background")

                    TOM

        Hurry!

A BEAT before the ignition catches, then the car starts up and skids away. Note that the character doesn't have to repeat any visual information, i.e., he wouldn't say, "Hurry, the figures are coming toward us!" We can assume that JANET sees the same thing he does.

When you have special sound effects, e.g., the waves crashing, the fire crackling, etc., you can place those directly in the scene description to add atmosphere and mood to the piece. Keep the action moving from scene to scene, and be sure your characters act and react like real people. Each one is unique, and must sound and behave like a credible, identifiable person. Once the script is finished, be sure to:

All effects visual and sound are incorporated into the scene description

                              FADE OUT.

This is the last direction in the script. The screen image fades to black

                Format Distinctions

The industry-standard font is Courier (12 point, nonproportional), Pica on a typewriter. These are some other distinctions in a film script.

1. If a scene is continued on a new page, that is indicated by a "(CONTINUED)" at the bottom right-hand page of the script, and "CON-TINUED" at the top left of the following page.

2. If dialogue is broken at the end of a page, it should end with a full sentence. Then "(MORE)" is added under the broken dialogue, and "(CONT'D)" is typed on the following page, after the character's name.

3. Words are generally capitalized to identify NEW SCENES, NEW

CAMERA ANGLES or SHOTS, SPECIAL EFFECTS, and scene transitions like CUT TO or DISSOLVE TO.

4. The names of CHARACTERS are also capitalized to indicate who is performing in the scene, and who is speaking at the moment. If a character is simply mentioned by another, there is no need for capitalizing. There is some latitude about capitalizing a character's name throughout the script. Some writers will only capitalize it the first time the character appears in the script. Others will capitalize the name throughout each scene in the script. Both ways are acceptable.

Page Margins

A film script usually abides by these margin guidelines.

Page margins. One and a half inches from the left, one inch from the right.

Dialogue. Three inches from the left, two inches from the right.

Characters' names. Four inches from the left.

Top of the page. One inch from the top of the page.

Bottom of the page. One inch from the bottom.

Page numbers. A half inch from the top, one inch from the right.

Computer Software for Script Format

Script formatting can be made a lot easier by using a specially designed computer program for screenwriters. Among the more trusted and enduring programs for IBM compatible users are Movie Master™, Scriptware™, and Scriptor™. For Macintosh users, consider Scriptor™ or Final Draft™. (See "Resources for Screenwriting Software" in the Bibliography.) Before investing in software, do research. Ask for a demonstration disk, and be certain the program is compatible with your needs.

How to Set Up Camera Angles

Most film scripts are written without complicated, extensive camera directions. There is no need to clutter scripts with OVER-THE-SHOULDER SHOTS, REVERSE ANGLES, MEDIUM SHOTS, TWO SHOTS, or

CRANE SHOTS. The director will make all those decisions in pre-production planning. It's the writer's responsibility to merely suggest the potential for camera coverage without complicating or over-directing the script.

Here are a few angles that are particularly helpful in scripting:

WIDE ANGLE
This provides full-screen coverage of all the ensuing action. It's also called a FULL SHOT.

NEW ANGLE
This suggests that some other perspective is needed, but does not necessarily pinpoint that coverage.

CLOSEUP
This is the magnified coverage of a person's face or a specific object on the screen. An ECU stands for extreme close-up.

BACK TO SHOT
This is a way of suggesting that a previous angle is called for.

ANGLE ON
This might focus attention on a specific place or person, e.g., ANGLE ON HALLWAY or ANGLE ON JENNIFER.

The following is from a television film called "DEATH'S HEAD." You can see how simply the angles are set up for the opening sequence in the script.

"DEATH'S HEAD" SCRIPT SAMPLE

FADE IN:

INT. CAROL'S BEDROOM - NIGHT

It's late at night, and we can barely make out the figure of a woman sleeping alone in a king-size bed. She's cuddled up under the covers; the other half of the bed remains untouched. A shaft of light seeps in from the hall, highlighting her face as she stirs. CAROL MADDEN is a striking woman, early 30's, long blonde hair, soft, compelling features.

Over the steady rhythm of the air conditioner, we
hear a slight rustle. It doesn't seem to disturb her.
But then, after a BEAT, we hear another rustling
sound. Tired, CAROL opens her eyes, inquisitive at
first, not really sure if she's heard anything.

CLOSE ANGLE ON BED

A huge black spider is crawling across the covers,
gliding slowly and methodically toward her.

CLOSEUP CAROL

She sees it, recoils in fear.

                                        CUT TO:

INT. DOWNSTAIRS DEN - NIGHT

CLOSE ANGLE ON CRATE

The black furry legs of a spider can be seen trying
to climb the ledge of the crate. A hand gently cups
the insect, and adroitly puts it back into the crate,
closing the cover.

NEW ANGLE

We see CAROL's husband, STEVE, in the brightly lit
room downstairs. The wood-panelled den sports a
good many insect displays on walls and table. Exotic
butterflies, beetles, moths, all artfully pinned and
exhibited under glass. There's a peculiar beauty
about the whole collection. STEVE, a slightly built but
good-looking man in his late 40's, is straightening up
from the small wooden crate beside him. He glances
around, looking for something. One of the spiders is
missing.

If we analyze the script structure and camera angles, here's what we find:

1. The *slug line* identifies individual scenes (INT. CAROL'S BED-ROOM - NIGHT and INT. DOWNSTAIRS DEN - NIGHT).

2. Each scene is comprised of different shots or camera angles. So when we describe Carol's bedroom, then cut to a closeup of the spider on the bed, we are still in the same scene. We simply changed the viewing perspective.

3. Camera angles are suggested clearly. The description of CAROL'S BEDROOM is an implied WIDE ANGLE that establishes all the action in the scene. CLOSE ANGLES are used for special dramatic emphasis and impact. NEW ANGLES imply different perspectives within the same scene. Sometimes NEW ANGLES are implied by simply skipping a paragraph in the scene description.

4. The scene descriptions provide exact visual information about the set, character, and stage action. The descriptions tell us exactly what the camera sees.

5. The camera coverage and special effects are capitalized; so are the characters' names. Capitalizing is not mandatory, but it does help in pre-production breakdown of the script.

How to Structure Scenes

A scene is one link in a dramatic sequence of events. It is comprised of action and dialogue that occur in a single place and time. Once the location changes, so does the scene. The dictates of the story determine how long each scene will be, but many writers try to economize. Some scenes may run for a few sentences, others for as long as a few pages.

Here is a dramatic sequence that takes place at the airport. It is actually comprised of three separate scenes:

1. outside the airport
2. inside the terminal
3. inside the baggage compartment

Within each scene, a number of different camera angles and shots may be required to put the sequence together. But the general location remains the same, and the production crew will not have to move elsewhere.

"AIRPORT SEQUENCE" SCRIPT SAMPLE

EXT. AIRPORT - DAY

We're at L. A. Airport, clogged with traffic, the lines
of cars backed up as far as we can see. A large
707 sits waiting for take-off at one of the terminals.

INT. TERMINAL - DAY

As busy inside as it was outside. Lots of people
milling around, waiting for the crowd to board the
plane to Washington. A small coterie of FIRST CLASS
PASSENGERS make their way into the plane, obviously important. They're government VIPs.

In another section of the terminal, watching the
action, are THREE MEN near a food stand. One
wears a suit and tie, the others wear baggage handling outfits. The MAN IN THE SUIT slips open his
attaché and manages to pass a small packet to the
BAGGAGE HANDLER. A quick glance around. No one
has seen them. We HEAR a muffled call over the
P.A. system for all passengers to board the flight.
The MAN IN THE SUIT, attaché firmly in hand, waits
on line for the security check. He passes through
the gates without a problem.

INT. PLANE'S BAGGAGE COMPARTMENT - DAY

The two BAGGAGE HANDLERS work furiously to
attach electronic wiring to the wall of the compartment. One HANDLER opens a plaid piece of luggage,
exposing some kind of crude bombing device. Time is
pressing, but they complete their mission. One of
them reaches down into the luggage and hits a
switch. The countdown has begun. They scramble out
of the compartment and slam the door shut, leaving
us in darkness.

The first scene—outside the airport—is an establishing shot, which
provides a visual orientation to the viewer. When the scene is shot, the

director may use a number of different angles (a HIGH ANGLE of the airport, VARIOUS ANGLES of the traffic, a CLOSEUP of the large 707, etc.), but the actual scene location does not change (EXT. AIRPORT - DAY).

The second scene takes place inside the terminal. It identifies and focuses the action on some key characters. The director may use a number of different setups (camera angles and lighting changes) to achieve the total effect of passengers waiting, men interacting, passengers boarding, and so on.

The third scene takes place in the baggage compartment, and completes the dramatic action in the chain of events. The scene's action is specifically related to the previous scenes in the sequence.

Scenes can be viewed as links in the dramatic action chain, holding story sequences together with a clear purpose. They move the story forward with skill and maintain a tempo and rhythm for the entire script.

Master Scene Script Format

Most scripts submitted in the marketplace are in the *master scene* form. A master scene script is one that offers a vivid description of action within each scene, but does not break down specific camera angles or shots. Only when a script has been purchased and is ready for production is it ready to be put into shooting script form. The shooting script is the director's final blueprint for production, and has every shot numbered in the margins.

The master scene script allows latitude for the integration of character, action, and dialogue without the encumbrance of complex camera coverage. As an example, this is an excerpt from THE ELTON PROJECT. To set the scene, our leads, Mark and Tony, just escaped from a holding pen. Note the relative scarcity of camera shots and the strong visualization in the scene descriptions.

```
ANGLE DOWN THE CORRIDOR

At the far end of the corridor, the door is pulled
open and Lieutenant Mitchell coolly stands in his
familiar tan jumpsuit and helmet with raised visor.
He slowly unholsters his 9mm.
```

> LIEUTENANT
> (shouting over the alarm)
> Going for a little night air, gentlemen?

Tony grabs Mark's sleeve and yanks him towards the door at the other end.

> TONY
> This way!

They race the fifteen feet to the escape door and dive through it as a shot ricochets off the steel door frame.

> CUT TO:

INT. MOBILE HOME OFFICE OF H.S.I. - NIGHT

Kim sits in the kitchen area, red eyed, deeply concerned. Next to her, a somber Clem.

> KIM
> (pleading)
> Father, please. It's time for us to do something.

Clem breathes heavily, looks out at the night. Dark, ominous, no moonlight. He feels the pierce of his daughter's eyes.

> CLEM
> (staunchly)
> Not yet. We must wait.

He stares resignedly out at the night. The time will come. But not now. Outside, we hear the sound of coyotes wailing.

> CUT TO:

EXT. ENERGY SITE - NIGHT

It's late at night, but sections of the compound are brightly lit. The alarm bell is silent, but we hear the indecipherable voices of the Lieutenant and THREE other armed GUARDS in tan uniforms as they frantically search for Mark and Tony.

NEW ANGLE

Outside of the immediate area, other buildings are difficult to see in the distance. We can barely discern the figures of two people darting between the structures, hugging the walls for protection.

                    MARK
          We're going the wrong way for the
          gate!

                    TONY
          That's the idea. That's where they're
          expecting us to go.

ANGLE ON MARK AND TONY

Mark and Tony stop behind the walls of a prefabricated building, trying to get a better view of the darkened grounds. Beyond them, several hundred feet away, a large metal shed and another prefabricated office building.

                    MARK
          I remember that shed when I drove
          in...

Unfortunately, a huge flatbed tractor trailer obscures their view. Mark waves Tony on, and they dart toward the truck for a better look.

ANGLE ON TRACTOR TRAILER

It's military, but unmarked. From this perspective, they realize how huge the tractor trailer is. Next to it, an unmarked crane truck.

> TONY
> My God, look at the size of this thing.

Mark pulls Tony away from the truck and points back towards the building they just exited. Movement. There is the sound of something nearby. Footsteps?

> MARK
> (whispering)
> The guards!

ANGLE ON LIEUTENANT AND GUARDS

From behind the huge truck tires, Mark sees the Lieutenant searching the route they just came. Nearby, the other guards approach.

Tony quickly assesses the situation, points to the large metal storage shed nearby.

> TONY
> (whispering)
> Let's go.

ANGLE ON METAL STORAGE SHED

It's a large structure, unexceptional in every way. Mark and Tony carefully dart along the length of it, moving quickly toward the partially open sliding doors. They hear the Lieutenant and the guards getting closer.

No more motivation is needed. Mark and Tony slide open the door, slip into the shed.

> CUT TO:

INT. METAL SHED - NIGHT

Inside, they slide the heavy metal door closed. It's at least some protection from the danger outside. Mark closes his eyes, perspiring, breathing heavily. Tony is right beside him, trying not to picture what's out there - indistinguishable commands - yelling - doors slamming - engines revving up - trucks rolling by. Then, after an eternity, quiet.

> MARK
> Wanna try again?

Tony nods. They both know it's the only way out of this madhouse. And with that, they noiselessly slide the door open several inches.

THEIR POV - THROUGH THE SHED DOOR

The large truck is gone, and so is their cover. The doors are in direct view of a guard outside.

BACK TO SHOT

No questions asked, Tony slides the door shut again.

> TONY
> I think we're stuck here for a while.

They turn around to survey their temporary refuge.

ANGLE ON INSIDE OF SHED

For the first time, Mark and Tony get a real look at the inside of the shed. A dim small-wattage bulb provides the only source of light. The shed is remarkably large, more like a parking garage. In the far corner they see an army pick-up truck loaded with crates.

Mark notices that there are padded rails along the walls; he pounds them lightly with his fist.

> MARK
> Convenient. Just in case we wanna
> bang our heads til we get out.

NEW ANGLE

Without any warning, they hear a RUMBLE from
below, and the GROUND begins to SHAKE, VIBRATE.
A sudden shock of recognition flashes over Tony's
face.

> MARK
> It's an earthquake!

> TONY
> Worse! It's an elevator! We're in a god-
> damn freight elevator!

Before Mark can respond, the floor of the shed
begins to descend.

> CUT TO:

INT. UNDERGROUND CORRIDOR - NIGHT

Below ground, a WORKER in an army uniform
stands by the bottom of the elevator shaft, waiting
impatiently for the elevator. He's a young enlisted
man in his early 20's, average build, short cropped
hair. Finally, the elevator jolts to a stop, and he
punches a button that opens the wide freight gates.

> CUT TO:

INT. FREIGHT ELEVATOR - NIGHT

The worker heads onto the floor elevator and heads
toward the pickup. He jumps inside, starts the
engine.

ANGLE ON TRUCK

It lurches forward. In the back, under the tarp, we

see the shape of mismatched crates and the odd outline of two men. They don't dare look out.

> MARK (VO)
> Damn!

The truck leaves the elevator, bouncing the crates
and cargo in the back.

> CUT TO:

INT. UNDERGROUND CORRIDOR - NIGHT

The vehicle slowly travels several hundred feet, then
jerks to a stop on an underground roadway. We see
the uniformed worker jump out, head back towards
the elevator.

ANGLE ON BACK OF TRUCK

The tarp is pulled back by an anxious pair of
hands. We finally see Mark, then Tony. Completely
bewildered. It's another world they've entered.

> MARK
> My God, Dante's inferno.

We hear the sound of the elevator doors closing, and
the elevator as it rumbles upward.

> MARK (CONT'D)
> And there goes our only way out.

> TONY
> Let's go, before our Tour Guide gets
> back.

No argument about that. Mark jumps out, followed
by Tony. We hear the soldier heading back to the
truck. Before he arrives, Tony and Mark duck
behind a parked front-end loader.

> CUT TO:

The script relies on few camera directions. These are some of the camera angles referred to: ANGLE DOWN THE CORRIDOR, ANGLE ON MARK AND TONY, ANGLE ON TRACTOR TRAILER, ANGLE ON METAL STORAGE SHED, THEIR POV, BACK TO SHOT, ANGLE ON INSIDE OF SHED, ANGLE ON TRUCK. They are meant to give us the visual flavor of the scene, without directing the screenplay.

Special Techniques: Intercuts, Montages, Dreams, Flashbacks

Let's look at some special problems you may encounter in writing certain types of sequences in your script.

1. Intercuts

Intercutting is cutting back and forth between two or more scenes consecutively. For example, a script may call for parallel action and dialogue during a phone conversation. If you play the scene in one location, it could result in static dramatic action. If the script cuts back and forth between characters, it might result in awkward repetition of scene descriptions.

The most common solution to this kind of problem is to identify the ongoing scenes in advance by calling for an INTERCUT SEQUENCE. The appropriate scenes are defined, while action and dialogue are written as usual. The last scene concludes with: END INTERCUT SEQUENCE.

NOTE: INTERCUT SEQUENCE:

INT. LAURA'S APT - DAY

She's on the phone in the den, pictures scattered all over the floor.

EXT. PHONE BOOTH - DAY

It's raining cats and dogs as we see MIKE, drenched to the bone, talking to Laura.

                    LAURA
          (into phone)
     Hello?

MIKE
(into phone)
Hi, Laura, It's me. You o.k.?

LAURA
(into phone)
Fine, but I miss you somethin' awful.
When will you come back?

He takes a deep breath.

MIKE
(into phone)
Not for a long time.

LAURA's eyes widen. She didn't want to hear that.

END INTERCUT SEQUENCE.

The need for an intercut sequence is dictated by the length of the required scene and the importance of seeing consecutive dramatic action on the screen. The sequence allows the director to edit as he or she sees fit.

2. Montages

A *montage* is a succession of different shots that condense time, emotions, and action into just a few short scenes. The story may call for a quickly established romance, or an historical progression of images leading to the present time.

As with intercuts, the montage is identified in advance of the sequence and at its conclusion. The individual scenes are sometimes listed by number. If a writer needs to show a character undertaking different activities in a progression of time, the montage sequence is ideal. This is one way it would be set up.

MONTAGE SEQUENCE:

1. INT. CAROL'S ROOM - DAY

She's cleaning it up, carefully straightening the sheets on the bed.

2. EXT. SUPERMARKET - DAY

She wheels a basket down the aisles, quickly pulling food from the counter and piling it into the basket.

3. INT. CAROL'S KITCHEN - DAY

A bandanna over her head, she's polishing the oven fast and furiously.

4. EXT. CAROL'S PORCH - NIGHT

She's in her jeans, collapsed on the swinging porch bench, tired and weary.

END MONTAGE

There's no need to show Carol cleaning up everything in the room, or conversing with the cashier at the supermarket. The visual information in a montage implicitly gives the viewer that sense of completed action.

3. Dreams and Fantasies

In scriptwriting, *dreams* and *fantasies* are used interchangeably. They permit the viewer to enter the character's mind, to literally see imagination, daydreams, fantasies, nightmares. A "dream sequence" can be distinguished from "reality" to keep the production realities clear. Here is one way it can be done.

CU CAROL

She's fast asleep; a look of anxiety twists her face. Clearly disturbed, restless...

CU SPIDER (DREAM SEQUENCE)

It crawls toward her at an inscrutably slow pace...

CU CAROL (BACK TO REALITY)

She snaps her eyes open and looks around. There's
nothing there.

In this case, the dream sequence is almost a flashcut. It is a very fast insert
into the "real" world of Carol sleeping. The various angles and visual
descriptions help set the mood and atmosphere. Once the sequence is
over, the "real-time" sequence picks up the pace and helps sustain the
mood.

A longer sequence is generally identified in advance, and the first
"real" scene is also distinguished. Here's what a longer dream sequence
looks like. It is from the screenplay SONJA'S MEN. To set the scene, Aaron
has just taken a deposition from Ida, an elderly victim of the Holocaust.
She revealed how she escaped from a death train by jumping from a
bridge. It had a tremendous impact on him. The characters of Tyrowicz
and Osidatch are under investigation by his office as Nazi collaborators.

INT. HOTEL LOBBY - NIGHT

He walks to the revolving doors, and enters the
lobby entrance.

                                  DISSOLVE TO:

INT. AARON'S HOTEL ROOM - NIGHT

ECU AARON

Asleep. A fitful, deeply troubled sleep.

DREAM SEQUENCE:

EXT. UKRAINE TRAIN STATION - DAY (DREAM)

We see TYROWYCZ and OSIDATCH, barely in their
30's, in uniform, officiously directing the UKRAINIAN
POLICE as they forcefully push JEWISH CITIZENS
into the waiting train. We see men, women, children,
not sure what's happening. Once the doors are
locked, the train moves off.

INT. TRAIN - NIGHT (DREAM)

The train is crowded, dusty, noisy. We see a YOUNG
IDA KEMPNER, late teens, blonde, energetic, concerned. She reaches for the window, desperately trying to open it.

> IDA
> (in Yiddish)
> We've got to get out. They're going to
> kill us..!

The OTHERS look at her as if she's crazy.

> OLD LADY
> They're work camps. That's all.

ANGLE ON IDA (DREAM)

She struggles to open the window, with bars above.
No one helps.

She pries the window open, and tries to push herself
through the bars. Finally, one or two PASSENGERS
help her. She scrapes her way through the window
as the train passes over a river.

ANGLE ON AARON'S PARENTS (DREAM)

They, too, are passengers. They grab their son,
AARON, 10, and try to get him through the window
to safety.

EXT. TRAIN - NIGHT (DREAM)

The train crosses the bridge from Ukraine to Poland.
From the train window, we see IDA push her way
out of the open window and silently FALL twenty
feet below. We hear gunshots.

ANGLE ON AARON (DREAM)

The boy Aaron is FALLING from the train, down into
the water.

AARON'S POV - THE RIVER (DREAM)

We're falling, spiraling, down into the water. Water is rushing up toward us. We hear the sounds of rushing water and the sounds of gunshots.

END DREAM SEQUENCE

CUT TO:

INT. AARON'S HOTEL ROOM - NIGHT (REALITY)

ECU AARON

He sits bolt upright, grabs his chest, gasps for breath. He wakes with a start, catches himself in a silent scream. He tries to orient himself. The room is dark; there is no sound other than his own heart pounding. The clock reads 12:00 midnight. The dream was too real for him.

ANGLE

He turns on the table lamp.

4. Flashbacks

A *flashback* distinguishes "time remembered" from real time and is set up like the dream sequence. If a memory is very brief, the writer can parenthetically identify the FLASHBACK. For example:

CU RONALD

He remembers something; the memory plagues him.

INT. ATTIC - NIGHT (FLASHBACK)

It's a dingy place, no air, no light. In the corner, something moves...We can't make it out, but it's alive.

ANGLE ON RONALD (FLASHBACK)

He's on his knees, a flashlight in hand. He tries to switch it on, but the batteries are dead. He throws it toward the moving object and races toward the attic steps.

CU RONALD (REALITY)

Jarred by the memory.

If a flashback sequence is much longer, it would be written just like a lengthy dream sequence.

This might be the time to caution against the unnecessary use of flashbacks. The technique is helpful to provide some exposition about characters or to establish a "backstory" to the plot. However, if it's used too often, the effect can be detrimental to the story. The more a writer relies on flashbacks, the more he or she intrudes on the forward thrust of the plot. If a story begins in the present tense, then slips back in time, the viewer already knows the outcome. The audience is waiting to see the characters work their way out of the current situation. That action is forestalled with the intrusion of flashbacks. If you must use flashbacks, do so sparingly.

PART SIX

MARKETING
YOUR SCRIPT

12

How to Sell
Your Script

What You Should Know before Marketing

Marketing a script requires strategy, determination, and a realistic understanding of the industry. The marketplace is extremely competitive, and even the best projects written by established professionals can end up on the shelf or forever lost in development hell. Still, an excellent original script, submitted to the right person at the right time, might suddenly break through the barriers. The key word is "excellent." It makes no sense to submit a script unless it is in the most polished form, producible, and castable (and even then it will be subject to countless rewrites).

Your script represents the highest caliber of your creative potential. You might think producers and agents are inclined to see the masterpiece lurking behind a rough-draft script. More likely, they'll focus on the weaknesses, compare it to top submissions, and generalize about the writer's talents. So, if you feel uncertain about a script's professional quality, producibility, or castability, hold off on submitting it. Your next work might show you off to better advantage.

Selling scripts is an arduous task, and only perseverance pays off. Consider this reaction from Jeff Maguire when told of his nomination for best original screenplay (IN THE LINE OF FIRE) by the Writers Guild of America: "I'm still dazed . . . Two years ago, I was considering getting out of the business. I felt I was banging my head against a wall for quite awhile, unable to get a foothold. I had development deals and script sales, but nothing to my satisfaction. I was ready to move to New Hampshire and write a novel."[1] Perseverance is the key.

Registering Your Script and Joining the WGA

It's important to register your screenplay with the Writers Guild of America (WGA) before sending it into the marketplace. This service was set up to help writers establish the completion dates of their work. You don't have to be a member of the Guild to take advantage of this service. WGA registration doesn't confer statutory rights, but it does supply evidence of authorship that is effective for ten years, and is renewable after that.

Contact the WGA Registration Service for forms and fees. The WGA East is less expensive. Contact WGA East, 555 West 57th Street, New York, NY 10019, or WGA West, 8955 Beverly Boulevard, Los Angeles, California 90048-2456.

The Writers Guild of America protects writers' rights and establishes minimum acceptable arrangements for fees, royalties, credits, and so on. You are eligible to join the Guild as soon as you sell your first project to a signatory company, i.e., a production company that has signed an agreement with the Guild. A copy of your contract is automatically filed, and you will then be invited to join. Before you sell the next project, you have to be a member of the Guild. There is a one-time membership fee, dues are assessed periodically, and you pay a small percentage of your annual earnings as a film writer.

The Release Form or Submission Agreement

If you have an agent, there is no need to bother with release forms. But if you're going to submit a project without an agent, you may have to sign a release form—a submission agreement—in advance. Most production companies will return your manuscript if a submission agreement is not included. The waiver states that you won't sue the production company and that the company has no obligations to you. That may seem unduly lopsided, but millions of dollars are spent annually fighting potential lawsuits, and thousands of ideas are being developed simultaneously by writers, producers, studios, networks, cable, and pay TV companies.

The waiver is a form of self-protection for a producer who wants to avoid unwarranted legal action. But it also establishes a clear line of communication between the writer and producer, so if legal action is warranted, it can be taken.

A sample submission agreement appears below.

TITLE:

SUBMITTED BY:

AUTHOR:

DRAMA CATEGORY:

SUBMITTED TO:

CIRCA:

LOCATION:

PREMISE:

---

1. I request that you read and evaluate said material, and you hereby agree to do so, and if I subsequently make a written request, you agree to advise me of your decision with respect to the material.

2. I warrant that I am the sole owner and author of said material, that I have the exclusive right and authority to submit the same to you upon the terms and conditions stated herein, and that all of the important features of said material are summarized herein.

3. I understand that you have adopted the policy, with respect to the unsolicited submission of material, of refusing to accept, consider, or evaluate unsolicited material unless the person submitting such material has signed an agreement in a form substantially the same as this agreement.

4. I have retained at least one copy of said material, and I hereby release you of and from any and all liability for loss of, or damage to, the copies of said material submitted to you hereunder.

5. I enter into this agreement with the express understanding that you agree to read and evaluate said material in express reliance upon this agreement and my covenants, representations, and warranties contained herein, and that in the absence of such an agreement, you would not read or evaluate said material.

6. I hereby state that I have read and understand this agreement and that no oral representations of any kind have been made to me, and that this agreement states our entire understanding with reference to the subject matter hereof. Any modification or waiver of any of the provisions of this agreement must be in writing and signed by both of us.

7. If more than one party signs this agreement as submitter, then reference to "I" or "me" throughout this agreement shall apply to each such party, jointly and severally.

DATED:_____

_____
Signature

_____
Print Name

_____
Address

_____
City and State

_____
Telephone Number

Writing a Cover Letter

When you prepare to send out your project, craft a cover letter that is addressed to a specific person at the studio, production company, network, cable, or pay TV company. If you don't know who is in charge, look it up in the trade papers or call the studio receptionist. If the answer is "Ms. So and So handles new projects," ask how to spell the name. That courtesy minimizes the chance of embarrassment and maximizes the chance that the project will wind up at the right office.

The letter you write should sound professional. There's no need to offer apologies for being an unsold writer, or to suggest that the next draft will be ten times better than this one. If a cover letter starts off with apologies, what incentive is there to read the project?

Here's the tone a cover letter might have:

Dear _____

    I've just completed a screenplay called SURVIVING EVIDENCE, based on the book by Frank Tavares. I've negotiated all TV and film rights to the property. I think you'll find it an intriguing premise. It's based on fact, and offers unusual opportunities for casting.

    I look forward to your reactions. Thank you for your consideration.

Sincerely,

The letter doesn't say I'm an unsold writer in the Midwest or that Frank Tavares is my friend who let me have the rights for a handshake. Nor does it take the opposite route, aggressively asserting that it is the best project the studio will ever read. There's no need for such pretensions. The cover letter sets the stage in a simple and dignified manner. The project will have to speak for itself.

If your screenplay has won any awards, or is a finalist in a national competition, be sure to mention that in the cover letter. (For screenwriting competitions, see Chapter 13.)

How to Prepare Your Script for Submission

Your script should look professional, with the appropriate format and the right number of script pages. The paper should be three-hole punched, with metal brads fastened through. Put the script title and your name, address, and phone number on the title page. Do not create fancy covers or title designs. (For questions about format, refer to Chapters 10 and 11.)

Since unsolicited scripts tend to be lost or "misplaced" by production companies, it's a good idea to have a sufficient number of copies. Register one with the Writers Guild of America and reproduce five or six copies to submit to producers and agents. Keep the original to reprint for other submissions.

Submission Status Reports

It's helpful to keep a "submission status report," summarizing pertinent information about marketing contacts, dates, reactions and follow-ups to each project. That information can be kept in a computer or on paper.

Figure 12-1 shows one way it might be set up:

```
SUBMISSION STATUS REPORT
PROJECT TITLE:
DRAFT COMPLETED/REGISTERED:
SEND TO:      MAILED:       RESPONSE:    FOLLOW-UP:
1.
2.
3.
4.
5.
6.
```

Figure 12-1

Under the first column (*SEND TO*) you can preselect the names and addresses of agents, producers, studio executives, directors, and actors who might be interested in your project. If the first person turns down the project or doesn't respond in a reasonable period of time (four to six weeks), send it to the next person on the list. This preselected listing provides you with a planned strategy for an otherwise erratic marketplace.

The second column (*MAILED*) indicates when you forwarded—or plan to forward—the project to each person on the list.

In the next column (*RESPONSE*) you can summarize reactions received, e.g., "received letter from studio. They're not interested in this genre, but like my writing style. Asked to see more material."

The final column (*FOLLOW-UP*) leaves room for your initiatives, e.g., "if no word from studio, phone them," "sent copy of another screenplay, per their request."

Submission status reports can help keep track of strategies, problems, and solutions on a day-to-day basis.

How to Get an Agent

If you have no agent representing you, it's difficult to get projects considered by major producers. One of the best ways to make headway is to submit your work to an agent who represents a friend, a teacher, a long-lost relative. If you are recommended by someone known to the agency, it makes you less of an unknown commodity.

If you have no contact, the quest for representation can still be handled effectively through another type of marketing strategy. Contact the Writers Guild of America and request a list of guild-franchised agents. From that, work up a separate roster of potential agents for your project, and prioritize them in your submission status file.

You can send the project to one agency for consideration, or to a select number of agencies at the same time. There is nothing wrong with a limited, organized campaign that seeks representation for your project.

A brief cover letter might introduce you as a freelancer looking for representation on a specific project. If you don't get a response within six to eight weeks, you can follow up with a phone call or letter, and submit the project to the next agent on your list. Don't be discouraged if you get no response at first. Just keep the project active. If the script is good enough, you might eventually wind up with some positive and encouraging feedback from the agency.

If an agency is interested in your script, they'll ask for exclusive representation on that project. If the script is optioned or sold, the agent is entitled to a 10% commission for closing the deal. If the work elicits interest but no sale, you have at least widened your contacts considerably for the next project.

The larger agencies—William Morris Agency, Inc., Creative Artists Agency (CAA), and International Creative Management (ICM)—are virtually impenetrable to new writers. These agencies have a long list of clients in every field from variety and concerts to film, television, and the legitimate stage. They handle writers, producers, directors, actors, and even production companies.

For that reason, a major agency can package top clients into a new project with a massive price tag attached. If the package is appealing enough, the script may sell at a very lucrative price for the writer. The package is a strong way to present an original script, but it is not without its drawbacks. The process may take as long as three or four months to set up, and may stretch out for some additional months before getting a reading from the buyer.

The most erratic aspect of packaging is the marketplace response. An entire deal can be blown if a buyer dislikes any of the elements attached. If one actor is preferred to another, or if the director is disliked by any executive, months of waiting can explode into fragments of frustration. The project may never get off the ground.

The larger agencies offer an umbrella of power and prestige, but that advantage can be offset by the sheer size of the agency itself. Many clients inevitably feel lost in an overcrowded stable, and newcomers can hardly break into that race. In contrast, a smaller literary agency might provide more personalized service, and might be more open to the work of new talent.

If you're going to seek representation, the smaller agency is the better place to go. Many of these agencies are exceptionally strong and have deliberately limited their client roster to the cream of the crop. In fact, many smaller agents have defected from executive positions at the major agencies. So you'll have to convince them you're the greatest writer since

Shakespeare came on the scene—and that your works are even more saleable.

How do you prove that you have the talent? It's all in the writing. If your projects look professional, creative, producible, and castable, you're on the right track. Indeed, you can call yourself a writer. If the artistic content is also marketable and you back it up with determination and know-how, you just might become a *produced* writer.

Analyzing the Marketplace

Your submission strategy will depend on knowing the marketplace trends and organizing a campaign to reach the most appropriate people and places.

Networks, Cable, Pay TV

In network television, there is a network oligarchy at the top of the submission ladder: ABC, CBS, NBC, Fox, UPN, WB. If a project is submitted and "passed" (i.e., turned down), it's too late to move back down the ladder to producers. Their goal is to bring it back up to the networks.

The same is true of the cable and pay TV marketplace, where producers want to sell to a few key buyers, e.g., HBO, Showtime, Turner. Small companies can't compete with the deals offered by the larger companies. They are more likely to structure a modest licensing agreement for the rights to the show.

A visual model of the writer's marketplace in television is shown in Figure 12-2.

As that model shows, the closer a project comes to the top, the more limited the number of buyers. It faces stiffer competition and fewer alternatives. The marketplace is highly competitive, but not totally impenetrable.

Independent Producers

Independent producers represent the widest marketing potential for writers in television and motion pictures. If one producer turns down an idea, there are hundreds of others who might still find it fresh and interesting. However, the smaller independent producer is not likely to have the financial resources to compete with the development monies available at production companies and major studios.

THE WRITER'S MARKETPLACE IN TELEVISION

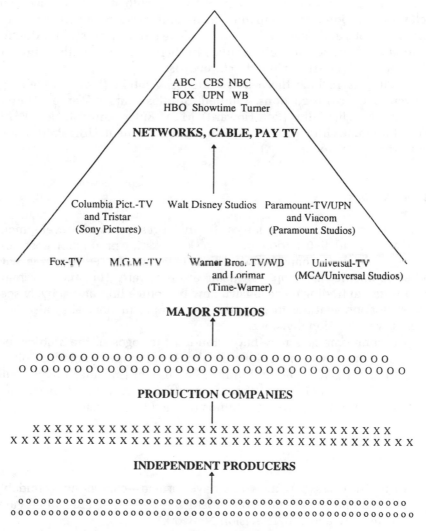

ABC CBS NBC
FOX UPN WB
HBO Showtime Turner

NETWORKS, CABLE, PAY TV

Columbia Pict.-TV   Walt Disney Studios   Paramount-TV/UPN
and Tristar   and Viacom
(Sony Pictures)   (Paramount Studios)

Fox-TV   M.G.M -TV   Warner Broo. TV/WB   Universal-TV
                             and Lorimar   (MCA/Universal Studios)
                             (Time-Warner)

MAJOR STUDIOS

o o o o o o o o o o o o o o o o o o o o o o o o o o o o o o o o o o o o o
o o o o o o o o o o o o o o o o o o o o o o o o o o o o o o o o o o o o o

PRODUCTION COMPANIES

x x x x x x x x x x x x x x x x x x x x x x x x x x x x x x x x x x x
x x x x x x x x x x x x x x x x x x x x x x x x x x x x x x x x x x x x

INDEPENDENT PRODUCERS

o o o o o o o o o o o o o o o o o o o o o o o o o o o o o o o o o o o o o o o o o o o o o o o o o o o o
o o o o o o o o o o o o o o o o o o o o o o o o o o o o o o o o o o o o o o o o o o o o o o o o o o o o

FREELANCE WRITERS

Figure 12-2

Production Companies

Production companies *do* have that bargaining power, and they represent the strongest marketing resource for new scripts. The distinction between independents and larger production companies is their relative financial stability and current competitive strength at the box office or on television. Production companies form and dissolve according to the financial ebbs and flows of the industry. The more successful production companies have become mini-studios in their own right, with features in development and triumphant track records.

Examples include these powerhouses: Amblin (Steven Spielberg), Steven Bochco Productions, Cannell Studios, Carsey-Warner, Hanna-Barbera, Imagine Films (Ron Howard), MTM Entertainment, New World Entertainment, Orion Pictures, Spelling Entertainment, UBU Productions (for others, see Appendix A).

Major Studios

Major studios have the largest financial resources for development, production, and distribution. But with skyrocketing production costs and a rough-edged economy, some studios have been forced to merge with other companies. Development deals are now rare. The studios remain committed to finding those elusive new box office hits, and actively seek co-production ventures to share the costs of production. They also have aggressive television divisions.

Corporate mergers may have clouded the logos of the studios, but these are currently the most identifiable: Sony Pictures (includes Columbia and Tristar), Walt Disney Studios, Paramount (includes merger with Viacom), Fox, M.G.M., Time-Warner (includes merger with Warner Bros. and Lorimar), MCA/Universal Studios (owned by Matsushita).

Other Avenues to Market

In recent years, new networks have formed—competing formidably for television projects. Among the most likely to flourish are United Paramount Network and WB Television Network.

O&Os (stations owned and operated by the networks) and group-owned stations should also be explored. They have been particularly active in program development. You can find background information in resources like *Television Factbook* or *Broadcasting and Cable Yearbook*.

A different avenue for new television projects is the advertising agency. Some larger agencies are heavily involved in program development activities for their clients. It is not unusual for major clients to commit to a number of television films, comedy shows, or variety specials—with the provision that the advertising agency find the product.

Many of the agencies buy into projects at an early stage and are almost guaranteed placement at the networks, in syndication, and with cable or pay TV. Some of the companies have their own production subsidiaries, but are still open to new programming concepts. The person to contact is the VP of programming (or some variant of that title)—*after* you have investigated their clients' demographic targets.

Marketing Strategies: Spec Scripts, TV Series Concepts, Motion Picture Screenplays, Interactive Programs

Each project requires its own marketing strategy, so marketing a script requires time. Ascertain which agents, producers, production companies, and studios would be interested in the type of project you've developed. You can begin by reading the trade papers and industry resources (see "Trade Publications and Periodicals" in the Bibliography). They provide clues to the current and future activities of key people, bringing you closer to making informed decisions about marketing your own script.

Spec Scripts for Television

If you wrote a spec script for any current television series, it would be effective to submit it first to an agent for representation. The idea is to get your script submitted to a prominent producer, story editor, or head writer of a similar-genre show. Remember that a spec script is meant to serve as a sample of your work, *not* to sell. A good script will get you invited to a pitch meeting, and that's where you can sell your new ideas.

The trades regularly publish lists of series contacts for current shows (see "Trade Publications and Periodicals" in the Bibliography). Another resource is *The Journal of the Writers' Guild of America*, which publishes a "Television Market List," identifying contacts for writing assignments, and indicating whether shows are open for submissions.

TV Series Concepts

If you've written a new television series concept, submit it to a producer or a production company that has been successful in developing those kinds of shows (see Appendix A). You can also submit it to the head of development for a major studio, since they have established track records with the networks. That will greatly enhance your credibility.

If the project is similar to one you've seen on cable or pay TV, send it to the head of programming for that company (see Appendix B).

Motion Picture Screenplays

If you have written a screenplay, try to market it as a *castable, producible, and low-budget motion picture.* Be creative and ingenious about getting the script to the right people. Read the trades to find out what film projects are in production and which are planned for the future. They provide the names of the executive producers, directors, actors, and other key people involved.

Try to get your script into the hands of a director who has done a similar film. The director is the one who has artistic control in theatricals. Look at the credits of films with comparable production values and characters. Write down the actors, production company, and executive producer. Get the script to them somehow.

Think about casting, and send it to actors who might be interested in playing the leads. Stars go on publicity tours and on location for shoots. Find out where they're staying. Send it to them with a personal note of appreciation.

You can also submit the screenplay directly to the head of feature development at a major studio or production company (for a list, see Appendix A). Since contacts change regularly, also check resources like *The Producer's Masterguide* for up-to-date marketing information.

If the script is small enough in scope and budget, think about marketing it as a television film. It can be set up for a deal at the networks, HBO, Turner, Showtime, or any other pay TV company that has the track record.

Interactive Programs

If you're developing projects for interactive or new technologies, investigate software companies and corporations that might be interested in exploring those ideas. Among the most significant Hollywood alliances are M.G.M.'s affiliation with Sega's CD-ROM to supply filmed interactive material, and MCA Universal's (owned by Matsushita) heavy investment in 3DOco.[2] Paramount Interactive entered into its first international partnership with NEC in Japan. NEC, a leader in CD-ROM, was given rights to distribute "Lenny's Music Toons," an interactive program that combines music, videos, puzzles, and games. The move was seen by insiders as an effort by Paramount to position itself as a global leader in developing, producing, and distributing interactive programs.[3]

Time Warner, Inc. has also set its sights on being a leader in interactive cable programming. Keep your eye on the trade papers for updates and leads.

Writers are now working under the WGA's Interactive Program Agreement for major multimedia players such as Electronic Arts, Sierra On-Line, Phillips Sidewalk Studios, Interplay, and Knowledge Adventure. Interactive producers and developers have been working under a "user-friendly" contract to establish compensation and groundrules for writing and designing for interactive multimedia.[4]

Business Deals and Contracts

If a producer is interested in a project, he or she will offer a deal. If you have no agent, this is the time to get one. Any agent will gladly close the deal for the standard 10% commission. An attorney would be equally effective. The need for counsel depends on the complexity of the proposed deal and the counter proposals you wish to present.

On the basis of your discussions, a *deal memo* is drawn up, outlining the basic points of agreement—who owns what, for how long, for how much, with what credits, royalties, rights, and so on. The deal memo is binding, although certain points may be modified if both parties agree. The contract is based on the terms of the deal memo and is the formal legal document.

If you're dealing with a producer who is a signatory to the Writers Guild (most established producers are), the contract will adhere to the terms of the *Minimum Basic Agreement (MBA)* negotiated by the Writers Guild of America.

Be sure to contact the Writers Guild of America for a copy of the most recent MBA, which outlines fees for every conceivable writing service. These are some of the areas covered for theatrical screenwriting: flat deals, payment schedules, purchase from a professional writer, optioned material, television release prior to theatrical release, week-to-week and term employment, narration, pension plan, and health fund.

For television, the MBA covers fees for: network primetime (story, teleplay, story & teleplay), made-for-pay television or video cassette/video disc, made-for-basic cable, informational programming, high budget other than primetime, rewrite and polish, plot outline (narrative synopsis of story), backup script, format, bible, narration, rerun compensation, foreign telecast compensation, week-to-week and term employment, noncommercial opening and closing, purchase of literary material, optioned material, sequel payment, character payment, low-budget minimum. It also covers comedy-variety, quiz and audience participation, serials (other than primetime), non-primetime nondramatic strip programs, documentary programs, and news programs.

Options and Step Deals

A producer can option your work, purchase it outright, or assign you to write new material. An *option* means that he or she pays for the right to shop it around. During the option period, you can't submit it to any one else. Typically, option money is relatively small, and is for a limited amount of time. But you will be paid a much greater sum if the project moves forward.

If the producer fails to exercise the option, the rights revert back to you. Some screenwriters find themselves earning tons of money in options—and never get to see their projects produced.

A *step deal* is the most common form of agreement between producers and freelance writers. It sets out fees for story and script in several steps. When you turn in a *story*, the producer pays for it. If you are retained to write the *first draft*, the producer exercises the first-draft option. When you turn in that draft, you receive the appropriate compensation. Now the producer has a third option, the *final draft*. Once you turn in the final draft, you are entitled to the balance of payment.

The step deal is a form of protection for the producer, who can respond to the quality of content and hold the writer to delivery dates. It also guarantees the writer that his or her work will be paid for, whether or not there is a cut-off.

Screen Credits and Arbitration

Screen credits equate to money in the bank. If a writer receives sole credit—WRITTEN BY—she or he is entitled to full residual payment as well as payment for story and script.

A CREATED BY credit entitles you to 100% of royalties every time a television show airs. That translates to thousands of dollars each week for a new television series.

If a producer hires another writer to revise a project—which happens more often than not—the credit problem is automatically referred to the WGA for arbitration. All material is reviewed by WGA members, anonymously. It's their job to decide who is entitled to what credit. If the final credit is sole story or teleplay (STORY BY or TELEPLAY BY), the residuals will be based on that contribution alone. If a credit is shared with another writer (STORY BY "A" AND "B"), so are the residual checks that come in the mail.

The issue of screen credits is so important and complex that many pages of legal definitions and regulations are included in the MBA. In an effort to stay on top of credit problems, the Guild requires the production company to send a "Notice of Tentative Writing Credits" to Writers Guild headquarters, and to all participating writers. If a writer protests the credits for any reason, the project automatically goes into the arbitration process.

ENDNOTES

1. "WGA Nominations Swing Into Action, Comedies," *The Hollywood Reporter*, Feb. 9, 1994, 19.
2. Andy Marx, "Hollywood Players Grapple for Interactive Paradigm," *Daily Variety*, April 28, 1994, 5.
3. Andy Marx, "Par Interactive Signs Pact," *Daily Variety*, April 5, 1994, 4.
4. For information on the Interactive Program Agreement, contact: Department of Industry Alliances, Writers Guild of America, West, Inc., 8955 Beverly Boulevard, West Hollywood, CA 90048 (310) 205–2511, (310) 550–8185 (FAX), CompuServe 73602,676.

13

Noncommercial Funding Sources

If you write high-quality drama or documentary projects, this chapter will help you wade through the maze of grant opportunities as well as screenplay competitions. Years ago, I served as senior program officer for the National Endowment for the Humanities (NEH), and know the intricacies of grant support for film and television projects. The bureaucracy is dreadful, and the financial rewards are relatively limited, but there is something notable about having your project supported by the NEA, NEH, CPB, or a foundation grant. (For national funding sources, see Appendix C.)

National Funding Sources: CPB, PBS, NEA, NEH

The Corporation for Public Broadcasting (CPB)

A quasi-government agency, CPB has a Program Fund to support independent filmmakers, TV writers, and public TV producers. It was designed to be insulated from political pressure, and remains one of the single most important sources for funding in the public television marketplace.

The Program Fund is a major funder of public television projects. The congressional mandate is to develop programs of high quality, diversity, creativity, excellence, and innovation. That's where you and your ideas fit in.

Independent producers, writers, and public TV stations can submit program proposals, and CPB encourages co-productions between independents and Public Broadcasting Service (PBS) stations. They also encourage submissions by women and minorities.

If you have an idea for development, write to them directly, or, more practically, set up a meeting with the head of programming at your local PBS station. Local stations are likely to know the program proposal requirements of CPB, and can help you put together a more competitive proposal if you mutually decide to pursue the idea.

CPB regularly publishes requests for proposals along with guidelines for submitting projects. Contact them for the latest guidelines and Program Fund announcements.

When you apply for funding, you fill out a basic information sheet, which is supplied with the program guidelines. That is the face sheet of the application, and describes the content of the show, costs, and key personnel involved. In addition, you'll need to write a short synopsis that shows how you plan to handle the subject matter for television. It's written in precisely the same way you would write a storyline for the networks. If you have completed a detailed treatment, that can be attached as well.

A budget is required for CPB applications, indicating how much money is needed for development or production of the television show. The budget is something a writer must deal with in grant applications. The funding agency needs to know where you plan to spend its money. For script development grants, the budget is usually very simple: writer's fees (these can be based on the Writers Guild of America's MBA), research fees, travel, and administrative costs.

CPB is an approachable agency. Whether your project is dramatic, cultural, special, children's, news or public affairs, contact them to find out how it fits in. You can also submit your project to the executive producer of a series currently funded by CPB.

Public Broadcasting Service (PBS)

PBS is primarily concerned with the acquisition of programs already produced, and functions as a distributor of public TV programs. Still, they get involved, peripherally, in the development of new shows for the system, and they have been involved with interactive programming initiatives.

The PBS Programming Department can be helpful in offering some backing for projects that might be of interest to their stations. That support usually comes in the form of a letter of endorsement rather than a banker's check. They will, however, help secure interest from appropriate funding sources, and, in some cases, will put up some seed money for development. The reality is that PBS funds are scarce.

Given the mandate to move PBS into a more aggressive program stance, Jennifer Lawson, Chief Program Executive, negotiated the rights to a high-quality NBC drama series, "I'll Fly Away," when it was canceled by NBC. In discussions I had with her, Jennifer Lawson said she wants to build a sense of quality drama that will bring new audiences to the network. The biggest problem is that PBS budgets can't compete with the big networks. The series was too expensive to produce, so she approved the purchase of reruns and the development of a new final episode.

In addition to targeting minority audiences, Jennifer Lawson wants to bring in younger audiences, like those targeted with documentaries on Paul Simon, Gloria Estafan, and Billy Joel.

For documentaries, PBS is the one place to seriously think about bringing a project. It has supported series like "Nova," Ken Burns' award-winning documentary series, "The Civil War," and his latest series, "Baseball."

With respect to development, they are now adding comedy to the mix. Jennifer Lawson initiated a groundbreaking comedy produced by Brandon Tartikoff with WYES in New Orleans ("The Steven Banks Show"). That half-hour series breaks a one-hour programming stranglehold that blocked half-hour shows from being developed at PBS. Lawson seeks to break away from the notion that PBS is a "humor-impaired network": "We take the stewardship of public funds seriously . . . But 'Steven Banks' is perfectly within the realm of what public television should explore. Humor and satire can be a way of looking at ourselves."[1] PBS is developing another half-hour show, "Future Quest," hosted by Jeff Goldblum, integrating sci-fi clips, TV shows, and cartoons. It gives a virtual-reality view from the perspective of animals.

When you develop a script or film project for public television, try to elicit interest from a local PBS station. They know the landscape and the players. And remember that PBS has very little money to award to projects. They are the place to help find funding, and to award a primetime spot to air your project.

National Endowment for the Arts (NEA)

The NEA was created by Congress to encourage and support the Arts in America. Its fundamental role is to support creativity at the highest level, and to stimulate the enjoyment of the arts in our country. The agency fulfills its mission through various grant-making programs, including one called Media Arts, designed for individuals and organizations in television, film, and radio.

The Media Arts Program offers support for individuals and nonprofit organizations in TV, film, and radio. The Independent Film and Videomaker Program offers grants for original productions that intrinsically deal with the Arts. Individuals can apply, but should have significant experience in television or film. Administered by the American Film Institute (AFI), the program provides funds for animation, documentary, experimental, and narrative projects. A maximum grant of $20,000 is awarded in each of those four categories. Applicants must submit a copy of a previously completed film or video (a superb example of your work) and a brief treatment (1-2 pages) for a documentary, or a completed script for the narrative category. You will also need a resumé of project principals (producer, director), and a detailed budget breakdown.

Panelists for the NEA give very serious consideration to the level of artistic and professional achievement exhibited in your sample project. Most of the film and video production grants are made to nonprofit organizations and are limited to a requirement for matching funds.

Programming in the Arts is a category for a limited number of PBS series, and requires substantial funding from other sources. Sample projects funded in the past include "American Playhouse" and "Great Performances."

The Regional Fellowship Program is important for writers and producers to know about. Independent film and video artists can apply for fellowships through a regional program set up by the NEA and state arts agencies. You can contact the agency nearest you to determine eligibility requirements. (There is a directory of state arts & humanities agencies in Appendix D.)

For a comprehensive look at all the programs at the NEA, write for a copy of their *Guide to NEA*.

The National Endowment for the Humanities (NEH)

The mission of the NEH is to encourage and support important works in the humanities, and to disseminate that information to the widest possible audience. The media program at the NEH has been one of the largest and most important funding sources for public television and film.

Within the Division of General Programs, the awkwardly titled Humanities Projects in Media is particularly relevant to freelance writers and independent producers. It supports the development and production of new television, film, and radio projects. The media program has funded such television projects as "Vietnam: The Television History," "Mark Twain Series," and "American Short Story."

The general themes that are relevant to the NEH shift with the incumbent administration's interpretation of the humanities. In the past, the NEH supported socially relevant projects tied to humanities themes, then shifted to a more conservative stance, supporting classical, scholarly subjects, e.g., "Masterworks of Civilization." You can keep up with the current trends by reading the media guidelines carefully and contacting staff members to determine eligibility.

A project that is submitted to the NEH for consideration should meet one or more of these basic NEH goals: provide an interpretation and appreciation of significant cultural works; help illuminate historical ideas, figures, and events; or provide an understanding of the disciplines of the humanities. Those disciplines have been defined by Congress, and are listed by academic fields in the guidelines.

The NEH media program encourages professional writers and producers to work in cooperation with scholars in particular program areas. The meeting of the minds between professionals and scholars creates a challenging atmosphere, and contributes to some mutually rewarding ideas about program development in the humanities.

Typically, the NEH offers these types of grants:

1. *Planning grants* to support writers, producers, and scholars seeking to develop innovative media humanities projects.
2. *Script development* to support the writing of scripts and series outlines. They cover appropriate research costs for treatment and scripts (travel, consultants) as well as other development costs (writer's fees, story conferences, typing and duplicating).
3. *Production grants* for single programs, pilots, or series episodes. Since production costs are so high, they usually require additional gifts and matching funds from other sources.

As for submission of proposals, the NEH strongly recommends a preliminary inquiry before each deadline. The staff can help determine the appropriateness of the project, and can help you prepare a more competitive proposal for submission. In addition, they can guide your project through formal evaluation procedures.

For a complete description of grants, write for a copy of the *NEH Guide to Humanities Projects in Media*.

State Funding Sources

State Arts and Humanities Agencies

One of the most practical places to look for seed money for the development of original scripts is the state arts and humanities agencies. Each state has money appropriated by the legislature for support of artistic and cultural work relevant to that state. The NEA and NEH also contribute block grants for re-granting purposes to the state agencies.

The arts and humanities agencies are separate and distinct from each other, operating within the same general mandate as their national counterparts. Since each agency has different guidelines, you should contact the staff to determine whether script development grants are possible. (For a list of state arts & humanities agencies, see Appendix D.)

State Film and Television Commissions

State film and television commissions are another resource for discussing your ideas and projects. Although they have no funding capabilities, these agencies are committed to the idea of nurturing new productions, and they can be helpful in the pragmatics of pre-production contacts. They know who is doing what in your state, and can often provide interesting leads. (For a list of state film and television commissions, see Appendix D.)

Private Foundations and Corporate Sources

Relatively few foundations are waiting to fund scriptwriters. However, several have been active in funding film and television projects, including the Annenberg/CPB Project, Ford Foundation, Guggenheim Foundation, Lilly, Mellon Foundation, Markle, Exxon, Sears Roebuck Foundation, and the Jerome Foundation (which funds screenwriters living in New York) (for a listing, see Appendix C).

One very helpful place to begin your search for appropriate funding is The Foundation Center, located in New York City and Washington, D.C. They have field offices and repository libraries in several parts of the country. The Center is the only nonprofit organization in the country designed to analyze and disseminate information about foundations.

One of its publications, *The Foundation Directory*, profiles thousands of foundations, and can help identify those organizations that support projects similar to your own. The directory identifies foundations that have supported film and video projects, as well as those interested in a vast array of catalogued subjects.

After determining the most appropriate possible contacts, tailor a letter to the specific interests of each foundation. You can define how your project relates to the mission of that organization, how you plan to carry out the project, what the television project might look like, and how your background fits in to guarantee the success of the project.

With respect to corporations, you can learn a great deal about their interests, objectives, and philosophies from their annual reports. You can also delve into a number of research directories available at your library to determine which ones support similar kinds of projects.

Annenberg/CPB Project

The Annenberg/CPB Project received $15 million over a ten-year period to support innovative projects that use new technologies—including television and film—to improve higher education. It's a very different and intriguing opportunity for writers and producers who want to collaborate with institutions of higher learning (and vice versa). For guidelines and more information about the program, write to the Annenberg/CPB project.

How to Write Grant Proposals

If you're planning to submit a project to any public agency, first write for the guidelines and application forms. The guidelines will give you a broad idea of the agency's needs, and your proposal will have to address those needs. A grant proposal is generally comprised of three parts:

1. the application form (called the *face sheet*)
2. the narrative proposal, which details your objectives and program format
3. the budget

In addition, a timetable is usually included, along with the vitae (resumes) of all key personnel are included.

The Face Sheet

The first page of the application is called a face sheet. It asks for identifying information about the applicant and the proposal. Most face sheets require an abstract, to be written in a paragraph or two, outlining the objectives and format of the show. They also ask for information about key personnel. A carefully worded synopsis is especially important when you consider the fact that some evaluators might only see that first page abstract.

Let's create a face sheet to identify some terms and to answer some questions about filling it out.

Item #1. Asks for the name of the individual applicant or project director. The project director is equivalent to an executive producer. This is the person responsible for creating the show and overseeing the total creative and administrative activities.

Item #2. Asks whether the proposal is new or was submitted in some other form. The application is considered new if it was never submitted to that agency. It is a revision if it was submitted and was rejected previously. It is a renewal if it is based on work done on an earlier grant (e.g., a request for production based on a script development grant). A supplemental request is one that is an extension of current grant activities.

Item #3. Asks the name of the program. This refers to the name of the division within the agency as it appears on the program announcement.

Item #4. Asks whether the applicant is an individual or an organization. If you are applying as a freelance writer or independent producer, you would specify "individual." If you are applying as a production entity or joint venture, you would check "institution," and specify the type of company (e.g., Television Production) as well as private or nonprofit status. Unless an agency specifically requests evidence of nonprofit status in advance, you can generally incorporate after a grant is awarded.

Item #5. Asks for the grant period, i.e., when the project will start and finish. As a rule, the start date should be several weeks after you expect to hear about the award decision. That assures you that your time won't be wasted waiting for a letter of confirmation while the grant period is already in effect. Similarly, the completion date ought to provide you ample time to finish the project. It is not unusual for script development requests to be six months long. That length of time serves as a contingency, since federal agencies are reluctant to authorize extensions later on.

Item #6. Asks you to define the intended audience. You can take your cue from the stated objectives of the agency. One might be primarily interested in reaching general adult audiences; others might be targeted for minority, handicapped, bilingual, or elderly audiences, or children.

Item #7. Asks for the amount of funds required to accomplish the project. Money requested directly from the agency is called an *outright grant.* The *gifts and matching* category refers to money that might be forthcoming from other sources. Some agencies require gifts and matching situation. They will offer money contingent upon your ability to raise a matching sum from another source. *Cost-sharing* refers to the contributions received in the form of service, facilities, and similar donations from your own production company.

Item #8. Asks for the field of the project. This refers to the specific subject category as it relates to the agency's announcement.

Item #9. Asks for the chief location in which most of the work will be accomplished during the grant period. It is a curious category for free-lance writers, and can generally be listed as your home state. The purpose of this type of question is to provide the agency with a broad base of data to determine how effectively they serve their constituencies.

Item #10. Asks for the public issues of the project. This refers to the thematic issues of relevance to the agency.

Item #11. Asks for the topic title. This is the complete working title of the project.

Item #12. Asks for a description of the proposed project. This is an extremely important item, since it defines the objectives and approach in a paragraph or two. The synopsis should clearly and succinctly define the intentions, the filmic approach, the proposed content, and the key personnel involved. You'll be able to flesh out all that information later in the attached narrative proposal.

The Narrative Proposal

The *narrative* is the body of your request. It fully details the concept and filmic approach of the show. The narrative may run 20-100 pages or more, depending on the nature of the project. The narrative section expands upon the ideas proposed in the abstract. Objectives are clarified, approaches are defined, and sample visual treatments are provided. In a request for script development funds, a fully detailed pilot story or treatment may also be included. If a production grant is sought, the full script is needed, and a budget breakdown is required.

A well-written narrative generally covers each of these areas in depth:

1. the nature and scope of the project
2. the importance of the project to target audiences and general audiences
3. the selected format and visual approach for television or film
4. the timetable for research, development, and/or production
5. the background and expertise of key personnel
6. the budget

Some applications ask for a detailed synopsis of the project on a continuation sheet. This is the time to address the points above in a condensed version of the entire proposal. A continuation sheet provides significant background information on the nature and scope of the project, the personnel, and the relevance of the project to specific agency goals.

As an example, if this project were for the NEH to support a film script based on a book, the description of the book would be minimal, compared to a larger discussion of issues and themes relevant to the humanities. The treatment itself would appear in the narrative section of the proposal.

If this project were designed for another agency, e.g., the CPB, this page would offer a straightforward synopsis of the dramatic storyline, instead of focusing exclusively on the historical and cultural background.

The narrative section of the proposal begins after the application forms are completed. This is the heart of the grant proposal. Objectives need to be stated clearly and the program content should be relevant to those goals.

A well-written treatment is particularly important, since it gives the reader a specific sense of the program you have in mind. It's the basis for determining how you intend to script the project. Treatments for grants are written precisely the same way as those for network television or features. The format and structure are identical, and so is the dramatic storytelling technique.

The Budget

A budget is an integral part of a grant proposal. It demonstrates the creator's ability to plan accurately, realistically, and professionally. Moreover, it assures the funding agency that the money will be spent reasonably.

"But wait!" you say, "I'm a writer! What do I know about budgets?" That's a reasonable, plaintive cry, but the fact is, in grantsmanship, the creator must be equipped to think like a hyphenate (writer-producer).

The budgetary needs of projects differ considerably. However, certain elements do tend to appear regularly. For example, in script development, the budget generally includes costs for scriptwriting, research, travel, consultant fees, typing and duplicating, administrative overhead, and so on. The actual cost for each item is dependent upon the development needs of a particular show.

This is not to suggest that there are no budget guidelines for research and development. You can refer to the Writers Guild of America MBA for appropriate fees for writing services. You may need to budget consultants into your project. These are academic or technical advisors who are experts in their fields. You may find that one or two will be sufficient for the project, or that a full-fledged ten-member advisory board is necessary. Consultants usually receive a per diem honorarium. The number of days must be clarified in the budget, and their responsibilities clarified in the narrative.

As for travel costs incurred in researching or developing a script, it's necessary to know who must travel where, and for how long. Funding agencies will support travel, but the costs must be justified in the budget. Airplane trips should be coach fare, and per diem costs should be within standard federal guidelines. The funding agency itself can offer per diem guidelines for travel in both domestic and foreign cities.

Production budgets are much more difficult to determine than script costs. If you are seeking funds for production on the basis of a completed script, it is essential to get some professional help. At the local level, a production manager at a station or production house can supply you with rate sheets, i.e., the established costs for using facilities and personnel.

If the script to be produced is more complex, an independent producer or production manager can help break down costs for above-the-line (talent and creative staff) and below-the-line items (technical services and facilities).

The Directors Guild of America might help you locate specific people for the purpose of budgeting the show. In addition, other key guilds and unions can provide you with up-to-date information concerning going rates. (Those guilds are listed in Appendix F.)

How Projects Are Evaluated

Every agency has a different review system, but the general process remains the same. PBS and CPB review projects in cooperation with each other and will try to find support and distribution for the projects of the highest merit. CPB usually pre-selects projects for review by an advisory panel of experts. They base their evaluation on the relevance of the project to the priorities of CPB and PBS, the credentials of the production team, and the innovation and diversity the project offers to the PBS schedule. It is likely that your local PBS station has a similar evaluation process or can initiate that process with your project ideas.

Some federal agencies who publish RFPs (requests for proposals) literally have a point system for ranking proposals. Various segments of the proposal are judged according to specified criteria in the guidelines. The proposal with the highest ranking receives the award. Unfortunately, some outstanding projects get left in the dust because they miss out by two-hundredths of a point on some technicality.

One of the most rigorous evaluation systems is set up by the National Endowment for the Humanities. The NEH might select outside reviewers who are scholarly experts in various fields to look at the proposal and comment on its intellectual soundness. Whether or not the proposal receives this outside review, it is submitted to a specially convened panel who represent a wide range of experience and interests in academics and television or film. The panel might be comprised of a Hollywood writer, a studio executive, a philosopher, an anthropologist, a cultural historian, an archaeologist, and a documentary filmmaker. The panel meets for two days, much like a sequestered jury, discussing each proposal on its own merits and in comparison with other projects submitted in that cycle.

The NEH staff forwards the recommendations of reviewers and panelists to the National Council on the Humanities. The Council is comprised of presidential appointees who generally endorse the recommendations of reviewers, panelists, and staff. The Council then recommends action to the Chairman of the Endowment, who has sole legislative authority to make final decisions about funding. Most often, those decisions are consistent with the advice received from the evaluation process.

The process sounds terribly cumbersome, but in fact the applicant gets a definitive word in three or four months from the submission deadline. In addition, if you request the information, the staff will provide you with complete copies of the reviews and a summary of the panelists' comments.

The National Endowment for the Arts has a similar, though less complicated, review process. The staff reviews the applications and refers them to the appropriate advisory panel. The panel's comments are reviewed by members of the National Council on the Arts, and they in turn recommend approval or disapproval to the Chairman of the Endowment. Once again, the Chairman has sole legislative authority to make final decisions, but will most often act on the advice and recommendations of the Council. The applicant is notified of acceptance or rejection by the Chairman's office.

Rights, Profits, and Royalties

If a project is funded, the creative rights are usually retained by the writer or project director. However, the question of rights should be fully investigated—and negotiated—before the signing of any agreement. As a reference, keep the Writers Guild's MBA by your side.

Try to get complete information about a particular agency's stance on royalties, profits, and rights. The NEH, for example, gives the grantee total control over the project and total ownership of creative rights. That's a very critical and important right for any creative writer. If the policies seem carved in stone, there's probably no room for negotiation. However, if there is some latitude, it can't hurt to negotiate.

Screenwriting Festivals,
Competitions, and Professional Workshops

Submitting your script to national competitions is a wonderful way of giving it exposure. Recognized competitions are usually judged by established producers, agents, and writers.

These are a sample of the competitions that are currently available. Since they tend to change frequently, contact the appropriate places for rules, deadlines, applications, and entry fees. (See "Screenwriting Festivals, Competitions, and Professional Workshops" in Appendix E.)

For other opportunities, be sure to investigate resources like *Grants and Awards Available to American Writers; Gadney's Guide to International Contests, Festivals, and Grants in Film, Video; The Writer's Handbook;* and *Writers Market.* (See "Marketing Resources" and "Grants and Noncommercial Funding" in the Bibliography.)

Don and Gee Nicholl Fellowships in Screenwriting

The Academy of Motion Picture Arts & Sciences Foundation awards up to five $20,000 fellowships each year to new writers (writers who have not sold or optioned to film or television).

When I was a regional coordinator for the Nicholl fellowships, judges received scoring sheets that rated these elements of a screenplay: story, characterization, dialogue, and structure. The judges are seeking an original story and exceptional craft—crisp dialogue, compelling dramatizations, and interesting characters.

Since Academy members are the judges, it's a unique way of getting your original screenplay exposed to the right people. Several of my students placed as semi-finalists, and obtained top agents to represent them. Contact the Academy Foundation for application rules, entry fee, and deadline date. Screenplays must be in the appropriate form.

Academy of Television Arts & Sciences

The Academy of TV Arts & Sciences has student internship programs in television scriptwriting. They provide college students with an opportunity for in-depth exposure to the industry. Winners receive a stipend; those from outside Los Angeles are awarded a small travel/housing allowance to the city. The internship includes an overview of comedy or drama writing, idea inception, story meetings, revisions, and production.

Applicants submit an opening scene of a spec script written for a comedy or dramatic series on the air. Finalists will be asked to submit the complete script. Contact the Academy for requirements and deadlines.

Black Independent Film, Video, and Screenplay Competition

Black Filmmakers Hall of Fame, Inc. sponsors this competition to recognize outstanding African-American screenwriters, producers, and directors. Before the deadline, submit a full-length screenplay. Finalists are invited to a prestigious reception in Oakland, California. Get application materials and information from the Black Filmmakers Hall of Fame.

The Chesterfield Film Company—Writer's Film Project

The Writer's Film Project is co-sponsored by Universal Studios. Up to ten $20,000 screenwriting fellowships are awarded for a one-year period (for living in Los Angeles). Each writer is assigned a mentor and takes part in screenwriting workshops to complete two feature-length screenplays, receiving feedback from professional writers, producers, and directors.

Chesterfield Film Company plans to produce the best of each year's work, and will pay no less than WGA minimums. Acceptance is based on storytelling talent. Screenplays must be in the appropriate form, with a synopsis, no more than 3-4 sentences. Contact Chesterfield Film Company for information about application, deadline, and entry fee.

The Walt Disney Studios Fellowship

These are fellowships for ten to fifteen culturally and ethnically diverse new writers to work full time developing their craft at the Walt Disney Studios. Fellowships are open in the feature and television divisions, with a focus on hiring African Americans, Latinos, Asians, Native Americans, and women. A $30,000 salary is provided for a one-year period. Fellows outside of Los Angeles will be provided with air fare and one month's accommodations.

For features, submit a full-length motion picture screenplay. For television, submit a spec half-hour comedy script for shows like "Mad About You," "Roseanne," or "Seinfeld." Submissions are evaluated by Disney executives. Contact Disney Studios for application forms, requirements, and deadlines.

Sundance Institute

The Sundance Institute was founded by Robert Redford and other professionals to provide a resource center for writers, directors, and producers interested in exploring film projects with strong humanistic content. The Institute has combined script development and production assistance programs into one division—the Independent Feature Program. This allows them to consider projects on an ongoing basis.

The program is designed to support development and production of independent feature films. Script Development is a five-day screenwriter's lab. Participants have access to an accomplished writer or producer who serves as script advisor. The Institute provides travel and room and board for the lab. A project must be, at minimum, a first-draft screenplay. The Institute seeks low-budget, fictional, feature-length films with compelling, original stories that explore unique perspectives of the human condition, regionalism, or the life, legends, and diverse culture of America.

Warner Bros. Writer's Workshop

Warner Bros. Writer's Workshop is a recognized leader in developing new television writers. Their Comedy Writer's Workshop in Los Angeles is one of the most comprehensive programs in the industry. Ten to fifteen writers are selected, and spend ten weeks pitching ideas and writing teleplays, with feedback from top Warner Bros. producers and executives.

This is a prime entry point into the industry, with a lot of success stories. Two of my students from a regional workshop were selected for the Comedy Writers Workshop, and were signed to contracts as writers of "Roc" and "The Fresh Prince of Bel Air."

Applicants submit a spec half-hour comedy script from a current television series. Scripts need to reflect an understanding of the structure, characters, and dialogue of existing television shows.

I was host and moderator of a regional workshop, and Warner Bros. conducts several regional workshops and teleconferences. Due to corporate mergers and budget cuts in 1995, the workshop may be threatened with cutbacks. Call their Writer's Workshop Hotline for information about activities and deadlines.

The Nate Monaster Memorial Writing Competition – UBU and UFVA

The Nate Monaster Memorial writing competition is co-sponsored by UBU Productions (Gary David Goldberg, Chair) and the University Film and Video Association (UFVA), a national organization of television and film professors. It's designed to foster television writing talent at college and universities.

Students submit a spec television script from a current series to a UFVA faculty member at their campus. Each faculty member selects one script to be submitted to the formal competition. Winners have an opportunity to work on a current television series.

UFVA Lee Rich Screenwriting Award

Each year, UFVA co-sponsors another competition for new screenwriters. The original screenplay must be nominated by a UFVA faculty member. Contact the UFVA or a UFVA faculty member for details.

ENDNOTES

1. Stuart Miller, "New Sked Stance Spurs Comeback," *Variety*, March 14-20, 1994, 32.

Appendixes:
Where to go Next

APPENDIX A

MAJOR STUDIOS

AND PRODUCTION COMPANIES

New motion picture scripts should be addressed to the head of Feature Development. Television projects should be submitted to the head of TV Program Development. Projects will stand the best chance of being read if they are submitted through an agent. Because addresses and phone numbers constantly change, you should check the current listings in the latest edition of *The Producer's Masterguide*.

ABC Broadcasting
2040 Avenue of the Stars
Los Angeles, California 90067
(310) 557-7777

A & M Films
335 North Maple Drive, Suite 350
Beverly Hills, California 90210
(310) 285-6200

Alive
8912 Burton Way
Beverly Hills, California 90211
(310) 247-7800

Irwin Allen Productions
400 Warner Boulevard
Burbank, California 91422
(818) 954-3601

Alliance Entertainment, USA
301 North Canon Drive, Suite 318
Beverly Hills, California 90210
(310) 275-5501

Amblin
(Steven Spielberg, President)
100 Universal City Plaza
Bungalow 477
Universal City, California 91608
(818) 777-4600

Warren Beatty Productions
5555 Melrose Avenue
Los Angeles, California 90038
(213) 468-5000

Steven Bochco Productions
1021 West Pico Boulevard

Building #1
Los Angeles, California 90035
(310) 203-2400

Mel Brooks Productions
10201 West Pico Boulevard
Los Angeles, California 90035
(213) 277-2211

Bill Burrud Productions
16902 Bolsa Chica Street
Suite 203
Huntington Beach, California
92649
(714) 846-7174

Cannell Studios
7083 Hollywood Boulevard
Los Angeles, California 90028
(213) 465-5800

Carolco Pictures
8800 Sunset Boulevard
Los Angeles, California 90069
(310) 859-8800

The Carsey-Werner Company
34-12 36th Street
Queens, New York 11106
(718) 706-5769

CBS Studio Center
4024 Radford Avenue
Studio City, California 91604
(818) 760-5000

Churchill Media
12210 Nebraska Avenue
Los Angeles, California 90025
(310) 207-6600

Dick Clark Productions
3003 West Olive Avenue

Burbank, California 91505
(818) 841-3003

The Cousteau Society
870 Greenbrier Circle
Suite 402
Chesapeake, Virginia 23320
(804) 523-9335

Crossroads Films
371 North La Cienega Boulevard
Los Angeles, California 90048
(310) 659-6220

Culver Studio
9336 West Washington Boulevard
Culver City, California 90230
(213) 836-5537

Dino De Laurentis Communications
8670 Wilshire Boulevard
Beverly Hills, California 90211
(213) 289-6100

Walt Disney Motion Pictures
500 South Buena Vista Street
Burbank, California 91521
(818) 560-1000

Disney/MGM Studios
P.O. Box 10,200
Lake Buena Vista, Florida 32830-
0200
(407) 560-7299

EUE/Screen Gems
222 East 44th Street
New York, New York 10017
(212) 867-4030

Fox, Inc.
10201 West Pico Boulevard

Los Angeles, California 90035
(310) 277-2211

Geffen Films
9130 Sunset Boulevard
Los Angeles, California 90069
(310) 278-9010

Samuel Goldwyn Company
10203 Santa Monica Boulevard
Los Angeles, California 90067
(213) 552-2255

Mark Goodson Productions
5750 Wilshire Boulevard
Suite 475 West
Los Angeles, California 90036
(213) 965-6500

Merv Griffin Enterprises
9860 Wilshire Boulevard
Beverly Hills, California 90210
(213) 461-4701

Group W Productions
3801 Barham Boulevard
Los Angeles, California 90068
(213) 850-3800

Jack Haley, Jr. Productions, Inc.
8255 Beverly Boulevard
Los Angeles, California 90048
(213) 655-1106

Hanna-Barbera Productions
3400 Cahuenga Boulevard
Hollywood, California 90068
(213) 851-5000

Imagine Films Entertainment, Inc.
(Ron Howard, Producer/Director)
1925 Century Park East, #2300
Los Angeles, California 90067
(213) 277-1665

ITC Entertainment
12711 Ventura Boulevard
Studio City, California 91604
(818) 760-2110

Norman Jewison Productions
9336 West Washington Boulevard
Culver City, California 90230
(213) 836-5537

Stacy Keach Productions
3969 Longridge Avenue
Sherman Oaks, California 91423
(818) 905-9601

Kings Road Productions
1901 Avenue of the Stars, #605
Los Angeles, California 90067
(213) 552-0057

Landsburg Productions
11811 West Olympic Boulevard
Los Angeles, California 90064
(310) 478-7878

Sherry Lansing
5555 Melrose Avenue
Los Angeles, California 90038

Malpaso Productions
(Clint Eastwood, Producer/
Director)
c/o Warner Bros.
4000 Warner Boulevard
Burbank, California 91522
(818) 954-1228

Maysles Films, Inc.
250 West 54th Street
New York, New York 10019
(212) 582-6050

MCA/Universal
100 Universal City Plaza
Universal City, California 91608
(818) 777-1000

McCann-Erickson Productions
6420 Wilshire Boulevard
Los Angeles, California 90048
(213) 655-9420

MGM
2500 Broadway
Santa Monica, California 90404
(310) 280-6000

MTM Entertainment
4024 Radford Avenue
Studio City, California 91604
(818) 760-5942

New World Entertainment
1440 South Sepulveda
Los Angeles, California 90025
(310) 444-8100

New World Entertainment
115 East 57th Street
New York, New York 10022
(212) 755-8600

New York Zoetrope
838 Broadway
New York, New York 10003
(212) 420-0590

Orion Pictures
1888 Century Park East
Los Angeles, California 90067
(310) 282-0550

Pakula Productions
445 Park Avenue
New York, New York 10022
(212) 664-0640

Paramount Pictures
5555 Melrose Avenue
Los Angeles, California 90038-
3197
(213) 956-5000

Playboy Enterprises
9242 Beverly Boulevard
Beverly Hills, California 90210
(310) 246-4000

Reeves Entertainment Group,
#500
3500 West Olive Avenue
Burbank, California 91505
(818) 953-7600

Republic Pictures
12636 Beatrice
Los Angeles, California 90066
(310) 306-4040

RKO Pictures
1801 Avenue of the Stars
Suite 448
Los Angeles, California 90067
(213) 277-0707

George Schlatter Productions
8321 Beverly Boulevard
Los Angeles, California 90048
(213) 655-1400

Showtime
10 Universal City Plaza
31st Floor
Universal City, California 91608
(818) 505-7700

Smith and Hemion Productions
1438 North Gower Street
Box 15
Los Angeles, California 90028
(213) 871-1200

Sony Pictures Entertainment, Inc.
(includes Columbia and Tri-Star):

TV: 3400 Riverside Drive
Burbank, California 91505
(818) 972-7000

feature films: 10202 West Washington Boulevard
Culver City, California 90232
(310) 280-8000

Spelling Entertainment
5100 Wilshire Boulevard
Los Angeles, California 90036
(213) 965-5700

Lyn Stalmaster and Associates
9911 W. Pico Boulevard
Suite 1580
Los Angeles, California 90035
(310) 552-0983

D. L. Taffner, Ltd.
5455 Wilshire Boulevard
Suite 1908
Los Angeles, California 90036
(213) 937-1144

Think Entertainment
(Shelley Duvall, President)
12725 Ventura Boulevard
Suite J
Studio City, California 91604
(818) 509-5982

Time/Telepictures
3300 Riverside Drive
Building 158
Burbank, California 91522
(818) 954-5305

Todd-AO/TAE Productions
201 Wilshire Boulevard
Suite 17-A
Santa Monica, California 90401
(310) 451-0011

Tribeca Film Center
375 Greenwich Street
#700
New York, New York 10013
(212) 941-4000

United Artists
450 North Roxbury Drive
Los Angeles, California 90210
(213) 239-0945

MCA/Universal
100 Universal City Plaza
Universal City, California 91608
(818) 777-1000

Universal Studios Florida
1000 Universal Studio Plaza
Orlando, Florida 32819
(407) 363-8000

Vertigo Films
16 West 56th Street
New York, New York 10019
(212) 262-6600

Viacom International, Inc.
1515 Broadway
New York, New York 10036
(212) 258-6000

Viacom Productions
10 Universal City Plaza
32nd Floor
Universal City, California 91608
(818) 505-7500

Warner Brothers, Inc.
4000 Warner Boulevard
Burbank, California 91522
(818) 954-6000

Robert Wise Productions
315 South Beverly Drive, #214
Beverly Hills, California 90212
(213) 284-7932

Witt-Thomas/Harris Productions
1438 North Gower
Building #35

4th Floor
Los Angeles, California 90028
(213) 464-1333

David Wolper Productions
4000 Warner Boulevard
Burbank, California 91522
(818) 954-1707

The Zanuck Company
202 North Canon Drive
Beverly Hills, California 90210
(310) 274-0261

APPENDIX B

TELEVISION NETWORKS, CABLE, AND PAY TV

Television Networks

Capitol Cities/ABC, Inc.
2040 Avenue of the Stars
Century City, CA 90067
(213) 557-7777

Capitol Cities/ABC, Inc.
77 West 66th Street
New York, NY 10023
(212) 456-7777

CBS, Inc.
7800 Beverly Boulevard
Los Angeles, CA 90036
(213) 852-2345

CBS, Inc.
51 West 52nd Street
New York, NY 10019
(212) 975-4321

Fox Television
205 East 67th Street
New York, NY 10021
(212) 452-5555

Fox TV Center
5746 Sunset Boulevard
Los Angeles, CA 90028
(213) 856-1000

NBC, Inc.
3000 West Alameda Avenue
Burbank, CA 91523
(818) 840-4444

NBC, Inc.
30 Rockefeller Plaza
New York, NY 10112
(212) 664-4444

Cable and Pay TV

American Movie Classics (Rainbow Programming)
150 Crossways Park West
Woodbury, New York 11797
(516) 364-2222

Arts & Entertainment
235 East 45th Street
New York, New York 10017
(212) 661-4500

Biznet
1615 H. Street, NW
Washington, DC 20062
(202) 463-5808

Black Entertainment Television
1232 31st Street, NW
Washington, DC 20007
(202) 337-5260

BRAVO (Rainbow Programming)
150 Crossways Park West
Woodbury, New York 11797
(516) 364-2222

The Cartoon Network
Box 105264
1050 Techwood Drive, NW
Atlanta, Georgia 30318
(404) 827-1717

Cinemax
1271 Avenue of the Americas
New York, New York 10020
(212) 522-1212

CNBC
2200 Fletcher Avenue
Fort Lee, New Jersey 07024
(201) 585-2622

CNN (Cable News Network)
1050 Techwood Drive, NW
Atlanta, Georgia 30318
(404) 827-1500

Comedy Central
1775 Broadway
New York, New York 10019
(212) 767-8600

Country Music Television (CMT)
2806 Opreyland Drive

Nashville, Tennessee 37213
(615) 871-5830

The Crime Channel
13601 Ventura Boulevard
Suite 103
Sherman Oaks, California 91423
(818) 907-5769

C-SPAN
(Cable Satellite Public Affairs Network)
400 North Capitol Street, NW
Washington, DC 20001
(202) 737-3220

The Discovery Channel (Discovery Networks)
7700 Wisconsin Avenue
Bethesda, Maryland 20814
(301) 986-1999

The Disney Channel
3800 West Alameda Avenue
Burbank, California 91505
(818) 569-7500

E! Entertainment Television
5670 Wilshire Boulevard
Los Angeles, California 90036
(213) 954-2400

ESPN
(Entertainment and Sports Programming Network)
ESPN Plaza
Bristol, Connecticut 06010
(203) 585-2000

Family Channel
1000 Centerville Turnpike
P.O. Box 64549
Virginia Beach, Virginia 23467

HBO (Home Box Office)
1100 Avenue of the Americas
New York, New York 10036
(212) 512-1000

Home Shopping Network, Inc.
Box 9090
Clearwater, Florida 34618
(813) 572-8585

The Learning Channel (Discovery Networks)
7700 Wisconsin Avenue
Bethesda, Maryland 20814
(301) 986-1999

Lifetime
36-12 35th Avenue
Astoria, New York 11106
(718) 482-4000

MTV
1515 Broadway
New York, New York 10036
(212) 258-8000

The Nashville Network
2806 Opryland Drive
Nashville, Tennessee 37214
(615) 889-6840

Nickelodeon
1211 Avenue of the Americas
New York, New York 10036
(212) 258-8000

Nostalgia Television
3575 Cahuenga Boulevard West
Suite 495
Los Angeles, California 90068
(213) 850-3000

The Playboy at Night
9242 Beverly Boulevard

Beverly Hills, California 90210
(310) 246-4000

Prism
225 City Avenue
Bala Cynwyd, Pennsylvania 19004
(215) 668-2210

QVC Network, Inc.
Goshen Corporate Park
Enterprise Drive
West Chester, Pennsylvania 19380
(215) 430-1000

Sci-Fi Channel (USA Networks)
1230 Avenue of the Americas
New York, New York 10020
(212) 408-9100

Showtime Networks, Inc.
1633 Broadway
3rd Floor
New York, New York 10019
(212) 708-1600

TBS
Box 105366
One CNN Center
Atlanta, Georgia 30348
(404) 827-1700

TNN: The Nashville Network
(Group W Satellite Communications)
Box 10210
250 Harbor Plaza Drive
Stamford, Connecticut 06904
(203) 965-6000

TNT: Turner Network Television
1050 Techwood Drive, NW
Atlanta, Georgia 30318
(404) 885-2402

The Travel Channel
2690 Cumberland Parkway
Suite 500
Atlanta, Georgia 30339
(404) 801-2400

USA Networks
1230 Avenue of the Americas
New York, New York 10020
(212) 408-9100

Viewer's Choice
909 Third Avenue, 21st Fl.
New York, New York 10022
(212) 486-6600

The Weather Channel
2600 Cumberland Parkway
Atlanta, Georgia 30339
(404) 434-6800

APPENDIX C
NATIONAL FUNDING SOURCES

Funding Agencies and Resource Groups

American Council for the Arts
1 East 53rd Street
New York, New York 10022
(212) 223-2787

American Film Institute (AFI)
2021 North Western Avenue
Los Angeles, California 90027
(213) 856-7600

Corporation for Public Broadcasting (CPB)
901 E. Street, NW
Washington, DC 20004
(202) 879-9600

The Foundation Center
79 Fifth Avenue
New York, New York 10003
(212) 620-4230
(800) 424-9836

The Foundation Center
1001 Connecticut Avenue, NW

Washington, DC 20036
(202) 331-1400

National Endowment for the Arts
1100 Pennsylvania Ave., NW
Washington, DC 20506
(202) 682-5400

National Endowment for the Humanities
1100 Pennsylvania Ave., NW
Washington, DC 20506
(202) 606-8438

National Public Radio
2025 M Street, NW
Washington, DC 20036
(202) 822-2000

WGBH-TV (National Productions)
125 Western Avenue
Boston, Massachusetts 02134
(617) 492-2777, ext. 4300

Private Foundations

Annenberg/CPB Project
901 E. Street, NW
Washington, DC 20004
(202) 879-9657

Ford Foundation
320 East 43rd Street
New York, New York 10017
(212) 573-5000

John Simon Guggenheim
Memorial Foundation
90 Park Avenue
New York, New York 10016
(212) 687-4470

Jerome Foundation
West 1050 First National Bank
Building

332 Minnesota Street
Saint Paul, Minnesota 55101
(612) 224-9431

Andrew W. Mellon Foundation
140 East 62nd Street
New York, New York 10021
(212) 838-8400

Sears Roebuck Foundation
Dept. 703
3333 Beverly Road
Hoffman Estates, Illinois 60179
(312) 875-2500

APPENDIX D
STATE FILM/VIDEO COMMISSIONS
AND STATE ARTS & HUMANITIES
AGENCIES

State Film/Video Commissions

Although film commissions are not in a position to fund scripts or productions, they are excellent resources for learning more about current and future television and film activities in your state.

Alabama Film Office
401 Adams Avenue
Montgomery, Alabama 36130
(800) 633-5898

Alaska Film Office
3601 C. Street
Suite 700
Anchorage, Alaska 99503
(907) 562-4163

Arizona Motion Picture Office
3800 North Central
Building D
Phoenix, Arizona 85012
(602) 280-1380

Arkansas Motion Picture Development Office
One State Capitol Mall
Little Rock, Arkansas 72201
(501) 682-7676

California Film Commission
6922 Hollywood Boulevard
Suite 600
Hollywood, California 90028
(213) 736-2465

Colorado Film Commission
1625 Broadway, #1975
Denver, Colorado 80202
(303) 572-5444

Connecticut Department of Economic Development
865 Brook Street
Rocky Hill, Connecticut 06067-3405
(203) 258-4301

Delaware Film Office
99 Kings Highway
Box 1401
Dover, Delaware 19903
(800) 441-8846

D.C. Office of Motion Picture
and TV Development
717 14th Street, NW
Washington, DC 20005
(202) 727-6600

Florida Film Office
107 West Gaines Street
Tallahassee, Florida 32399
(904) 487-1100

Georgia Film Office
P.O. Box 1776
Atlanta, GA 30301
(404) 656-3591

Hawaii Film Office
P.O. Box 2359
Honolulu, Hawaii 96804
(808) 586-2570

Idaho Film Bureau
700 West State Street
P.O. Box 83720
Boise, ID 83720-0093
(208) 334-2470

Illinois Film Office
100 West Randolph
Suite 3-400
Chicago, Illinois 60601
(312) 814-3600

Indiana Department of Commerce
1 North Capitol
Suite 700
Indianapolis, Indiana 46204
(317) 232-8860

Iowa Film Office
200 East Grand Avenue
Des Moines, IA 50309
(515) 242-4726

Kansas Film Commission
700 S.W. Harrison Street
Suite 1200
Topeka, Kansas 66603
(913) 296-4927

Kentucky Film Commission
2200 Capital Plaza Tower
500 Mero Street
Frankfort, KY 40601
(502) 564-3456

Louisiana Film Commission
P.O. Box 44320
Baton Rouge, Louisiana 70804
(504) 342-8150

Maine Film Commission
P.O. Box 8424
Augusta, Maine 04104
(207) 287-5710

Maryland Film Commission
601 North Howard Street
Baltimore, Maryland 21201
(410) 333-6633

Massachusetts Film Office
10 Park Plaza
Suite 2310
Boston, Massachusetts 02116
(617) 973-8800

Michigan Film Office
525 West Ottawa
P.O. Box 30004
Lansing, Michigan 48909
(517) 373-0638

Minnesota Film Board
401 North Third Street
Suite 460
Minneapolis, MN 55401
(612) 332-6493

Mississippi Film Office
1200 Walter Sillers Building
Box 849
Jackson, Mississippi 39205
(601) 359-3297

Missouri Film Office
P.O. Box 1055
Jefferson City, Missouri 65101
(314) 751-9050

Montana Film Office
1424 9th Avenue
Helena, Montana 59620
(406) 444-2654

Motion Picture Division/
Commission on Economic Development
3770 Howard Hughes Parkway
Suite 295
Las Vegas, Nevada 89109
(702) 486-7150

Nebraska Film Office
P.O. Box 94666
301 Centennial Mall South
Lincoln, NE 68509-4666
(402) 471-3368

New Hampshire Film & TV Bureau
172 Pembroke Road
P.O. Box 856
Concord, New Hampshire 03302-
0856
(603) 271-2598

New Jersey Motion Picture & Television Commission
P.O. Box 47023
153 Halsey Street
Newark, New Jersey 07101
(201) 648-6279

New Mexico Film Commission
1050 Old Pecos Trail
Santa Fe, NM 87501
(505) 827-7365

New York Governor's Office
for Motion Picture/TV Development
Pier 62
West 23rd Street & Hudson River
New York, NY 10011
(212) 949-0240

New York City Office of
Film/Theatre/Broadcasting
254 West 54th Street
13th Floor
New York, New York 10019
(212) 489-6710

North Carolina Film Office
430 North Salisbury Street
Raleigh, North Carolina 27611
(919) 733-9900

North Dakota Film Commission
604 East Boulevard
Bismarck, North Dakota 58505
(701) 224-2525

Ohio Film Commission
77 South High Street
29th Floor
Columbus, Ohio 43266-0101
(614) 466-2284

Oklahoma Film Office
440 South Houston
Room 505
Tulsa, Oklahoma 74127
(918) 581-2806

Oregon Film Office
775 Summer Street, NE

Salem, Oregon 97310
(503) 373-1232

Orlando Film & TV Office
200 East Robinson Street
Suite 600
Orlando, Florida 32801
(407) 422-7159

Pennsylvania Film Bureau
Forum Building
Room 449
Harrisburg, Pennsylvania 17120
(717) 783-3456

Puerto Rico Film Commission
P.O. Box 362350
San Juan, Puerto Rico 00936-2350
(809) 758-4747

Rhode Island Department of
Economic Development
Film Office
7 Jackson Walkway
Providence, Rhode Island 02903
(401) 277-3456

South Carolina Film Office
P.O. Box 927
Columbia, South Carolina 29202
(803) 737-0490

South Dakota Film Commission
711 East Wells Avenue
Pierre, South Dakota 57501-3369
(605) 773-3301

Tennessee
Film/Entertainment/Music
Commission
620 6th Avenue North
7th Floor
Nashville, Tennessee 37243-0790
(615) 741-3456

Texas Film Commission
P.O. Box 13246
Austin, TX 78711
(512) 463-9200

Utah Film Commission
324 South State Street
Suite 500
Salt Lake City, Utah 84111
(801) 538-8740

Vermont Film Bureau
134 State Street
Montpelier, Vermont 05602
(802) 828-3236

Virginia Film Office
P.O. Box 798
1021 East Cary Street
Richmond, Virginia 23206-0798
(804) 371-8204

Washington State Film and Video
Office
2001 6th Avenue
Suite 2700
Seattle, Washington 98121
(206) 464-7148

West Virginia Film Office
P.O. Box 50315
2101 Washington Street East
Charleston, West Virginia 25305-
0315
(304) 558-2286

Wisconsin Film Office
123 West Washington
6th Floor
Box 7970
Madison, Wisconsin 53707
(608) 267-3456

Wyoming Film Commission
I-25 & College Drive
Cheyenne, Wyoming 82002-0240
(307) 777-7777

State Arts & Humanities Agencies

Alabama Humanities Foundation
2217 Tenth Court South
Birmingham, Alabama 35205
(205) 930-0540

Alabama State Council on the
Arts
1 Dexter Avenue
Montgomery, Alabama 36130
(205) 242-4076

Alaska Humanities Forum
430 West 7th Avenue, Suite 1
Anchorage, Alaska 99501
(907) 272-5341

Alaska State Council on the Arts
411 West 4th Avenue, Suite 1E
Anchorage, Alaska 99501
(907) 279-1558

Arizona Commission on the Arts
417 West Roosevelt Avenue
Phoenix, Arizona 85003
(602) 255-5882

Arizona Humanities Council
Ellis-Shackelford House
1242 North Central Avenue
Phoenix, Arizona 85004
(602) 257-0335

Arkansas Arts Council
Heritage Center, Suite 200
225 East Markham
Little Rock, Arkansas 72201
(501) 324-9337

Arkansas Humanities Council
10816 Executive Center Drive
Suite 310

Little Rock, Arkansas 72211
(501) 221-0091

California Arts Council
2411 Alhambra Boulevard
Sacramento, California 95817
(916) 739-3186

California Council for
 the Humanities
312 Sutter Street, Suite 601
San Francisco, California 94108
(415) 391-1474

Colorado Council on the Arts
750 Pennsylvania Street
Denver, Colorado 80203
(303) 894-2617

Colorado Endowment for the
Humanities
1623 Blake Street, Suite 200
Denver, Colorado 80202
(303) 573-7733

Connecticut Commission on the
Arts
227 Lawrence Street
Hartford, Connecticut 06106
(203) 566-4770

Connecticut Humanities Council
41 Lawn Avenue
Wesleyan Station
Middletown, Connecticut 06457
(203) 347-6888

Delaware Division of the Arts
820 North French Street
Wilmington, Delaware 19801
(302) 571-3540

Delaware Humanities Forum
2600 Pennsylvania Avenue
Wilmington, Delaware 19806
(302) 573-4410

District of Columbia Commission
 on the Arts and Humanities
410 Eighth Street, NW
5th Floor
Washington, DC 20004
(202) 724-5613

D.C. Community Humanities
Council
1313 H. Street, NW
Suite 902
Washington, DC 20005
(202) 347-1732

Florida Arts Council
Department of State
The Capitol
Tallahassee, Florida 32399
(904) 487-2980

Florida Humanities Council
1514 1/2 East Eighth Avenue
Tampa, Florida 33605-3708
(813) 272-3473

Georgia Council for the Arts
530 Means Street, NW, Suite 115
Atlanta, Georgia 30318
(404) 894-9420

Georgia Humanities Council
1556 Clifton Road, NE
Emory University
Atlanta, Georgia 30322
(404) 727-7500

Guam Council on the Arts and
Humanities Agency

Office of the Governor
P.O. Box 2950
Agana, Guam 96910
011-671-477-7413 (must go through
overseas operator)

Guam Humanities Council
123 Archbishop Flores Street
Suite C
Agana, Guam 96910
011-671-472-4507 (must go through
overseas operator)

State Foundation on Culture
 and the Arts (Hawaii)
335 Merchant Street, Room 202
Honolulu, Hawaii 96813
(808) 586-0300

Hawaii Committee for
 the Humanities
First Hawaiian Bank Building
3599 Waialae Avenue, Room 23
Honolulu, Hawaii 96816
(808) 732-5402

Idaho Commission on the Arts
304 West State Street
Boise, Idaho 83720
(208) 334-2119

Idaho Humanities Council
217 West State Street
Boise, Idaho 83702
(208) 345-5346

Illinois Arts Council
State of Illinois Center
100 West Randolph
Suite 10-500
Chicago, Illinois 60601
(312) 814-6750

Illinois Humanities Council
618 South Michigan Avenue
Chicago, Illinois 60605
(312) 939-5212

Indiana Arts Commission
402 West Washington Street
Room 072
Indianapolis, Indiana 46204
(317) 232-1268

Indiana Humanities Council
1500 North Delaware Street
Indianapolis, Indiana 46202
(317) 638-1500

Iowa Arts Council
State Capitol Complex
1223 East Court Avenue
Des Moines, Iowa 50319
(515) 281-4451

Iowa Humanities Board
Oakdale Campus
University of Iowa
Iowa City, Iowa 52242
(319) 335-4153

Kansas Arts Commission
Jayhawk Tower
700 Jackson, Suite 1004
Topeka, Kansas 66603
(913) 296-3335

Kansas Humanities Council
112 West Sixth Street
Suite 210
Topeka, Kansas 66603
(913) 357-0359

Kentucky Arts Council
31 Fountain Place
Frankfort, Kentucky 40601
(502) 564-3757

Kentucky Humanities Council
417 Clifton Avenue
University of Kentucky
Lexington, Kentucky 40508-3406
(606) 257-5932

Louisiana Committee for
 the Humanities
The Ten-O-One Building
1001 Howard Avenue
Suite 3110
New Orleans, Louisiana 70113
(504) 523-4352

Louisiana Division of the Arts
900 Riverside North
P.O. Box 44247
Baton Rouge, Louisiana 70804
(504) 342-8180

Maine Arts Commission
55 Capitol Street
State House Station 25
Augusta, Maine 04333
(207) 289-2724

Maine Humanities Council
P.O. Box 7202
Portland, Maine 04112
(207) 773-5051

Maryland State Arts Council
601 North Howard Street
Baltimore, Maryland 21201
(301) 333-8232

The Maryland Committee for
 the Humanities
601 North Howard Street
Baltimore, Maryland 21201
(410) 625-4830

Massachusetts Cultural Council
80 Boylston Street, 10th Floor

Boston, Massachusetts 02116
(617) 727-3668

Massachusetts Foundation for
 the Humanities
One Woodbridge Street
South Hadley, Massachusetts
01075
(413) 536-1985

Michigan Council for the Arts
 and Cultural Affairs
1200 Sixth Avenue
Executive Plaza
Detroit, MI 48226
(313) 256-3735

Michigan Humanities Council
119 Pere Marquette Drive, Suite 3B
Lansing, Michigan 48912-1231
(517) 372-7770

Minnesota Humanities Commission
26 East Exchange Street
St. Paul, Minnesota 55101
(612) 224-5739

Minnesota State Arts Board
432 Summit Avenue
St. Paul, Minnesota 55102
(612) 297-2603

Mississippi Arts Commission
239 North Lamar Street
2nd Floor
Jackson, Mississippi 39201
(601) 359-6030

Mississippi Humanities Council
3825 Ridgewood Road, Room 508
Jackson, Mississippi 39211
(601) 982-6752

Missouri Arts Council
111 North 7th Street
Suite 105
St. Louis, Missouri 63101
(314) 340-6845

Missouri Humanities Council
911 Washington Avenue, Suite 215
St. Louis, Missouri 63101-1208
(314) 621-7705

Montana Arts Council
48 North Last Chance Gulch
Helena, Montana 59620
(406) 443-4338

Montana Committee for
 the Humanities
P.O. Box 8036
Hellgate Station
Missoula, Montana 59807
(405) 243-6022

Nebraska Arts Council
1313 Farnam-on-the-Mall
Omaha, Nebraska 68102
(402) 595-2122

Nebraska Humanities Committee
Lincoln Center Building, #225
215 Centennial Mall South
Lincoln, Nebraska 68508
(402) 474-2131

Nevada State Council on the Arts
329 Flint Street
Reno, Nevada 89501
(702) 688-1225

Nevada Humanities Committee
1034 North Sierra Street
Reno, Nevada 89503
(702) 784-6587

New Hampshire State Council on the Arts
40 North Main Street, Phenix Hall
Concord, New Hampshire 03301
(603) 271-2789

New Hampshire Humanities Council
19 Pillsbury Street
P.O. Box 2228
Concord, New Hampshire 03301-2228
(603) 224-4071

New Jersey Committee
 for the Humanities
73 Easton Avenue
New Brunswick, New Jersey 08901
(908) 932-7726

New Jersey State Council
 on the Arts
4 North Broad Street, CN 306
Trenton, New Jersey 08625
(609) 292-6130

New Mexico Arts Division
228 East Palace
Santa Fe, New Mexico 87501
(505) 827-6490

New Mexico Endowment
 for the Humanities
209 Onate Hall
Corner of Campus & Girard, NE
Albuquerque, New Mexico 87131
(505) 277-3705

New York Council
 for the Humanities
198 Broadway, 10th Floor
New York, New York 10036
(212) 233-1131

New York State Council on the Arts
915 Broadway
New York, New York 10010
(212) 387-7000

North Carolina Arts Council
Department of Cultural Resources
Raleigh, North Carolina 27611
(919) 733-2821

North Carolina Humanities Council
425 Spring Garden Street
Greensboro, North Carolina 27401
(919) 334-5325

North Dakota Council on the Arts
Black Building, Suite 606
Fargo, North Dakota 58102
(701) 239-7150

North Dakota Humanities Council
P.O. Box 2191
Bismarck, North Dakota 58502
(701) 255-3360

Commonwealth Council for
Arts and Culture (Northern Mariana Islands)
P.O. Box 553, CHRB
Saipan, MP 96950
011-670-322-9982 (must go through overseas operator)

Northern Mariana Islands Council
 for the Humanities
P.O. Box 1250
Saipan, MP 96950
011-670-235-4785 (must go through overseas operator)

Ohio Arts Council
727 East Main Street

Columbus, Ohio 43205
(614) 466-2613

Ohio Humanities Council
695 Bryden Road
P.O. Box 06354
Columbus, Ohio 43206-0354
(614) 461-7802

State Arts Council of Oklahoma
Jim Thorpe Building, #640
2101 North Lincoln Boulevard
Oklahoma City, Oklahoma 73105
(405) 521-2931

Oklahoma Foundation for
the Humanities
Festival Plaza
428 West California, Suite 270
Oklahoma City, Oklahoma 73102
(405) 235-0280

Oregon Arts Commission
550 Airport Road, SE
Salem, Oregon 97310
(503) 378-3625

Oregon Council for the Humanities
812 S.W. Washington, Suite 225
Portland, Oregon 97205
(503) 241-0543

Pennsylvania Council on the Arts
216 Finance Building
Harrisburg, Pennsylvania 17120
(717) 787-6883

Pennsylvania Humanities Council
320 Walnut Street, #305
Philadelphia, Pennsylvania 19106
(215) 925-1005

Institute of Puerto Rican Culture
Apartado Postal 4184

San Juan, Puerto Rico 00905
(809) 723-2115

Fundacion Puertorriquena de las
Humanidades
Apartado Postal S-4307
San Juan de Puerto Rico 00904
(809) 721-2087

Rhode Island Committee for the
Humanities
60 Ship Street
Providence, Rhode Island 02903
(401) 273-2250

Rhode Island State Council on the
Arts
95 Cedar Street
Suite 103
Providence, Rhode Island 02903
(401) 277-3880

South Carolina Arts Commission
1800 Gervais Street
Columbia, South Carolina 29201
(803) 734-8696

South Carolina Humanities
Council
1610 Oak Street
Columbia, South Carolina 29204
(803) 771-8864

South Dakota Arts Council
108 West 11th Street
Sioux Falls, South Dakota 57102
(605) 339-6646

South Dakota Humanities Council
Box 7050, University Station
Brookings, South Dakota 57007
(605) 688-6113

Tennessee Arts Commission
320 6th Avenue, North
Suite 100
Nashville, Tennessee 37243
(615) 741-1701

Tennessee Humanities Council
P.O. BOX 24767
Nashville, Tennessee 37202
(615) 320-7001

Texas Commission on the Arts
P.O. Box 13406
Capitol Station
Austin, Texas 78711
(512) 463-5535

Texas Committee for the Humanities
3809 South Second Street
Austin, Texas 78704
(512) 440-1991

Utah Arts Council
617 East South Temple Street
Salt Lake City, Utah 84102
(801) 533-5895

Utah Humanities Council
10 West Broadway, Suite 505
Salt Lake City, Utah 84101
(801) 531-7868

Vermont Council on the Arts
136 State Street
Montpelier, Vermont 05633
(802) 828-3291

Vermont Council on the Humanities
P.O. Box 58
Hyde Park, Vermont 05655
(802) 888-3183

Virginia Commission for the Arts
223 Governor Street
Richmond, Virginia 23219
(804) 225-3132

Virginia Foundation for the
Humanities
145 Ednam Drive
Charlottesville, Virginia 22903
(804) 924-3296

Virgin Islands Council on the Arts
41-42 Norre Gade
P.O. Box 103
St. Thomas, Virgin Islands 00804
(809) 774-5984

Virgin Islands Humanities Council
P.O. Box 1829
St. Thomas, Virgin Islands 00803
(809) 776-4044

Washington Commission for the
Humanities
615 Second Avenue, Suite 300
Seattle, Washington 98104
(206) 682-1770

Washington State Arts
Commission
110 9th and Columbia Building
Mail Stop GH-11
Olympia, Washington 98504
(206) 753-3860

West Virginia Department of Education and the Arts
Arts and Humanities Section
Division of Culture and History
Capitol Complex
Charleston, West Virginia 25305
(304) 348-0240

West Virginia Humanities Council
723 Kanawha Boulevard
Suite 800
Charleston, West Virginia 25301
(304) 346-8500

Wisconsin Arts Board
131 West Wilson Street
Suite 301
Madison, Wisconsin 53702
(608) 266-0190

Wisconsin Humanities Committee
716 Langdon Street

Madison, Wisconsin 53706
(608) 262-0706

Wyoming Council of the Arts
2320 Capitol Avenue
Cheyenne, Wyoming 82002
(307) 777-7742

Wyoming Council for the Humanities
Box 3643, University Station
Laramie, Wyoming 82701-3643
(307) 766-6496

APPENDIX E
SCREENWRITING FESTIVALS,
COMPETITIONS, AND
PROFESSIONAL WORKSHOPS

For up-to-date information about these and other opportunities, refer to resources like *Grants and Awards Available to American Writers*; *Gadney's Guide to International Contests, Festivals, and Grants in Film, Video*; *The Writer's Handbook*; and *Writers Market*. If you are interested in submitting productions for festival consideration, consult the latest edition of *The Producer's Masterguide*. (See "Marketing Resources" and "Grants and Non-Commercial Funding" in the Bibliography.)

Academy of Television Arts
& Sciences
Student Internship Program
5220 Lankershim Boulevard
North Hollywood, CA 91601
(818) 754-2830

America's Best Writing
Competition
The Writer's Foundation
1801 Burnet Avenue
Syracuse, New York 13206

American Independent
Screenplay Competition
P.O. Box 58529
New Orleans, Louisiana 70158-
8529

Black Independent Film, Video,
and Screenplay Competition
Black Filmmakers
Hall of Fame, Inc.
405 14th Street
Suite 515
Oakland, CA 94612
(415) 465-0804

The Chesterfield Film Company
Writer's Film Project
Universal Studios
100 Universal City Plaza,
Building 447
Universal City, CA 91608

The Christopher Columbus
Screenplay Discovery Awards

433 North Camden Drive
Suite 600
Beverly Hills, CA 90210
(310) 288-1881

The Walt Disney Studios Fellowship
The Walt Disney Studios
500 South Buena Vista Street
Burbank, California 91521
(818) 560-6894

International Film & Television
Workshops
2 Central Street
Rockport, Maine 04856
(207) 236-8581

The Nate Monaster Memorial
Writing Competition
c/o The University Film and Video
Association
Communications Arts Department
Loyola Marymount University
Loyola Boulevard and West 80th
Street
Los Angeles, CA 90045
(310) 338-1855

Nicholl Fellowships in
Screenwriting
Academy Foundation

Academy of Motion Picture Arts
and Sciences
8949 Wilshire Boulevard
Beverly Hills, CA 90211
(310) 247-3000

Sundance Institute
P.O. Box 16450
Salt Lake City, Utah 84116
(801) 328-3456

The Squaw Valley Community of
Writers Workshops
P.O. Box 2352
Olympic Valley, CA 96146

Lee Rich Screenwriting Award
c/o The University Film and Video
Association
Communications Arts Department
Loyola Marymount University
Loyola Boulevard and West 80th
Street
Los Angeles, CA 90045
(310) 338-1855

Warner Bros. Writer's Workshop
Warner Bros.-TV
4000 Warner Boulevard
Burbank, CA 91522
(818) 954-2933 (Warner Bros.
Writers' Workshop Hotline)

APPENDIX F

PROFESSIONAL UNIONS AND ASSOCIATIONS

Academy of Motion Picture Arts
and Sciences
8949 Wilshire Boulevard
Beverly Hills, California 90211
(310) 274-3000

Academy of Television Arts and
Sciences
5220 Lankershim Boulevard
North Hollywood, California
91601
(818) 754-2800

Actors' Equity Association
165 West 46th Street
New York, New York 10036
(212) 869-8530

Alliance of Motion Picture and TV
Producers
15503 Ventura Boulevard
Encino, California 91436
(818) 995-3600

American Federation of Television
and Radio Artists (AFTRA)
6922 Hollywood Boulevard

8th Floor
Hollywood, California 90028
(213) 461-8111

American Film Institute (AFI)
John F. Kennedy Center for the
Performing Arts
Washington, DC 20566
(202) 828-4000

American Film Institute (AFI)
2021 North Western Avenue
Los Angeles, CA 90027
(213) 856-7600

Broadcast Education Association
1771 N Street, NW
Washington, DC 20036
(202) 429-5355

Directors Guild of America, Inc.
110 West 57th Street
New York, New York 10019
(212) 581-0370

Directors Guild of America, Inc.
7920 Sunset Boulevard

Hollywood, California 90046
(310) 289-2000

International Radio and Television
Society
420 Lexington Avenue
New York, NY 10170
(212) 867-6650

Motion Picture Association of
America (MPAA)
15503 Ventura Boulevard
Encino, CA 91436
(818) 995-6600

National Academy of Television
Arts and Sciences
Suite 1020
111 West 57th Street
New York, NY 10019
(212) 586-8424

National Association of Broadcast-
ers (NAB)
1771 N Street, NW
Washington, DC 20036
(202) 429-5300

PEN (Poets, Playwrights, Essayists,
Editors, and Novelists)
Pan American Center
568 Broadway
New York, NY 10012
(212) 334-1660

Producers Guild of America
292 South La Cienega Boulevard

Beverly Hills, CA 90211
(301) 557-0807

Screen Actors' Guild (SAG)
1515 Broadway
New York, New York 10036
(212) 944-1030

Screen Actors' Guild (SAG)
5757 Wilshire Boulevard
Hollywood, CA 90046-3600
(213) 549-6400

Story Analysts, Local 854, IATSE
Suite 301
13949 Ventura Boulevard
Sherman Oaks, CA 91423
(818) 784-6555

Women in Film
Suite 530
6464 Sunset Boulevard
Hollywood, CA 90028
(213) 463-6040

Writers Guild of America, East,
Inc.
555 West 57th Street
New York, NY 10019
(212) 767-7800

Writers Guild of America,
West, Inc.
8955 Beverly Boulevard
West Hollywood, California 90048
(310) 550-1000

ANNOTATED AND SELECTED BIBLIOGRAPHY FOR THE TELEVISION- AND SCREENWRITER

Adler, Stella. *The Technique of Acting* (with a preface by Marlon Brando). New York: Bantam Books, 1988. A legendary actress and teacher, Adler had a profound influence on American acting. She was a student of Stanislavski and based her technique on his Method acting, with emphasis on analyzing the writer's text.

Armer, Alan A. *Writing the Screenplay: TV and Film.* Belmont, Calif.: Wadsworth Publishing Company, 1993. Emmy Award-winner Alan Armer takes aspiring writers through the essential steps leading to good screenwriting: visual thinking, characters and plotting, story structure and conflict, dialogue, and formats.

Berman, Robert A. *Fade In: The Screenwriting Process.* Stoneham, Mass: Focal Press, 1988. Berman presents a clear, concise method for turning a story concept into a successfully completed screenplay.

Blacker, Irwin R. *The Elements of Screenwriting.* New York: Macmillan Publishing Co., 1986. Blacker was the preeminent teacher of screenwriting at USC. This book outlines his theories, based on Aristotelian and classical dramatic theory. He discusses the elements necessary for writing quality marketable scripts. The book is based on his lectures, published posthumously.

Blum, Richard A., and Richard D. Lindheim. *Inside Television Producing.* Boston and London: Butterworth Publishers – Focal Press, 1991. Breaks through the confusion surrounding both the role and the activities of a creative writer-producer by taking an in-depth look at the development of two brand-new shows, a half-hour situation comedy ("Coach") and a one-hour dramatic series ("Law & Order"). The entire developmental process is detailed and presented along with insightful comments by creators Barry Kemp ("Coach") and Dick Wolf ("Law & Order"). Complete pilot scripts for both shows are included.

———. *Primetime: Network Television Programming*. Boston and London: Butterworth Publishers – Focal Press, 1987. An analysis of who does what in primetime television, including chapters on developing series concepts, pitching, pilot production, network decision-making strategies, developing TV miniseries, movies, and specials, and constraints on creativity.

Blum, Richard A. *Working Actors: The Craft of Television, Film, and Stage Performance*. Boston and London: Butterworth Publishers – Focal Press, 1989. This book features interviews with twelve actors in television and film, some of whom were trained in variations of the Method, others who can't stand it. They talk about their individual approaches to finding the character from the given circumstances of the text provided by the writer.

———. *American Film Acting: The Stanislavski Heritage*. Ann Arbor: UMI Research Press, 1984. This book traces the history and impact of Stanislavski's system on American film acting.

Egri, Lajos. *The Art of Dramatic Writing*. New York: Simon and Schuster, 1966. This is an important and useful book for any writer of television or film. Egri deals with the theory and technique of character development, premise construction, and conflict building. His theories are at the heart of "COLLABORATOR II," idea development software for screenwriters.

Field, Syd. *Selling the Screenplay*. New York: Dell, 1989. An informed look at the elements necessary to write a marketable screenplay. This is one of Syd Field's most practical and useful books.

———. *Screenplay*. New York: Delacort, 1982.
This is Field's paradigm for writing a screenplay, looking at the structure of screenplays, and writing marketable scripts.

———. *Screenwriter's Workbook*. New York: Dell, 1984. A practical guidebook for writing a marketable screenplay.

Froug, William. *Screenwriting Tricks of the Trade*. Los Angeles: Silman-James Press, 1992. A practical guide in which Froug, a renowned screenwriter, encourages every new writer to develop his or her own style of writing.

Garfield, David. *A Player's Place: The Story of the Actors' Studio*. New York: Macmillan, 1980. An authoritative history of the Actors' Studio and the Method, by a member of the Studio.

Goldman, William. *Adventures in the Screen Trade*. New York: Warner Books, 1983. Excellent resource about the industry from one of its foremost screenwriters.

Haag, Judith, and Hillis R. Cole. *The Complete Guide to Standard Script Formats.* North Hollywood: CMC Publishing, 1991. Several versions available, with individual volumes dedicated to formats for teleplays and screenplays.

Haugue, Michael. *Writing Screenplays That Sell.* New York: Harper Collins, 1991. This is an effective, straightforward book about how to write marketable screenplays.

Hunter, Lew. *Screenwriting 434.* New York: A Perigee Book, 1993. Lew Hunter teaches screenwriting at UCLA. This book is an insider's guide to the process of developing marketable scripts, including ideas, characters, outlines, and scripts. Very good insights.

Josefsburg, Milt. *Writing Comedy for Television and Hollywood.* New York: Harper & Row, 1987. Important information on writing comedy for TV and film.

King, Viki. *How to Write a Movie in 21 Days: The Inner Movie Method.* New York: Harper and Row, 1988. A good basic approach that takes you through the process of writing in manageable phases.

Kosbert, Robert, and Mim Eichler. *How to Sell Your Idea to Hollywood.* New York: Harper Perennial, 1991. Deals with practical issues like concepts and pitching in the industry.

Mehring, Margaret. *The Screenplay: A Blend of Film Form and Content.* Boston: Focal Press, 1990. Argues that film writing is an art form that should blend artistic content and form.

Sautter, Carl. *How to Sell Your Screenplay.* Ferndale, California: New Chapter Press, 1992. Important book on marketing your script.

Seger, Linda. *Making a Good Script Great.* Hollywood: Samuel French, 1989. Excellent analysis of tools you will need for rewriting the script.

_____. *Creating Unforgettable Characters.* Hollywood: Samuel French, 1990. An important tool for understanding and developing credible characters in your scripts.

_____. and Edward Jay Whetmore. *From Script to Screen: The Collaborative Art of Filmmaking.* Henry Holt, 1993. An informative look at the collaborative nature of screenwriting.

Trottier, David R. *Correct Format for Screenplays and Teleplays.* Anaheim, California: The Forbes Institute, The Screenwriting Center, 1991. A precise resource for script formatting.

Walter, Richard. *Screenwriting: The Art, Craft, and Business of Film and Television Writing.* New York: New American Library, 1988. Head of the UCLA screenwriting program Walter discusses the importance of turning a good story into a highly marketable script. A very informative resource.

Whitcomb, Cynthia. *Selling Your Screenplay.* New York: Crown, 1988. A useful and pragmatic guide to breaking into the business.

Wolff, Jurgen and Kerry Cox. *Successful Scriptwriting*. Cincinnati, Ohio: Writers Digest Books, 1988. A good resource for the process of scriptwriting.

Where to Find Sample Television Scripts and Screenplays

Larry Edmonds Books, 6658 Hollywood Boulevard, Hollywood, CA 90028 (213) 463-3273. Specializes in books on film and television, trade journals, and screenplays.

Samuel French Books is a reliable resource for thousands of books and scripts. They have catalogues available and can be reached at 1-800-822-8669 or in California, 1-800-722-8669.

Script City, 8033 Sunset Boulevard, Box 1500, Los Angeles, California 90046 (213) 871-0707. A valuable resource for ordering television scripts and motion picture screenplays.

Resources for Screenwriting Software

The Writer's Computer Store, 11317 Santa Monica Boulevard, Los Angeles, CA 90025. A knowledgeable resource for scriptwriting software and computer hardware.

The Journal of Writers Guild of America West, 8955 Beverly Boulevard, Los Angeles, CA 90035. Watch for monthly articles written by James Tugend ("Tools"), a professional screenwriter and computer expert. Tugend objectively evaluates all the latest hardware and software for television and screenwriters.

"The Write Stuff Catalogue," 21115 Devonshire Street, #182-143, Chatsworth, CA 91311. This is a discount catalogue listing books and computer software programs for television and screenwriters.

These are some of the most utilized software packages.

Movie Master™
Comprehensive Cinema Software
148 Veterans Drive
Northvale, New Jersey 07647
(800) 526-0242
A well documented software program, reliable.

Scriptor™
Screenplay Systems
150 East Olive Avenue, Suite 203
Burbank, CA 91502

(818) 843-6557
A little difficult to learn, but a powerful tool.

Scriptware™
Cinovation
204 West 20th Street, Suite 37
New York, New York 10011
(800) 788-7090
Very easy to use and learn, excellent software for writers.

Trade Publications and Periodicals

Academy Players Directory
c/o Academy of Motion Pictures
8949 Wilshire Boulevard
Beverly Hills, CA 90211-1972

Advertising Age
220 East 42nd Street
New York, NY 10017

Backstage
1515 Broadway
New York, NY 10036

Broadcasting and Cable
1705 DeSales Street, N.W.
Washington, D.C. 20036

Current
1612 K Street, N.W.
Washington, D.C. 20006

Daily Variety
Suite 120
5700 Wilshire Boulevard
Los Angeles, CA 90036

Editor and Publisher
11 West 19th Street
New York, NY 10011

Emmy
Academy of Television Arts and
Sciences
5220 Lankershim Boulevard
North Hollywood, CA 91601

Entertainment Weekly
1675 Broadway
New York, NY 10019

Film Quarterly
University of California Press
Berkeley, CA 94720
The Hollywood Reporter
5055 Wilshire Boulevard
Los Angeles, CA 90036

*The Journal of Writers Guild
of America West*
Writers Guild of America
8955 Beverly Blvd.
Los Angeles, CA 90048

*Kemps International Film & TV
Year Book*
c/o Expanding Horizons
6725 Sunset Boulevard, #402
Los Angeles, CA 90028

Millimeter Magazine, Inc.
826 Broadway, 4th Fl.
New York, NY 10003

The Producer's Masterguide
330 West 42nd Street, 16th Fl.
New York, NY 10036-6994

Ross Reports
Television Index, Inc.
40-29 27th Street
Long Island City, NY 11101

Television Quarterly
National Academy of
Television Arts and Sciences
Suite 1020
111 West 57th Street
New York, NY 10019

Variety
475 Park Avenue, South
New York, NY 10016

The Writer   Writer's Digest
120 Boylston Street   1507 Dana Avenue
Boston, MA 02116   Cincinnati, OH 45207

Marketing Resources

Broadcasting and Cable Yearbook, 1735 DeSales St., N.W., Washington, DC 20036. This is an annual compilation of facts and figures about the television, cable, and pay TV industry. It is a major resource to consult.

DVE Productions' Hollywood Personnel Directories, 3017 Santa Monica Boulevard, Suite 149, Santa Monica, CA 90404. Lists all the names, titles, addresses, and phone numbers of current development and production personnel at the studios and networks, as well as independents.

Pacific Coast Directory, 6331 Hollywood Blvd., Hollywood, CA 90028. A quarterly listing of all production companies in California and fifteen other states. Includes lists of agents, advertising agencies, producers, TV stations, and film commissions. A very useful directory for finding names, addresses, and phone numbers.

The Producer's Masterguide, 330 West 42nd Street, 16th Fl., New York, NY 10036-6994. An excellent resource for names and contacts in film and television, including a list of film contests.

Ross Reports, Television Index, Inc., 150 Fifth Ave., New York, NY 10011. A monthly publication on the East Coast that lists all national production activity, including film, network, cable, and pay TV programming. Lists names, addresses, and contacts for all the current productions.

Television Factbook, 1836 Jefferson Pl., NW, Washington, D.C. 20036. A major annual directory that encompasses the entire spectrum of the television industry. It includes a list of all networks, cable and pay TV, group-owned stations, network O&O's, and advertisers.

The Writer's Handbook, The Writer, Inc., Boston, Mass. Annual compilation of thousands of markets for manuscript sales.

Writers Market and *Writers Year Book*, 1507 Dana Avenue, Cincinnati, OH 45207. Annual compilation of thousands of markets for writers in every realm.

Grants and Noncommercial Funding

Annual Register of Grant Support. Chicago: Marquis Academic Media. This annual register offers information on writing proposals and provides an index to grant programs catalogued by subject.

Catalog of Federal Domestic Assistance. Washington, D.C.: U.S. Government Printing Office. This is an annual compilation of all RFPs (requests for proposals); available in libraries with U.S. government publications.

Foundation Center National Data Book. New York: Foundation Center. Annual information on all nonprofit organizations in the U.S.

Foundation Directory. New York: Columbia University Press. Exceptionally useful cross-indexed resource of thousands of foundations and subjects funded. Revised editions written by The Foundation Center, New York.

Gadney's Guide to International Contests, Festivals, and Grants in Film, Video. Glendale, CA: Festival Publications. A cross-indexed reference for worldwide grants and competitive events in film, video, writing, and broadcasting.

Grants and Awards Available to American Writers. N.Y. PEN. Annual compilation of grants and awards for writers. Compiled by PEN (Poets, Playwrights, Essayists, Editors, and Novelists), American Center, New York.

Index